FABULOUS!

FABULOUS!

A PHOTOGRAPHIC DIARY OF STUDIO 54

BOBBY MILLER

ST. MARTIN'S PRESS

NEW YORK

FABULOUS! A PHOTOGRAPHIC DIARY OF STUDIO 54. Copyright © 1998 by Bobby Miller. All rights reserved. Printed in the United States of America. No part of this book may be used or reproduced in any manner whatsoever without written permission except in the case of brief quotations embodied in critical articles or reviews. For information address St. Martin's Press, 175 Fifth Avenue, New York, N.Y. 10010.

Library of Congress Cataloging-in-Publication Data

Miller, Bobby.
    Fabulous! : a photographic diary of Studio 54 / Bobby Miller.—1st ed.
        p.   cm
    ISBN 0-312-19567-2
    1. Celebrities—Portraits.   2. Portrait photography.   3. Studio 54 (Nightclub).   I. Title.
    TR681.F3M55   1998
    779'.2'092—dc21   98-26377
                                                                         CIP

Design by Elissa Stein

First Edition: September 1998

10 9 8 7 6 5 4 3 2 1

DEDICATION

To my mother, Dorothy Miller, who always encouraged me to be myself and to believe that I could be whatever my heart desired. I treasure so many memories of her, including one glorious night when we danced together at Studio 54.

To all those whose names and stories I missed or got wrong in the disco haze, I apologize profusely, and to the many others whom I mention in this book and who are no longer here to tell their version of the story . . . this is for you, too.

ACKNOWLEDGMENTS

Bobby Miller would like to thank:

God
Basil Twist
Amy Trachtenberg
Jordy Trachtenberg
Dana Albarella
Sid Kaplan
Jim Smith
Fred Bernstein
Chi Chi Valenti
Johnny Dynel
Verbal Abuse Staff
Tina Paul
Victor Bockris
Lisette Model
Hilda Charleton
Merlin Fahey
My Mother
The Miller Family
The Twist Family
The Jackie Family
The Tasty Family
Friends and Extended Family
Smitty the Dog (1980–1998)

FURIOUS DAYS
AND GLORIOUS NIGHTS

I have always wanted to transport my readers back to the Seventies, and in particular their peak years, 1977–1979. I see that Bobby Miller has beat me to it, and he has done it in the most magic way, with photographs that freeze a moment forever, allowing one to see deeper into it with repeated viewings.

Ever since Ken Burns gave us his marvelous television series on the Civil War, people have been given the ability to see photographs differently. They can see them moving, even hear music behind them. At least that is what happened to me looking through this book. When I first saw the photographs, which I whipped through the way one often does when first looking at a book of photographs in a shop, I felt as if a hand had wrapped itself around my neck and yanked me into that giant room that was Studio 54, its balcony, the stairs leading to the balcony, the couches on the mezzanine. The images that subsequently flashed by transported me back to some glorious nights those privileged to gain regular entrée to the world of Studio 54 experienced. Many images filled me with mixed emotions—ambition, hunger, joy—but most of all the *fun* that was the essence of Studio 54.

The first time I ever stood at the edge of the dance floor watching the beauties winding and grinding through marvelous-to-behold visual contortions in

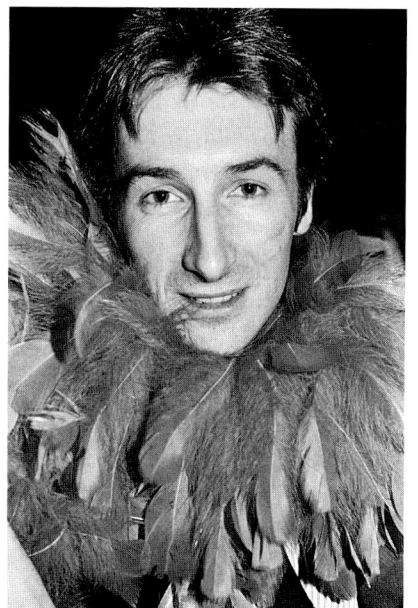

grace, large flakes of snow suddenly began to fall profusely onto the dance floor. This, I flashed, was a tiny, magic kingdom of its own in the midst of Manhattan, and it symbolized what was then the atomic, electric, radiant capital of the world.

Bobby Miller was and is a fiercely independent man. That is one of the factors that makes his photographs such strong sculptural evocations of an era. Although many of the players in this pageant are still famous twenty years later, for me one of the most moving photographs is, perhaps appropriately, the photographer Marcia Resnick dancing, her Egyptian arms, her face aglow with the knowledge of her own beauty, and all the anonymous hands seeming to grab at her, accenting that wonderful sense of being the center of attention that all Miller's subjects possess. Another such example is the photograph of the model Iman. On her first visit to Studio 54 she seems to be emerging from darkness into the light of New York, represented in the right-hand foreground by the garishly lit face of Andy Warhol. And yet it is undoubtedly Iman who rules the photo, Iman to whom one's eyes are drawn again and again.

There is no need to look through more than a few of the photographs to know that Mr. Miller has a complete portrait of the place. Furthermore, one can tell by talking to him for a few minutes that he is not a product of Studio 54. He is the kind of person who made Studio into what it was. Indeed, his photographs helped mold the place into what it became. His pictures of Disco Sally, Disco Granddad, a never-again-as-handsome Christopher Walken, and a ferocious Eartha Kitt are, for example, instant icons.

But Mr. Miller's book is more than a pageant; it is a book of photographs in the best sense of the word, perhaps in the old-fashioned sense of the word—the record of one witness's view of a whole new aura and era, of an exploding society colored by the essence of who Mr. Miller is.

On arriving in New York, he was rapidly discovered by a few of the central figures of New York's art-photo-social scene in the three magic years this book covers, encompassing the late Seventies from the highlights of disco to the low lights of punk. This was shortly after then-President Ford had told New York to drop dead and it had become the Berlin of America—an alienated city, cut off, on its own, especially and spectacularly Manhattan. In that time, those who arrived from elsewhere were embraced and assimilated into the cause. Perhaps some will think me overdramatic (I am! I am!) in comparing this circle-the-wagons feeling to being at the Alamo on that memorable occasion when Colonel Bowie (from whom David Bowie took his name) drew a line in the sand and said, "Any man who wants to stay and fight step over this line and join me in saving the Alamo and Texas!" (Years later a film was made of this event, and as I recall there was not a dry eye in the house when it was

screened; every one of Bowie's men stayed and fought.) For me, in those days, if Manhattan was one vast ocean liner on an endless voyage to astonish and astound, then Studio 54 was the bridge on which one could often find Andy Warhol, Halston, or Bianca Jagger at the helm.

The essence of this book was crafted before the grim reaper visited Manhattan with his scythe. It pursues life and happiness, its photos echoing with the laughter of beautiful voices. If you've read every one of F. Scott Fitzgerald's books, you'll recognize that rather than being full of cash those voices were full of splendor in the grass.

When I got to there, even though I owed my allegiance to CBGB's and then the Mudd Club, I also belonged to the church-school of Andy Warhol, and our crowd attended services at Studio as well as classes at the Factory. For me, there was no getting away from it. Mr. Miller, however, did get away with it by remaining his own man, and taking his own photographs.

That is why Bobby Miller has a great future.

In memory of the war paint . . .

Victor Bockris

New York City, 1998

INTRODUCTION

Upon moving to New York City in 1973, I resumed a hairdressing practice which I had begun at the tender age of fourteen and which eventually afforded me the wonderful opportunity to meet and work with many of the great fashion photographers of the decade. It was during this period that I became interested in taking photos myself. At first I tried to make it in the fashion world by creating portfolios for amateur models out of my apartment. Beginning with a standard makeup and hair makeover, I transformed a variety of women into stunning versions of themselves and then photographed them. But I soon lost interest in taking pictures of "pretty models" in a controlled setting and began to wonder if this was the career move I was looking for. Being cooped up in a hot studio taking the same type of picture day after day was repetitive and unrewarding, and I soon realized it wasn't for me. I decided to start taking pictures all the time, everywhere, and I began carrying my camera constantly. Soon I found myself taking pictures of everything: shoes, hats, people on the street, people in museums, people in department stores. It was as if my once-closed eyes were suddenly opened wide,

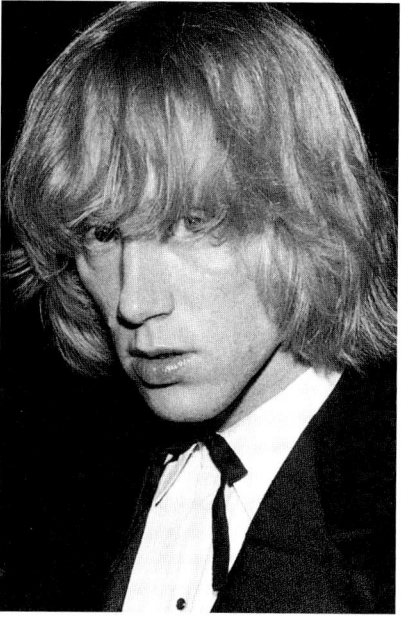

and I developed an insatiable appetite to photograph and document the world around me. And then 1977 gave birth to Studio 54, and there I was with a camera around my neck.

You see, all hell broke loose when Studio 54 opened its doors. How could I *not* have photographed it? I *had* to. I had already started taking nighttime pictures at a few of the smaller nightclubs, and I felt secure enough to stick a camera in someone's face. While there had been some great New York clubs up until then, none had the magic, the promise of surprise, and the always dependable excitement of Studio 54. There were small clubs where people could dance and have a drink or even see a show, but there were no huge emporiums where you could dance, have a drink, see a show, be at a private party, be secluded, and have sex in the basement or balcony, all under one roof. Most clubs offered the same-old-same-old to their clientele week after week, and most weren't hard to get into. But Studio was about exclusivity, and every night it celebrated the in crowd. The unnatural selection process began at the front door, where only the beautiful people were allowed in (with many strange and unusual exceptions thrown in for good measure).

With its world-famous reputation, Studio promised a never-ending parade of superstars and freaks from every walk of life, night after night. Those who passed through the red, black, and bronze doors were hand-picked for their appearance. Being rich, famous, or sexy could get you in, but none of those qualities alone guaranteed admission. Though there were the regulars whom you'd see every night, and certain others who showed up only for the special parties, there were always the new ones who clamored to get inside. Having made it past the watchful eyes of doorman Mark Benecke or owner Steve Rubell, into the club they'd come, wandering wide-eyed, looking to see Liza or Andy or Calvin or Bianca. And they'd find them behind a wall of exploding flashbulbs, sitting on those eternal silver couches, smiling, posing, and willing to be worshiped. Still, it was an unwritten rule at Studio that the "real" people had to give the stars some space. You could look at them, watch them, breathe the same rarefied air, but you didn't touch them or talk to them. And somehow it worked—for the most part, people paid homage to their legends from a respectable distance.

Except me! I talked to everyone I got close to: I asked Truman Capote for a dance, which he declined; Gloria Swanson gave me a lecture on the evils of sugar; Martha Graham shared a brief discourse on how she thought her modern dancers looked discoing on the dance floor; Andy Warhol frequently asked me to tell him which other famous people had come in the door before him; Salvador Dalí inquired about the identity of a certain drag queen descending the stairs; a look-alike Elvis tried to seduce me in the men's room.

Oh, the drugs that flowed over tongues and up noses and into the brains and nerve centers of the frenzied . . . so many nights . . . so many stories . . . So many photographs! I took more pictures at Studio than anywhere else because it seemed like the center of the universe at the time. We were on a cocaine-Quaaludes-Tequila-Sunrises-always-rolling-another-joint high . . . heading off into deep space on an acid trip . . . wearing sequins and feathers . . . or a tuxedo . . . and so I went night after night until I felt the disco fire begin to fade. It had burst like a rocket across the horizon and fizzled out in a crash-boom at the end of its ride. So many people went with it. But many more survived to tell its tale. This is my photographic diary through the eternally long and fabulous night that was Studio 54.

FABULOUS!

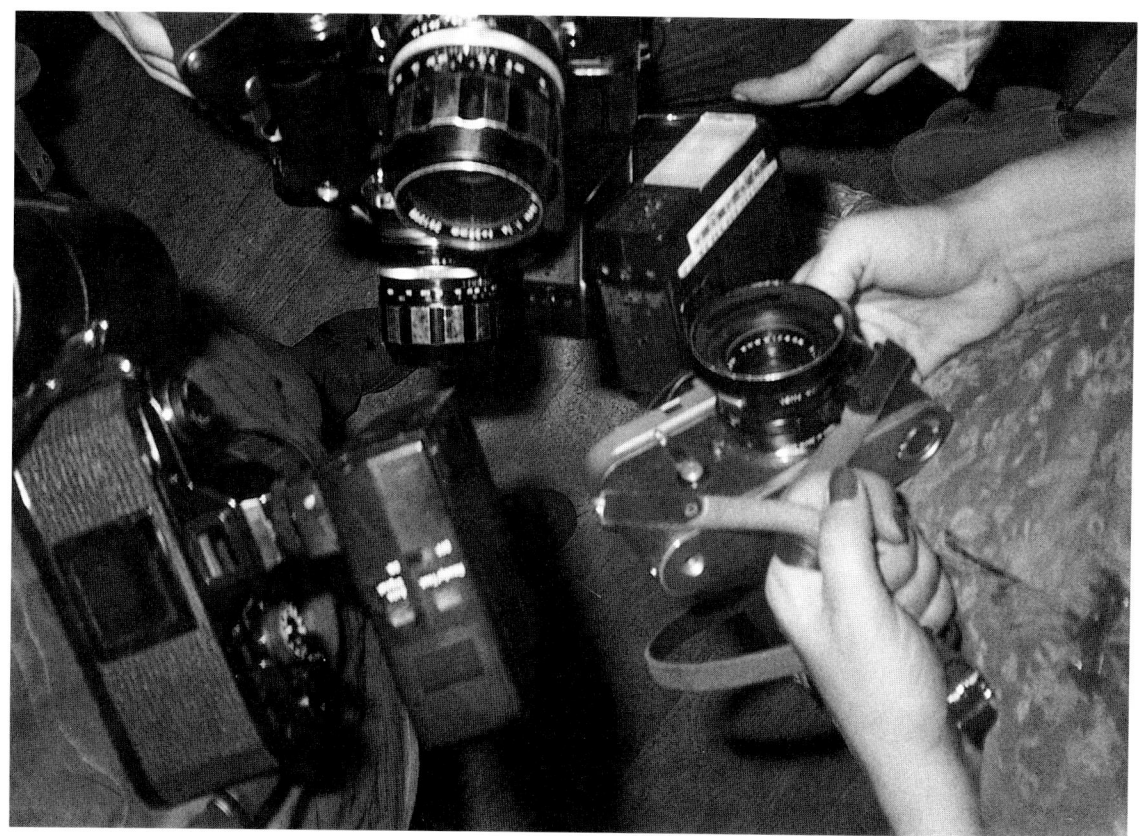

PRESS POOL

There was a small pool of photographers who worked regularly at Studio 54. Most were friendly with one another and shared tips for getting the best shots. For a young, inexperienced photographer there was a lot to learn. I remember my first night out with a camera around my neck. I went rushing headfirst into the fray with my elbows sticking out to the sides as I shot. Met with angry glares and forceful nudges, I quickly learned to keep my elbows down at my sides and to become as thin and invisible as possible. I also learned to carry more than one camera with me at all times, because if I ran out of film in one camera I would always be prepared with a second or third. Among the masters with whom I was fortunate to work alongside were Sonia Moskowitz, Robin Platzer, Felice Quinto, RPM, Rose Hartman, Bill Cunningham, and the legendary Ron Galella. There were more whose names are lost in the disco haze, but I think of them and their long nights giving chase in search of the perfect shot.

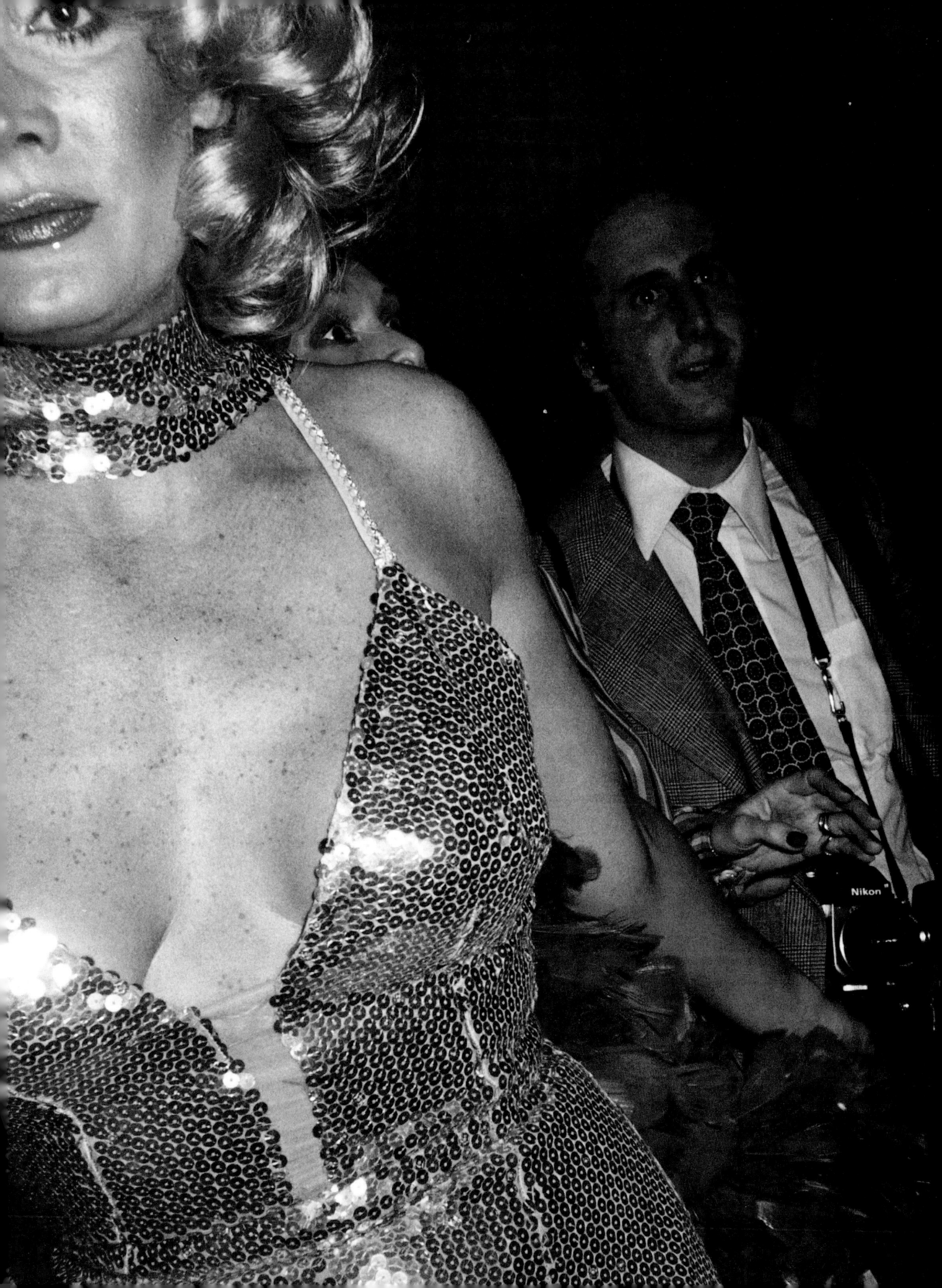

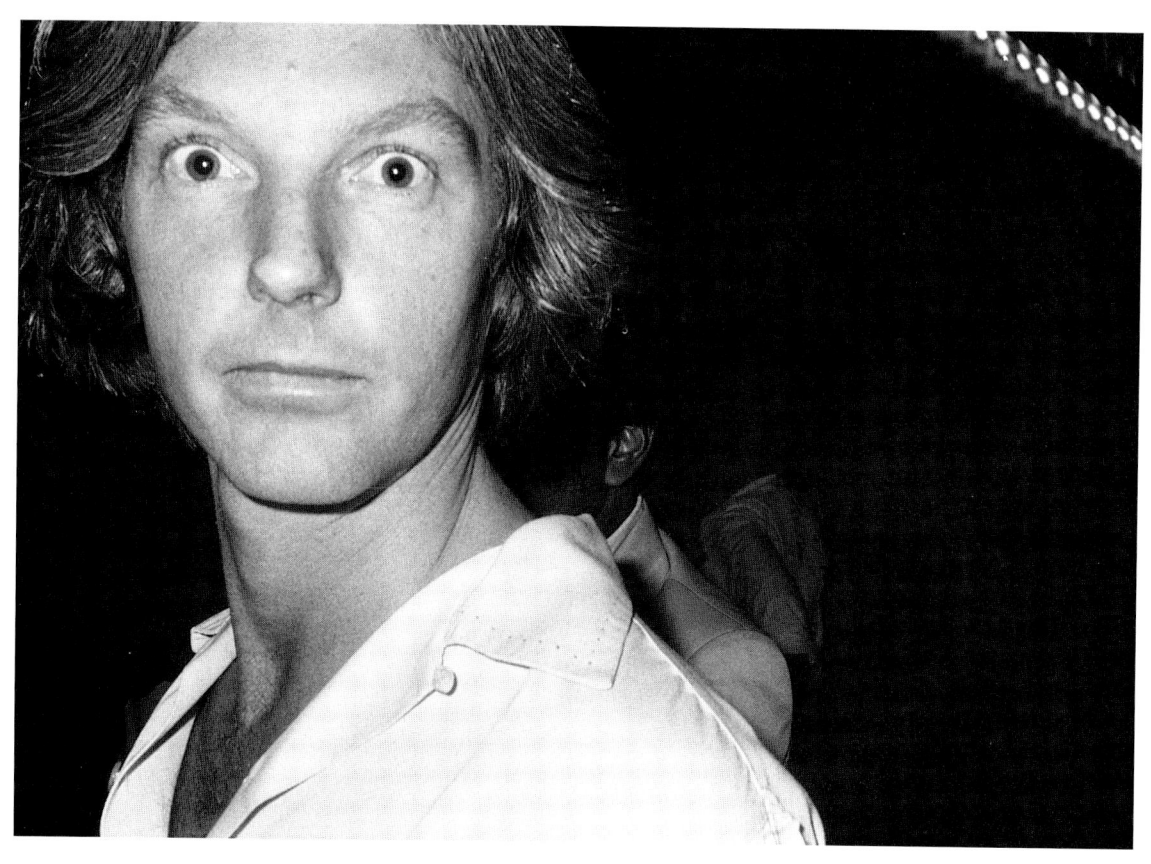

LYNN THE DOORMAN

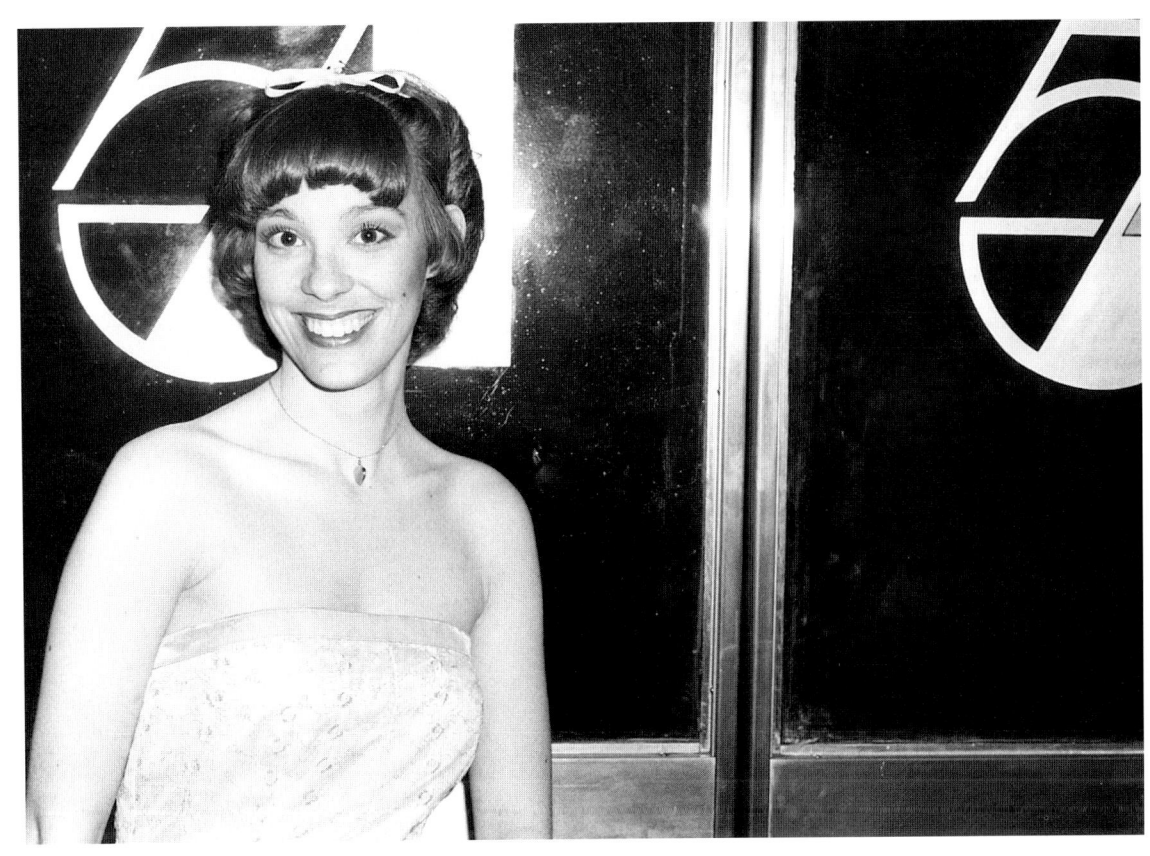

MYSTERY GIRL

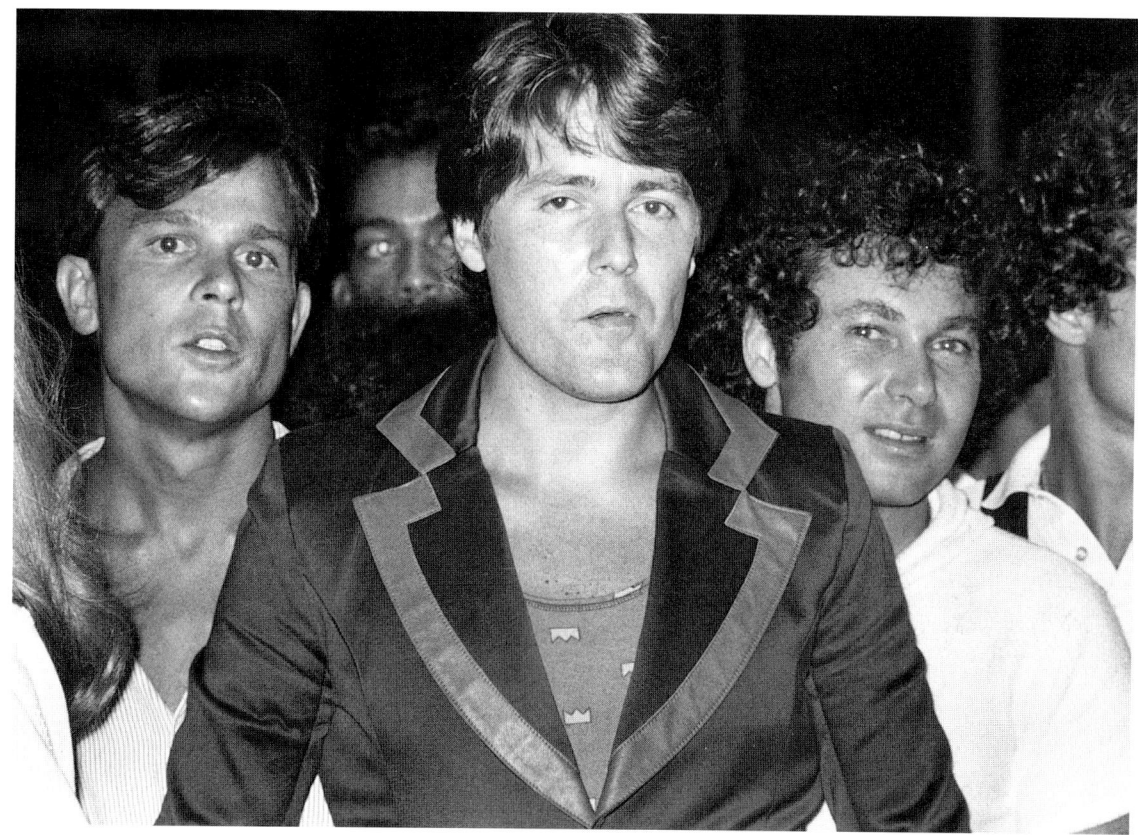

WAITING TO GET IN

Many nights when the club was slow or it was still early, I would go and hang out at the front entrance with the doorpeople who had become my friends. Standing with them behind the velvet ropes I would watch people arrive and try to get in. Sometimes they were whisked straight in, other times they were forced to wait a little while, and often they were never let in at all. The exclusive standard that was set by Studio 54 in the Seventies has continued to this day—almost every one of the current slew of clubs embraces that same velvet-rope rule. I hated the concept then, and I am still uncomfortable with its practice today. These are just some of the masses who played the Studio waiting game.

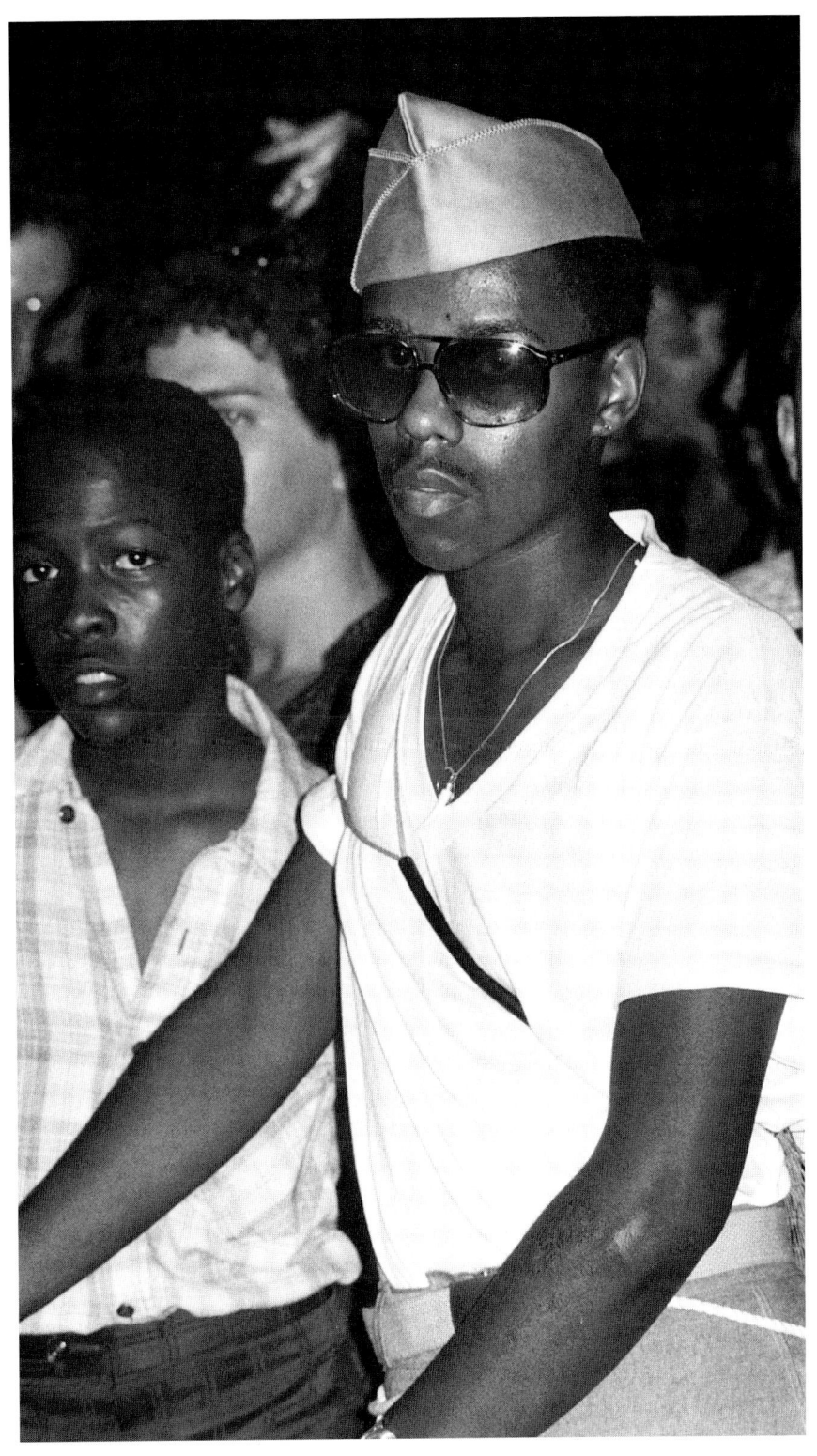

CHRISTOPHER WALKEN

Most of the celebrities who came to Studio on a regular basis knew that press photographers would be inside working the club, and thus it was a real boon to an actor's career to be seen there. Just being on the "scene" cast them in a hip and glamorous light, and as a result most were friendly and accommodating. Others who were already hip and glamorous were less accommodating and a little less friendly—Christopher Walken was among this group. Still, after following him around the room several times, he finally surrendered and let me take this photo.

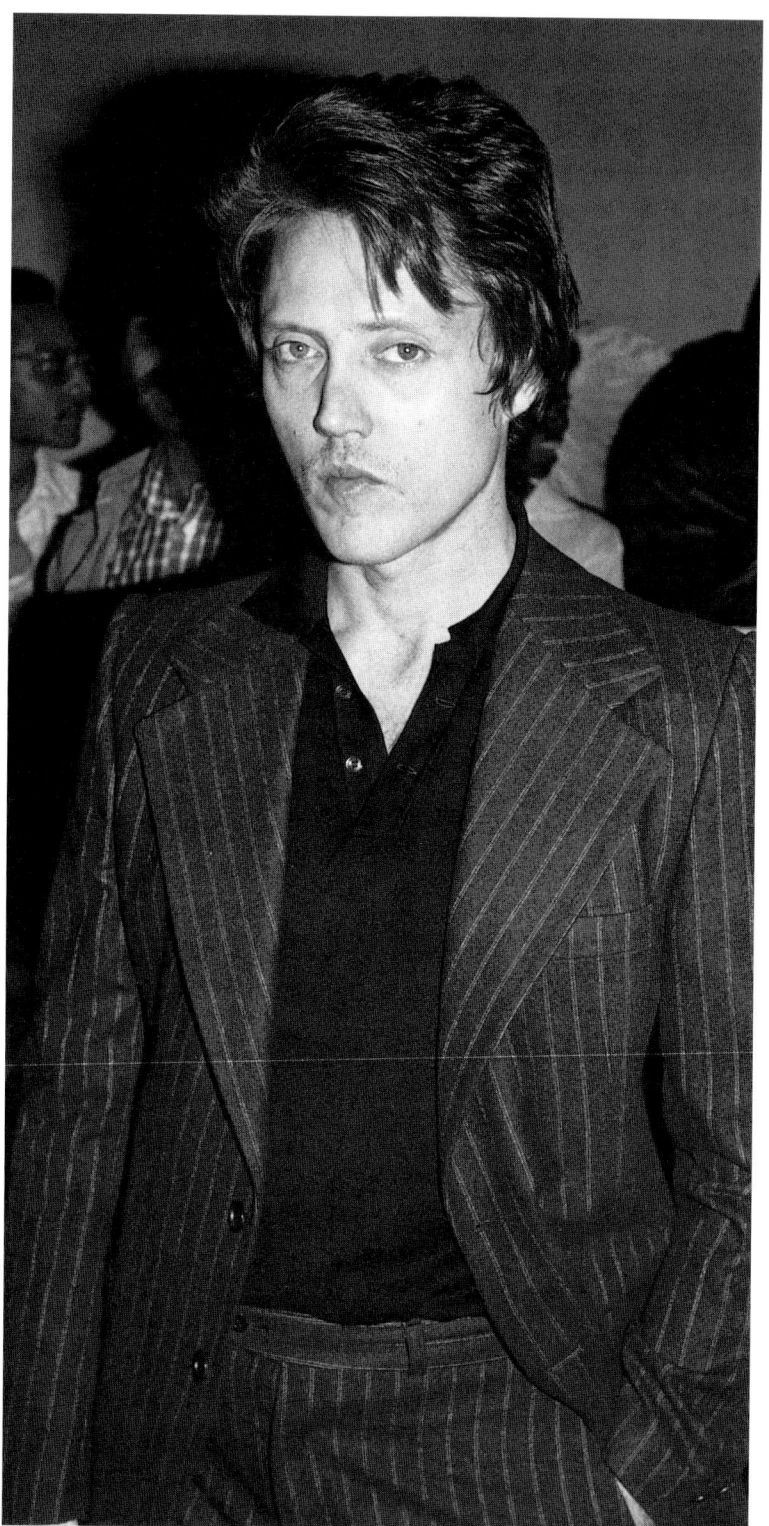

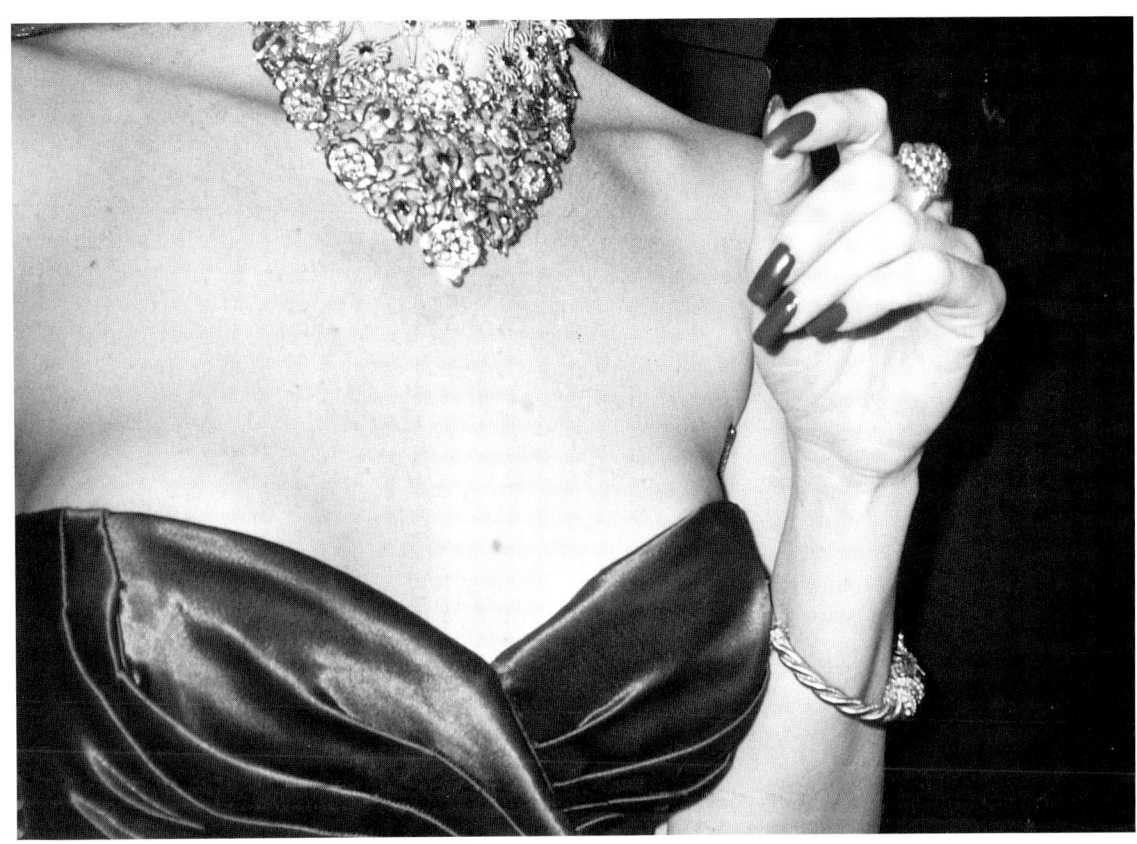

NECKLACE

Studio catered to a diverse clientele, from shop girls to debutantes, and the fashions they sported on any given night ranged from blue jeans and cowboy hats to satin bustiers and baubles. The bejeweled neck in this photo belonged to a rich New York debutante who asked me not to take her picture because she didn't want to be seen in the paper as someone who might frequent a nightclub. We compromised with this headless shot of her jewelry.

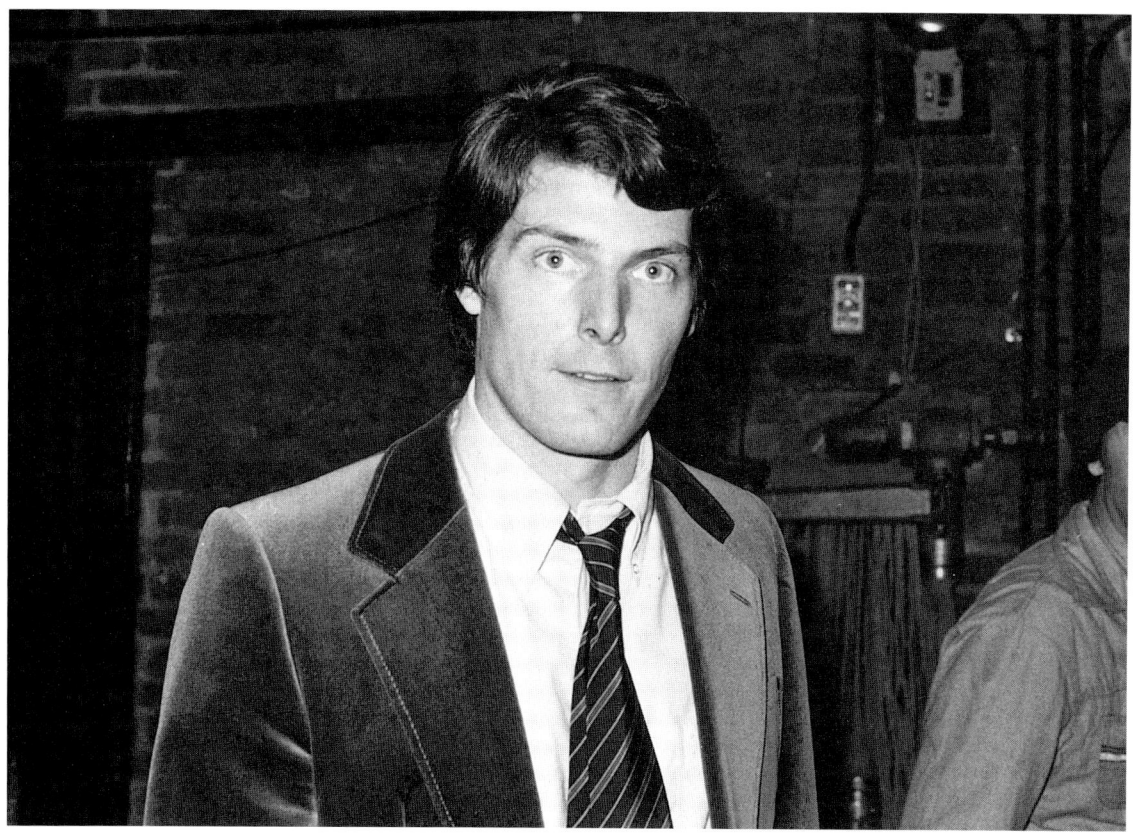

CHRISTOPHER REEVE

Superman, the movie, had only been out for a short while when Christopher Reeve first came to Studio. The paparazzi had a tendency to hang out at the front entrance like piranhas waiting for the big fish to arrive, but like many celebrities Reeve wanted to avoid the crush at the door and planned a quiet entrance through the back. Luckily I found a friend in one of the doormen, who made a point of telling me who was coming in what door—he had advanced warning over his walkie-talkie. If I was standing at the front entrance, he would signal me to head toward the rear and vice versa. Such was the case with this photo—I was the only camera waiting for Mr. Reeve when he came in quietly through the back.

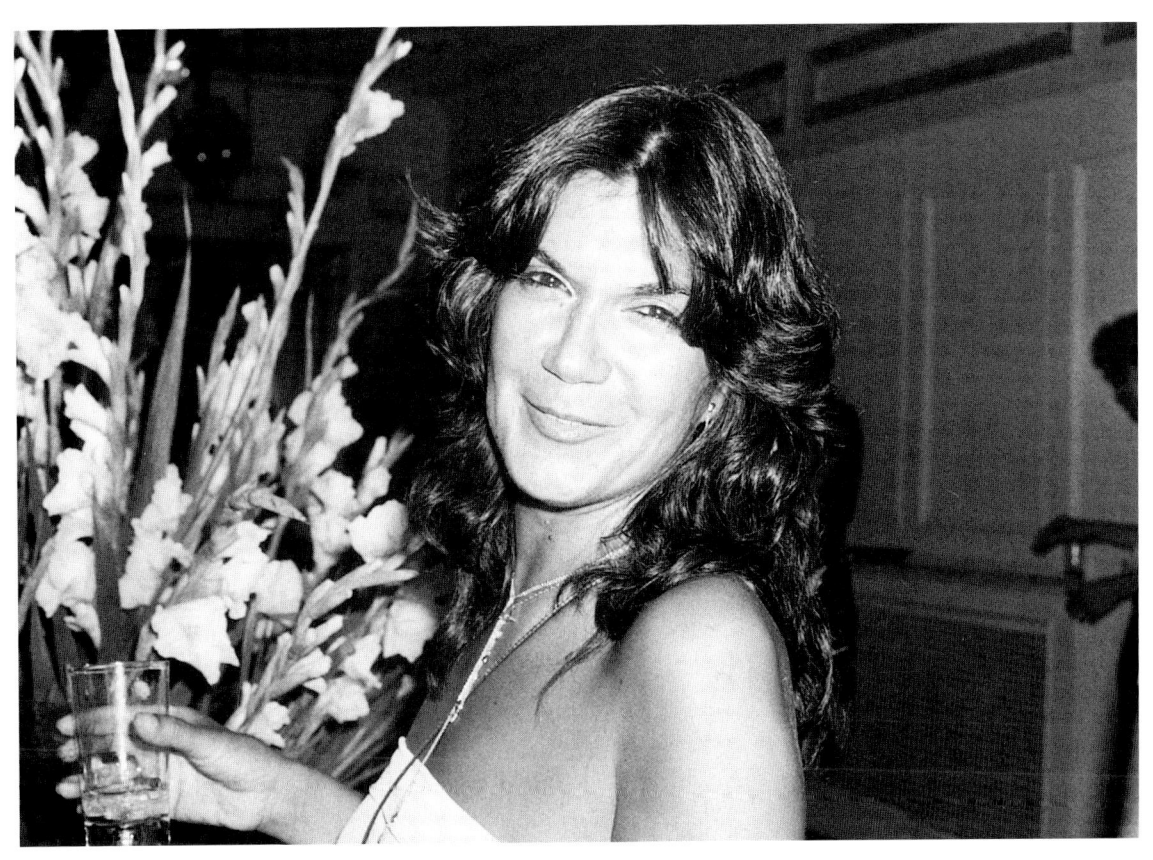

CARMEN D'ALESSIO

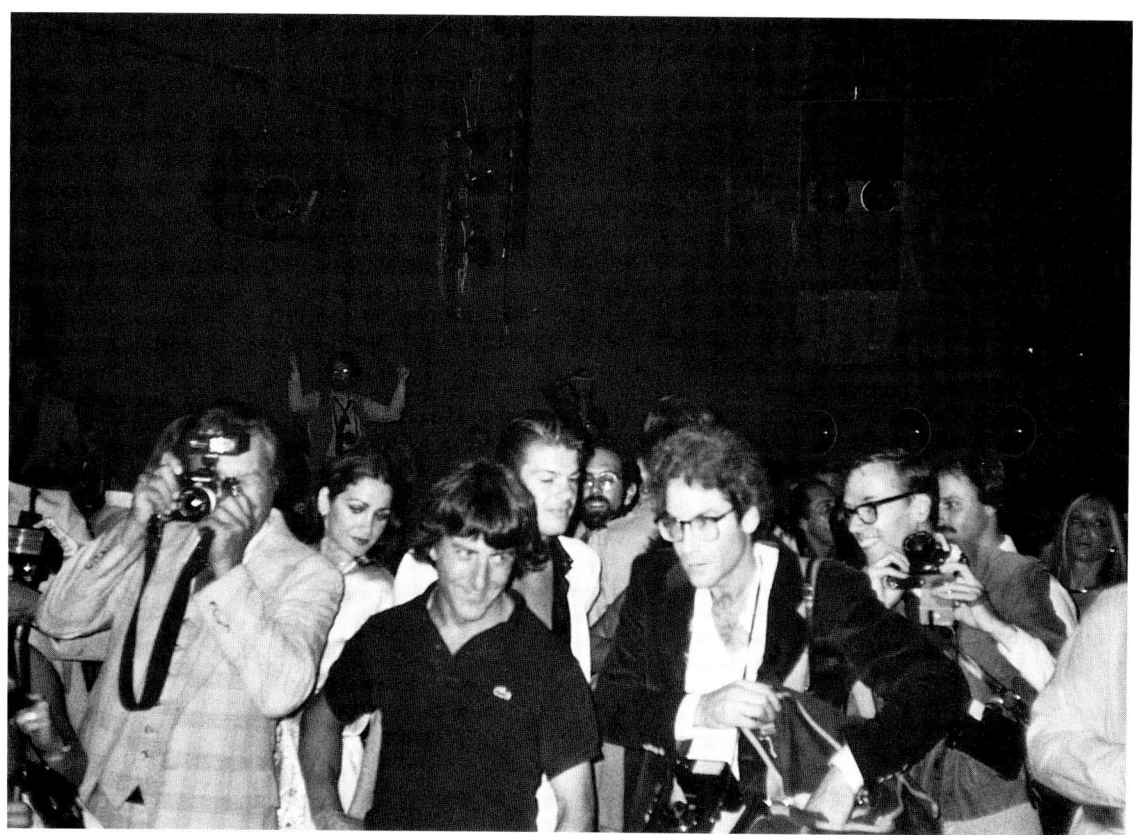

DUSTIN HOFFMAN

Only seconds before this picture was taken, I was standing in the very spot that Dustin Hoffman occupies in this photo. I was shooting a group of celebrities posed just opposite this press pool when Dustin grabbed me and switched places so that I would be the only one to have this shot of him. The next day in the *New York Times*, a picture ran of me with the celebrities, sans Dustin.

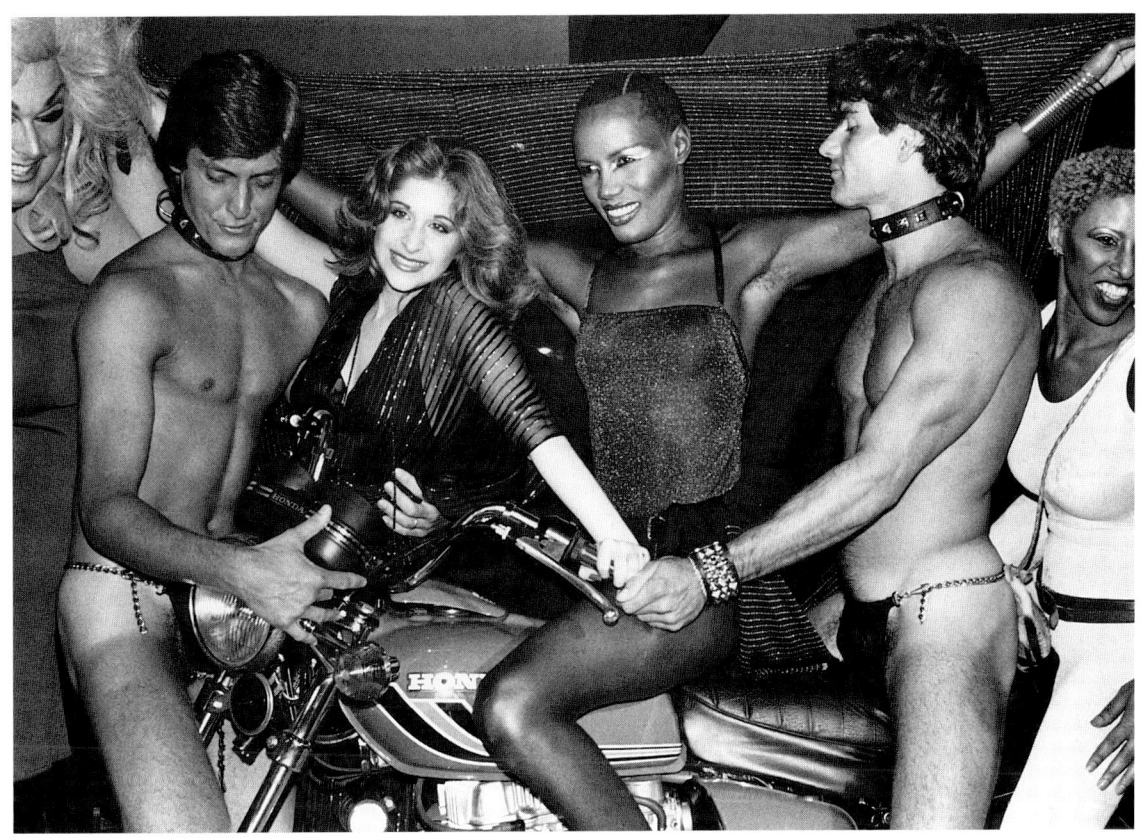

Perhaps more than any other person, Grace Jones personified the spirit of Studio 54: outrageous, glamorous, and beautiful. She grew to fashion-model stardom in Paris with Jerry Hall and Pat Cleveland, and that was just the beginning. Always a striking figure, Grace could wear either couture or street fashion and carry them off with flair—her outfits were both shocking and chic. Once she crossed over into the music world, her understanding of style and fashion contributed greatly to her performances. Her live shows at Studio on New Year's Eve and Halloween had thousands waiting in the streets to get in to see her. Those who made it in were awed by what they saw. Her tremendous personal style coupled with her vibrant personality made her one of my favorite people to photograph. She was always gracious and a pleasure to shoot, and during Studio's reign I captured her image many times. Here is just a small sampling:

Grace straddling a Harley with Divine, Julie Budd, Nona Hendryx, and two cute go-go boys.

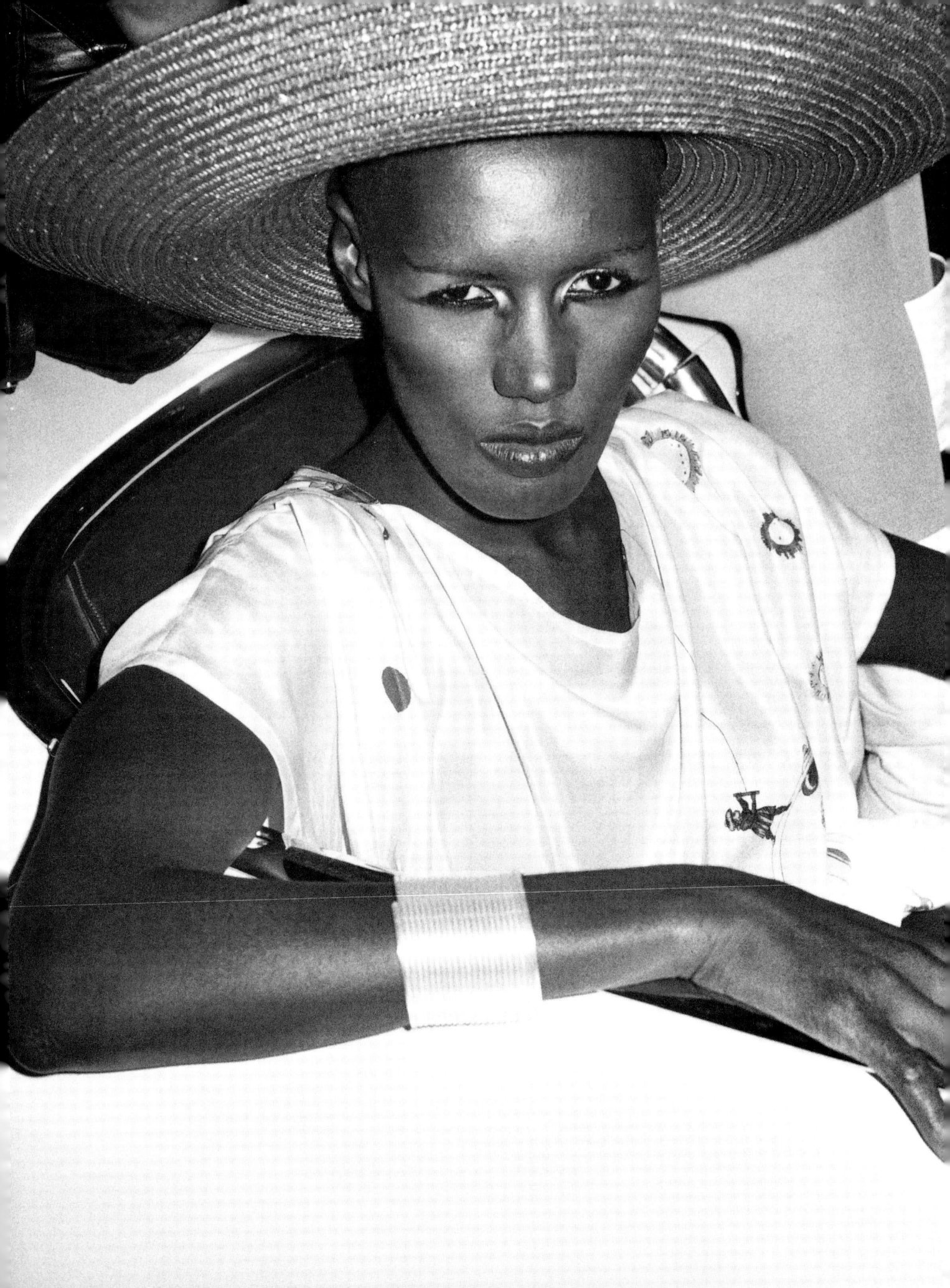

Grace in a wide-brimmed straw hat, sitting in a small sports car just off the dance floor, receiving guests and posing for photos.

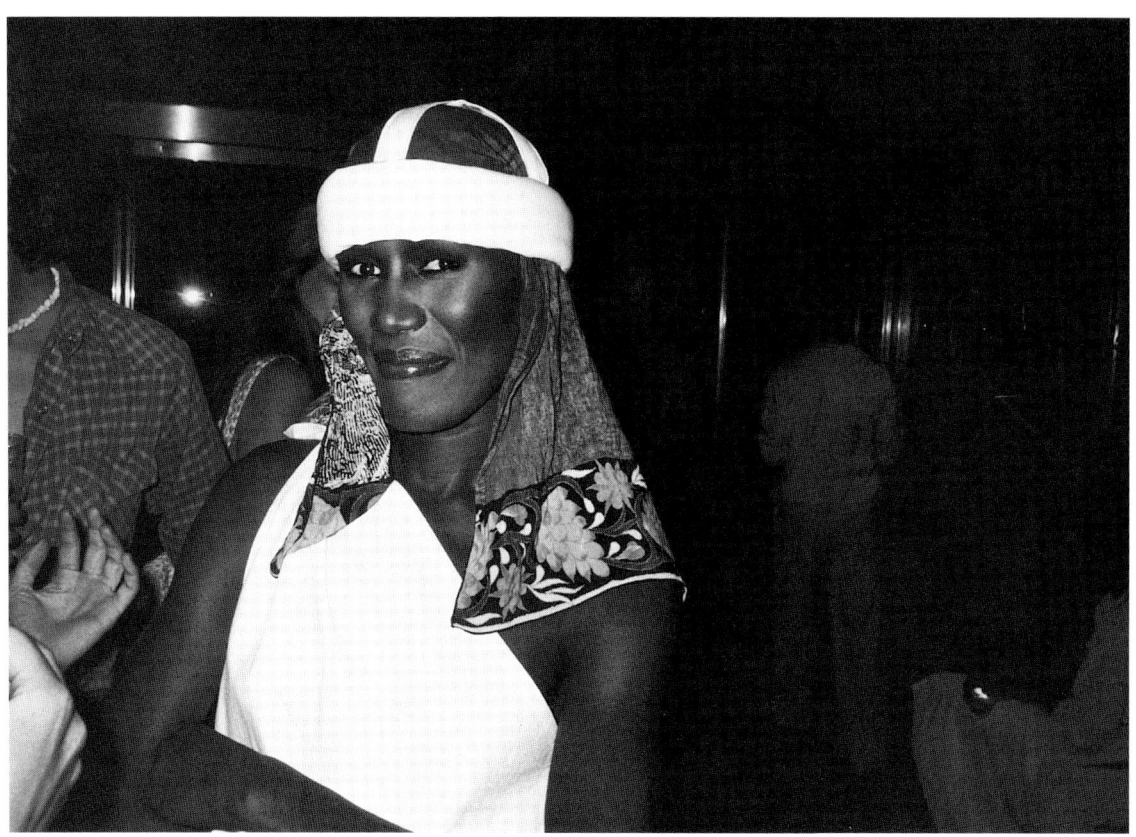

GRACE JONES

Grace in a white asymmetrical summer top and a soft-sculpted pith helmet with a neck shade in an African print.

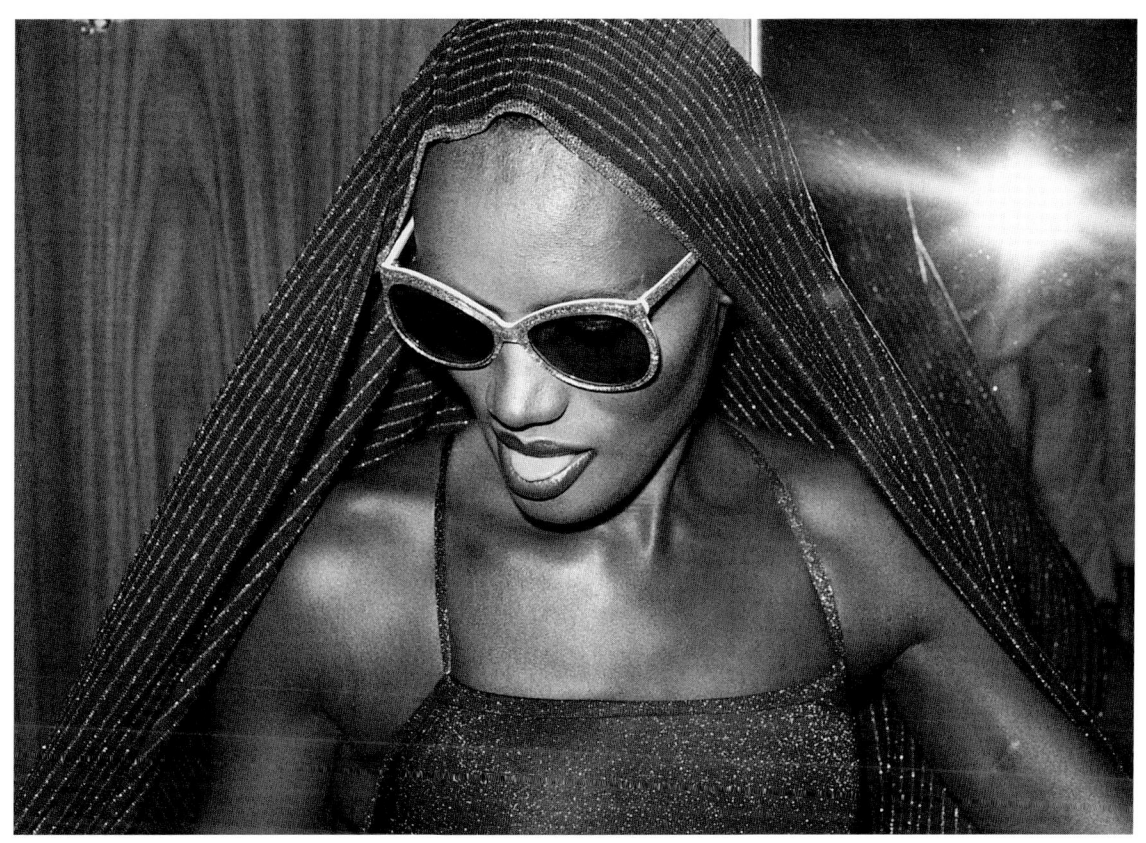

Grace in black-and-gold stretch Lurex with a matching pinstriped hooded cape, which created a true disco Madonna look. (That's me in the mirror's reflection.)

JACQUES BELLINI AND TONI TUCCI

On any given night there were hordes of beautifully attired people at Studio. So many of us had come through the hippie late Sixties and funky early Seventies, and we'd had enough of dressing down. Studio offered an opportunity to be glamorous for the first time in a decade. Many of the currently successful designers got their start around that time. Some careers that began then are now at their apex. Jacques Bellini was a great French designer with a small private salon on East Sixtieth Street in New York. He made gorgeous clothes for the rich and very rich. Here he is entering the club's foyer with his model and muse Miss Toni Tucci.

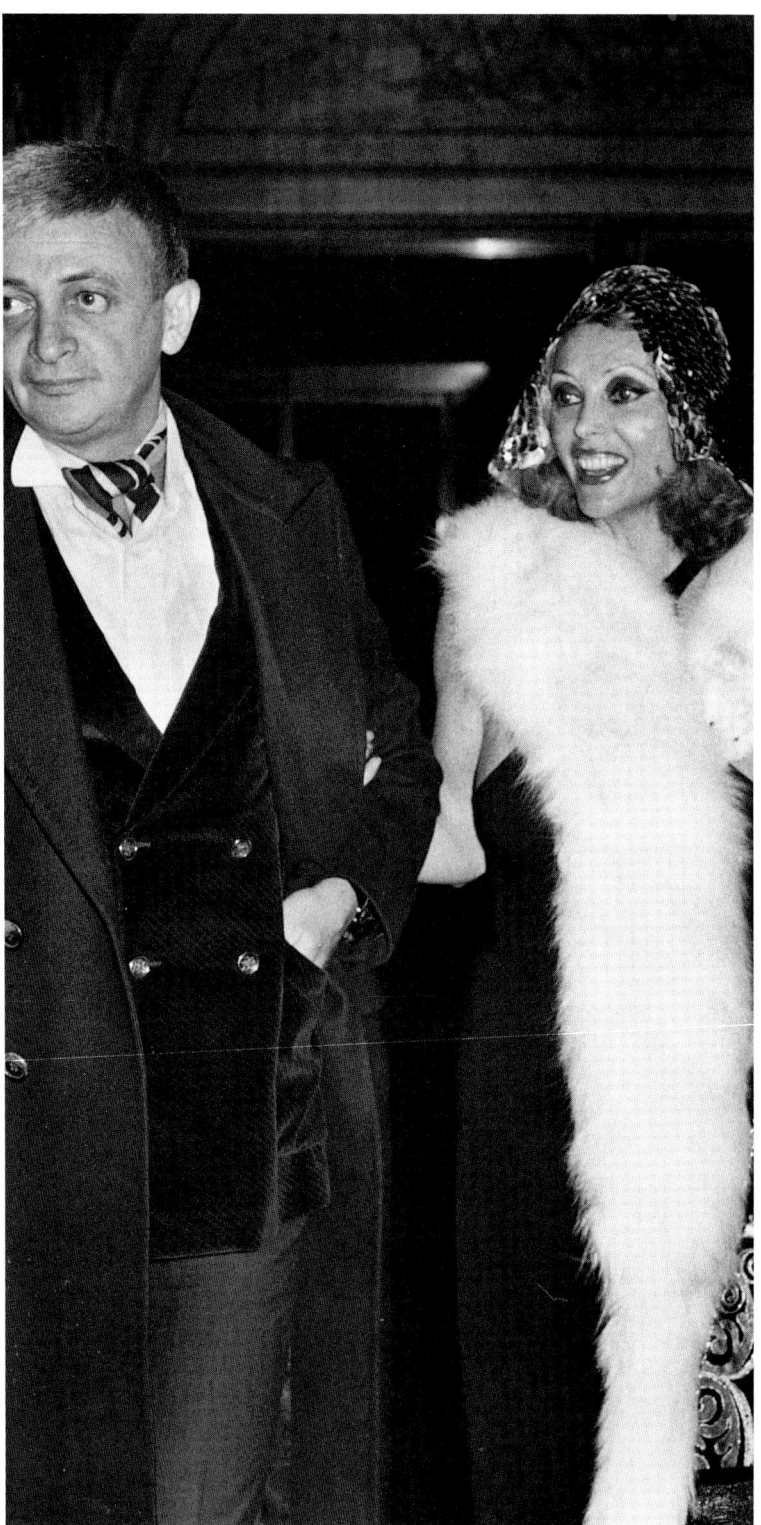

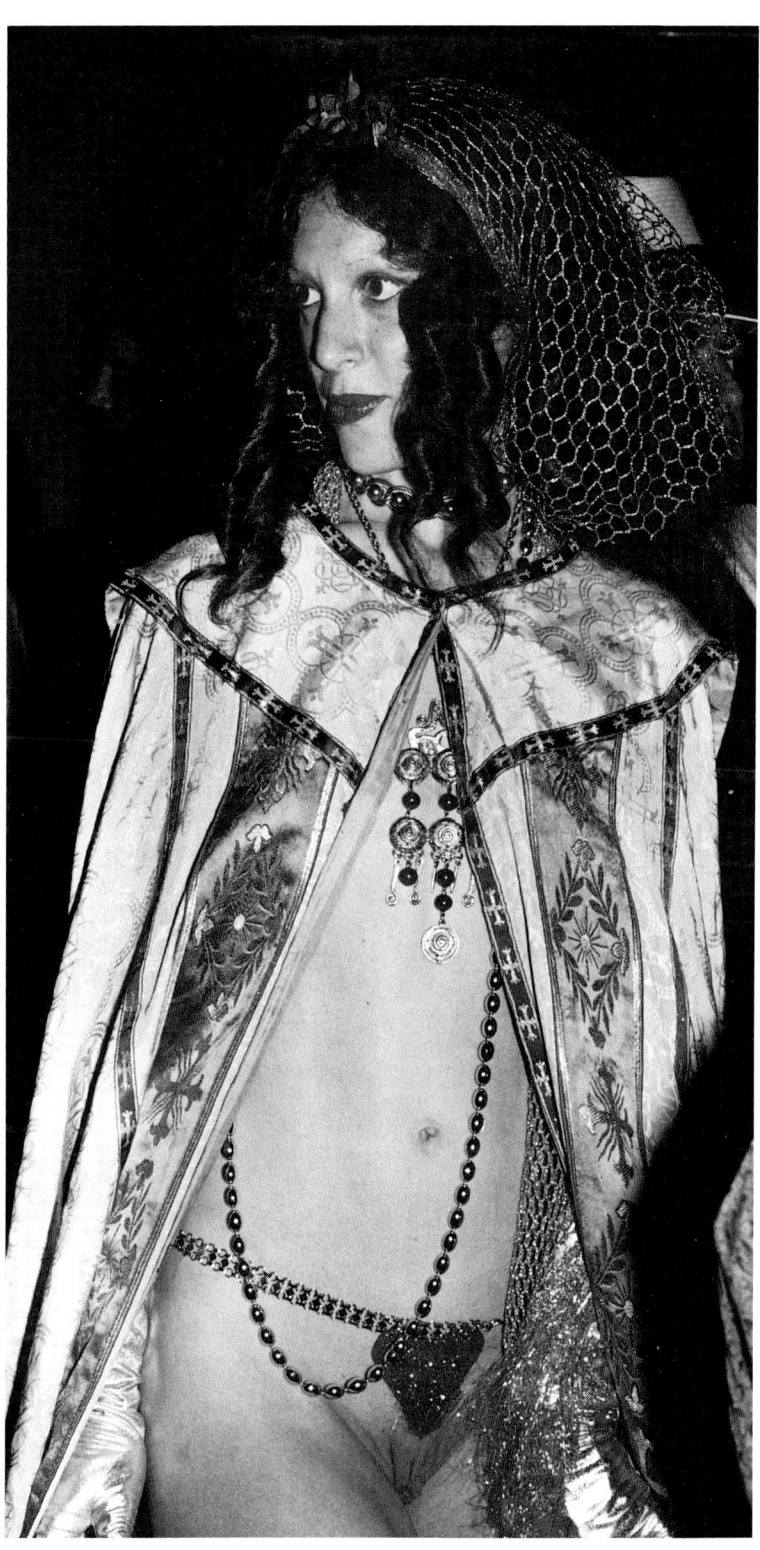

This woman was a regular sight at Studio 54 and always came decked out in costumes similar to the one shown here. Her signature style consisted of a shaved vagina, silk cape, and a Ping-Pong ball or cork protruding from her butthole, which she revealed with a flip of her cape to passersby.

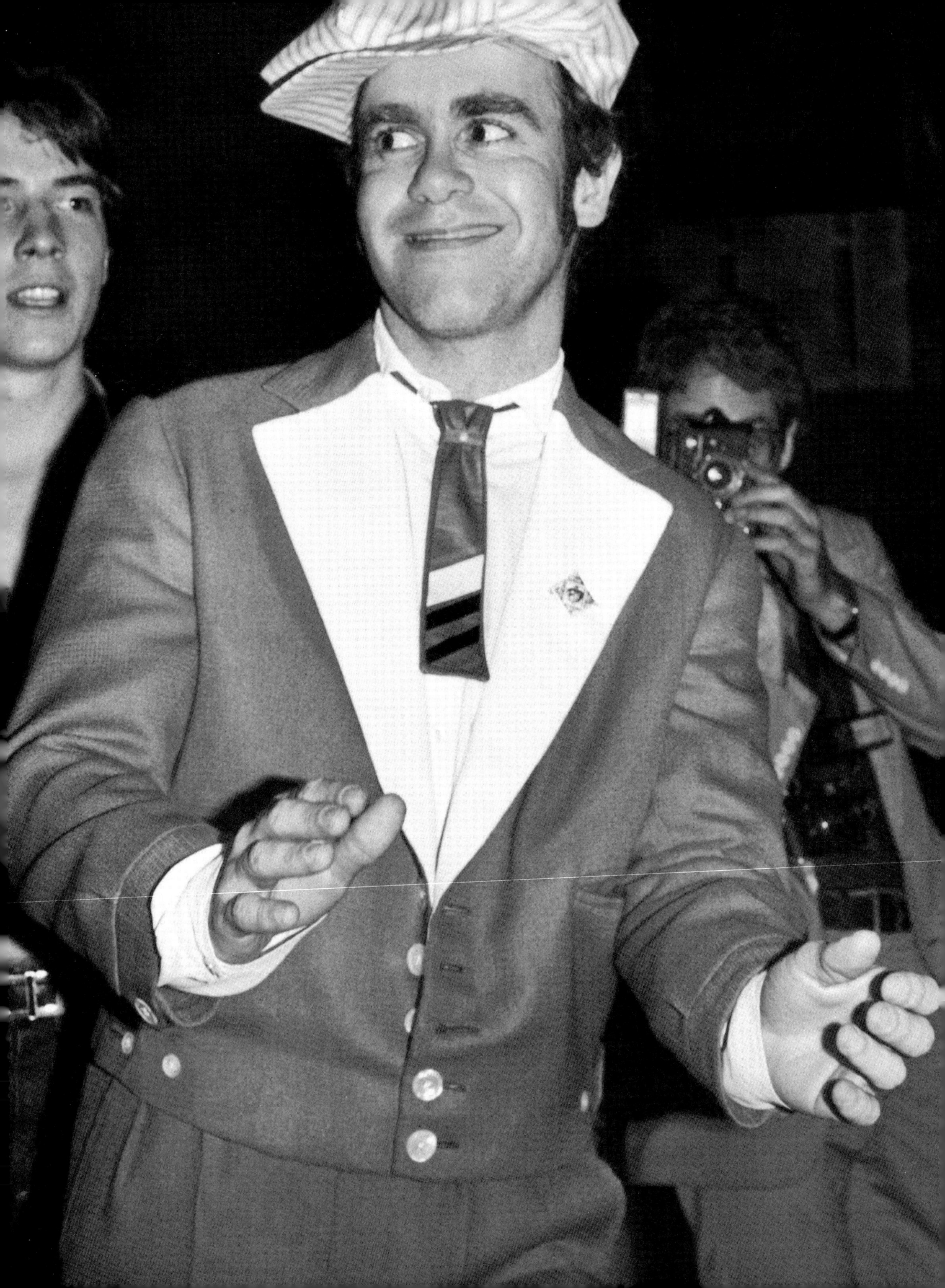

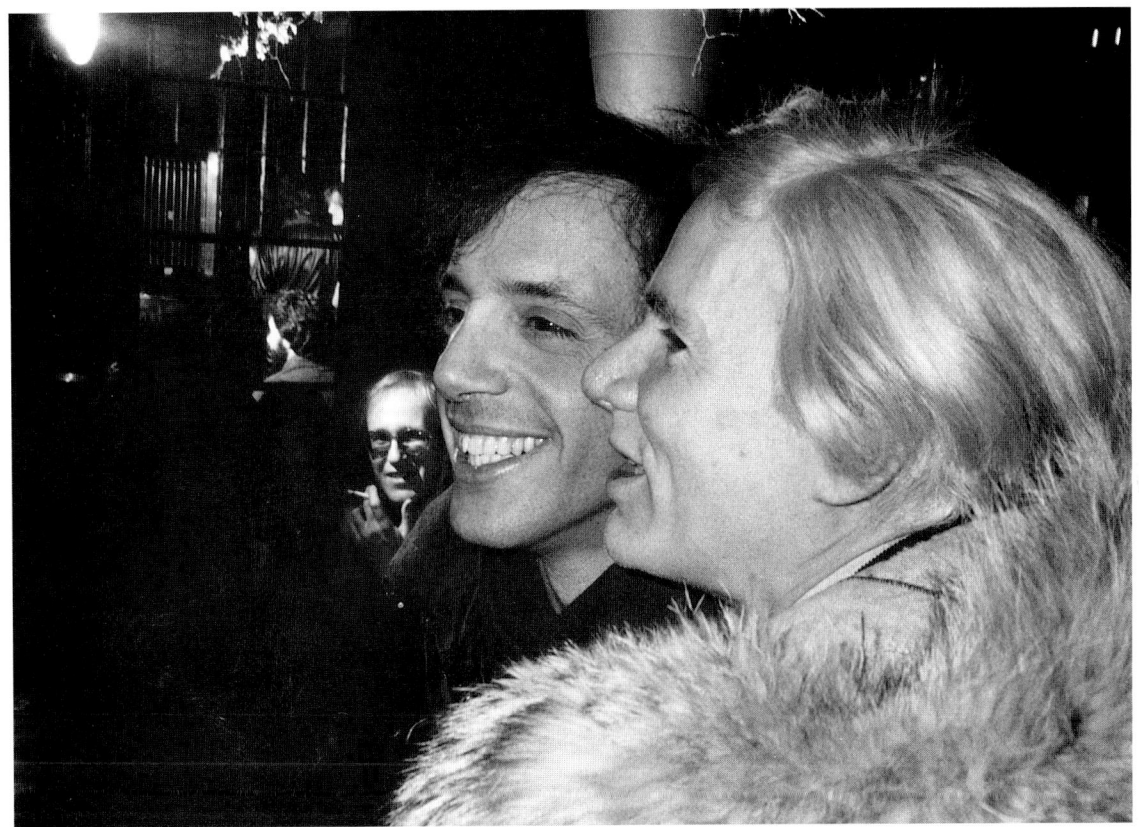

STEVE RUBELL AND ANDY WARHOL

Steve Rubell and Ian Schrager were the co-owners and masterminds of Studio 54. While Ian stayed out of the limelight, rarely showing his face at the club, Steve loved the attention and the celebrities that were Studio regulars. Here he is posing with Andy Warhol for another photographer's camera. Andy loved to have his picture taken, too, and was always an easy pose for anyone pointing a camera in his direction.

ANGEL JACK

Angel Jack was a traveling performer with the Angels of Light, a performance troupe from San Francisco founded by Hibiscus and considered part of the extended family of the Cockettes. In the late Sixties, Hibiscus and the Cockettes made underground films such as *Tricia's Wedding* and gained notoriety as hippie drag queens with glittered beards. Angel Jack always wore sequins and feathers and beautiful pumps, which made him well over six feet tall and quite surreal. He survived the Seventies and was often seen in the nightclubs of the Eighties, still wearing the same simple, but brilliantly glamorous, costumes.

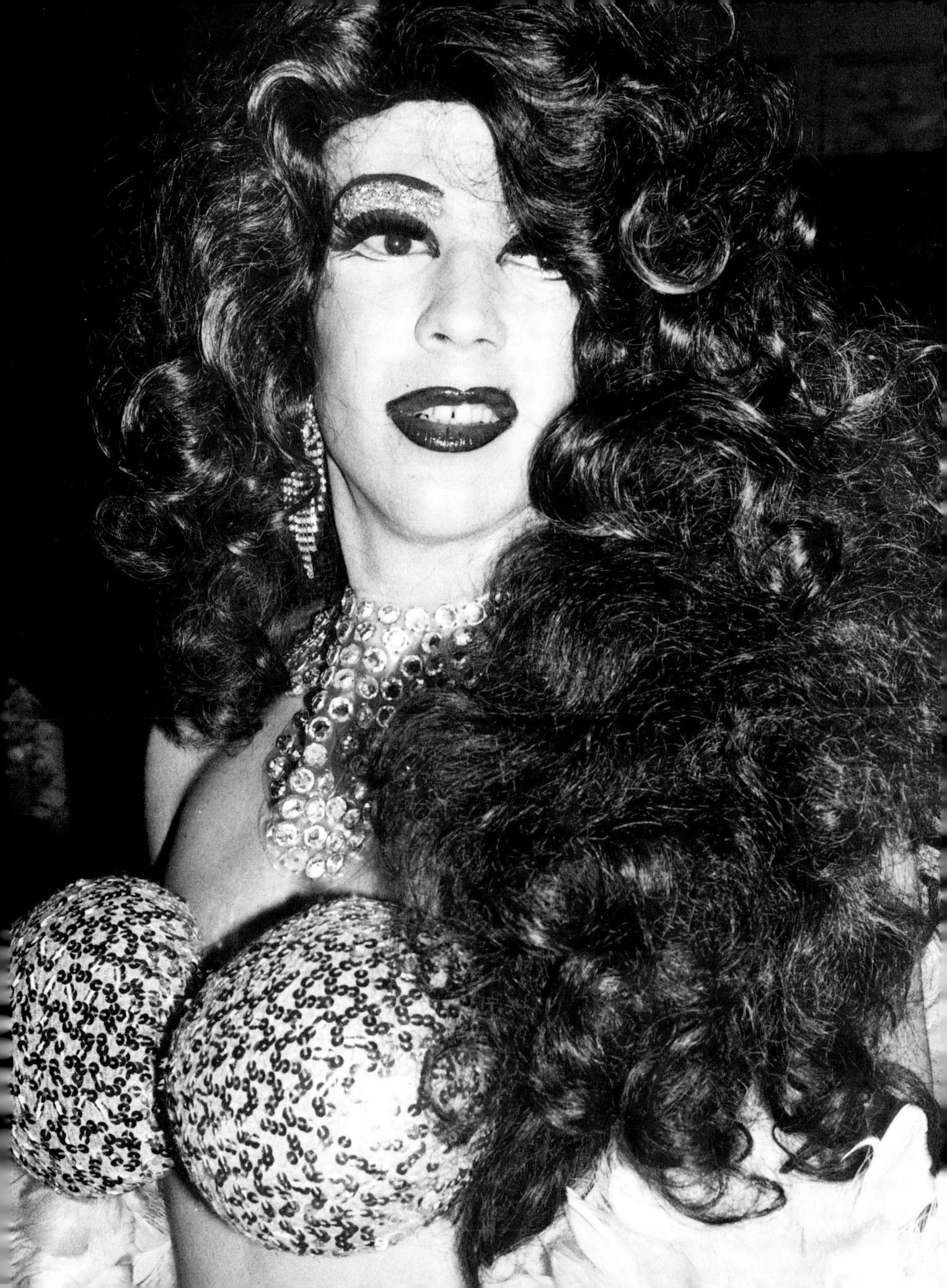

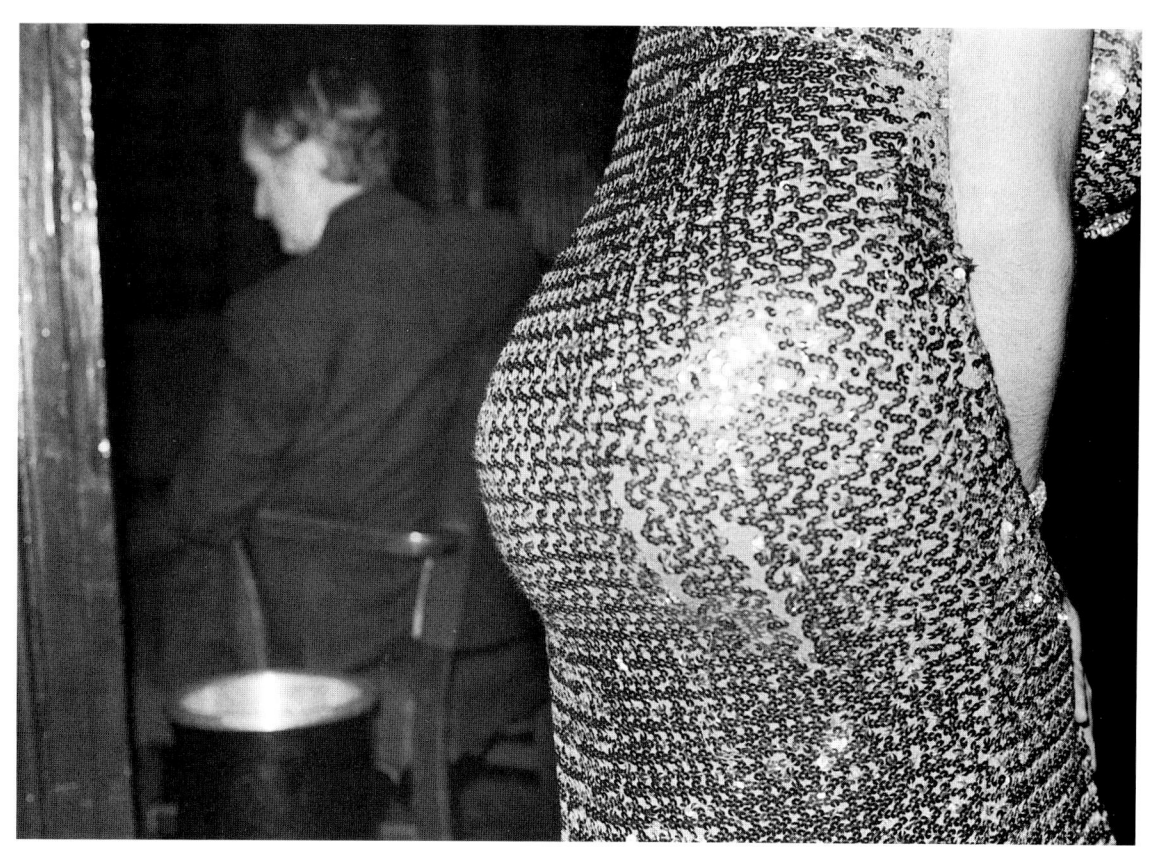

ANGEL JACK

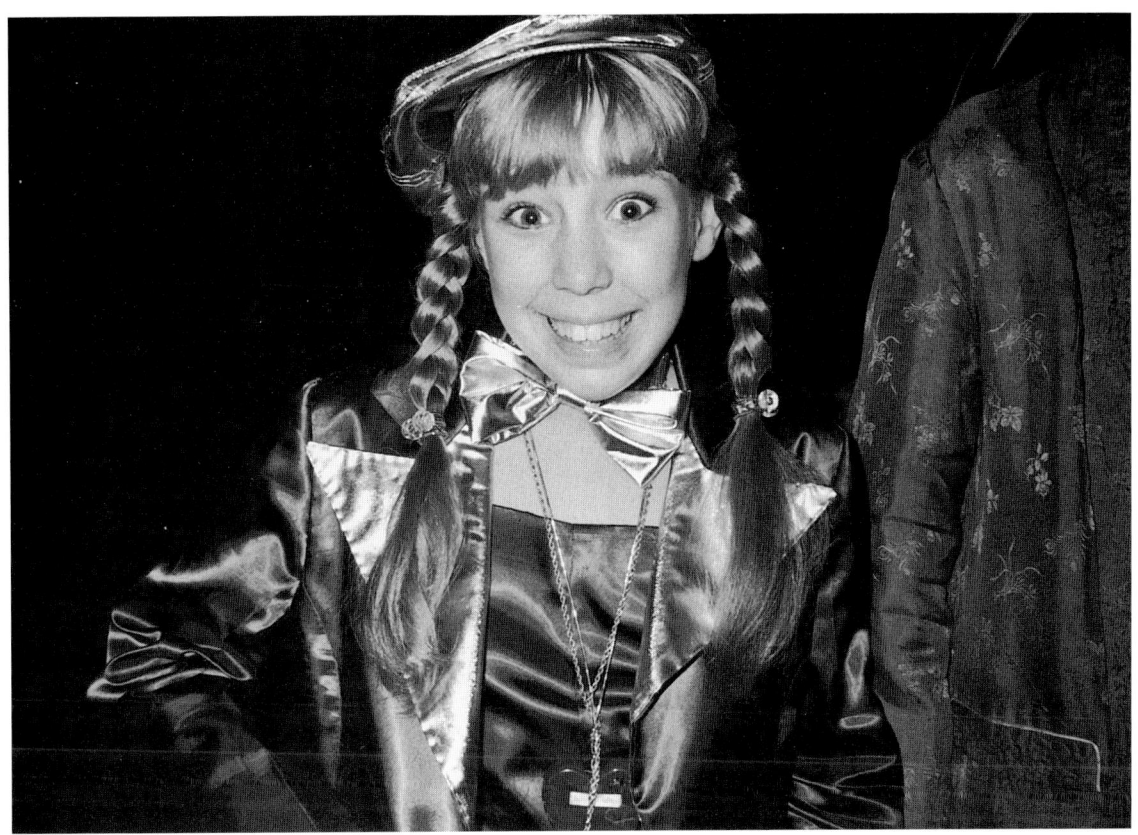

Children were rarely seen at Studio, but Diana Barrows, an actress from the original Broadway production of *Annie*, was most welcome. As the paparazzi surrounded her to take her picture, she posed easily and purposefully while her guardian waited by her side. Her radiance and energy mirrored the excitement seen in the faces of adults after an evening at Studio.

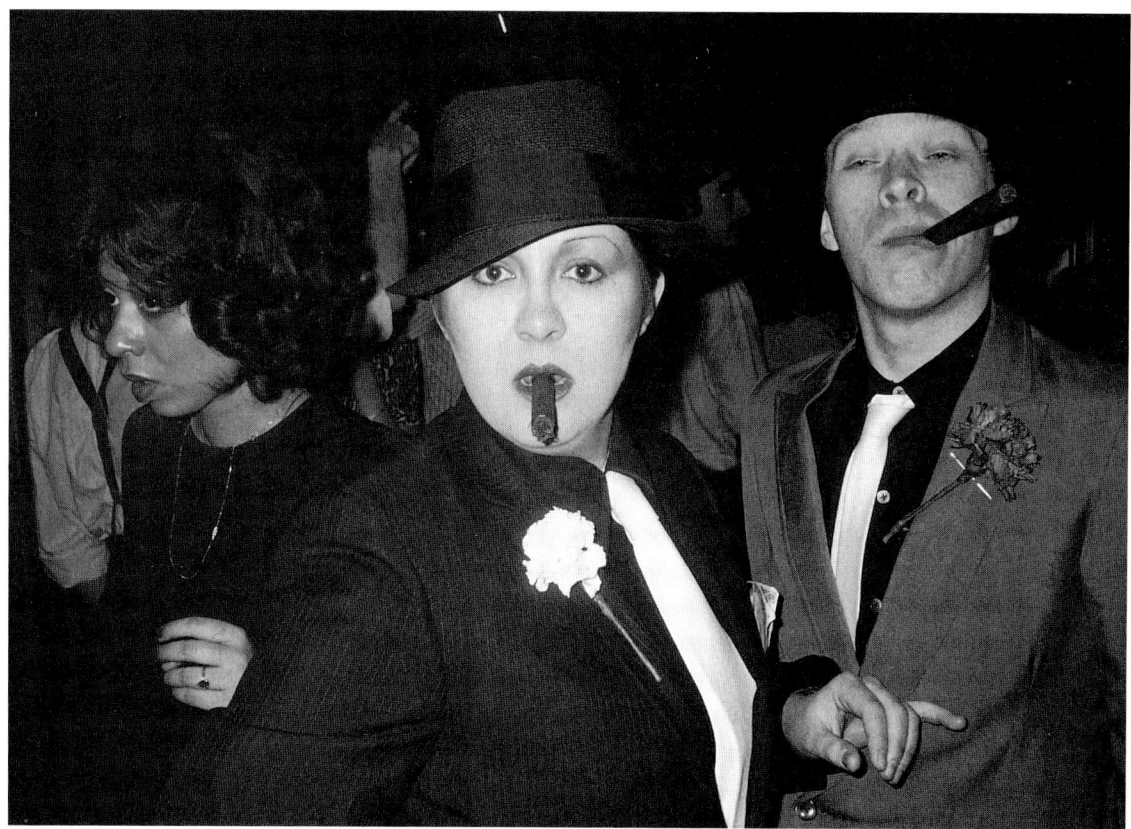

MIRA AND MATTHEW

Mira and Matthew were the original club kids. Mira was a design student and Matthew a young budding photographer, but at nighttime they were fixtures at Studio, arriving each evening dressed in a different theme. They always stayed in character throughout the night, sporting accents and actions to match the evening's persona. They were amazing and fresh and everyone loved them. On one occasion they set up camp in the middle of the dance floor, complete with pup tent, Sterno campfire, sleeping bags, and pajamas. At the end of the night, after the dance floor had thinned out, they extinguished their campfire, crawled into their sleeping bags, and went to sleep. I was fortunate to photograph them in so many different costumes, and they always gave the camera their best. Here they are as gangsters, as tennis players, as early NYC punks, as terrorists, and as symbols of young Hollywood.

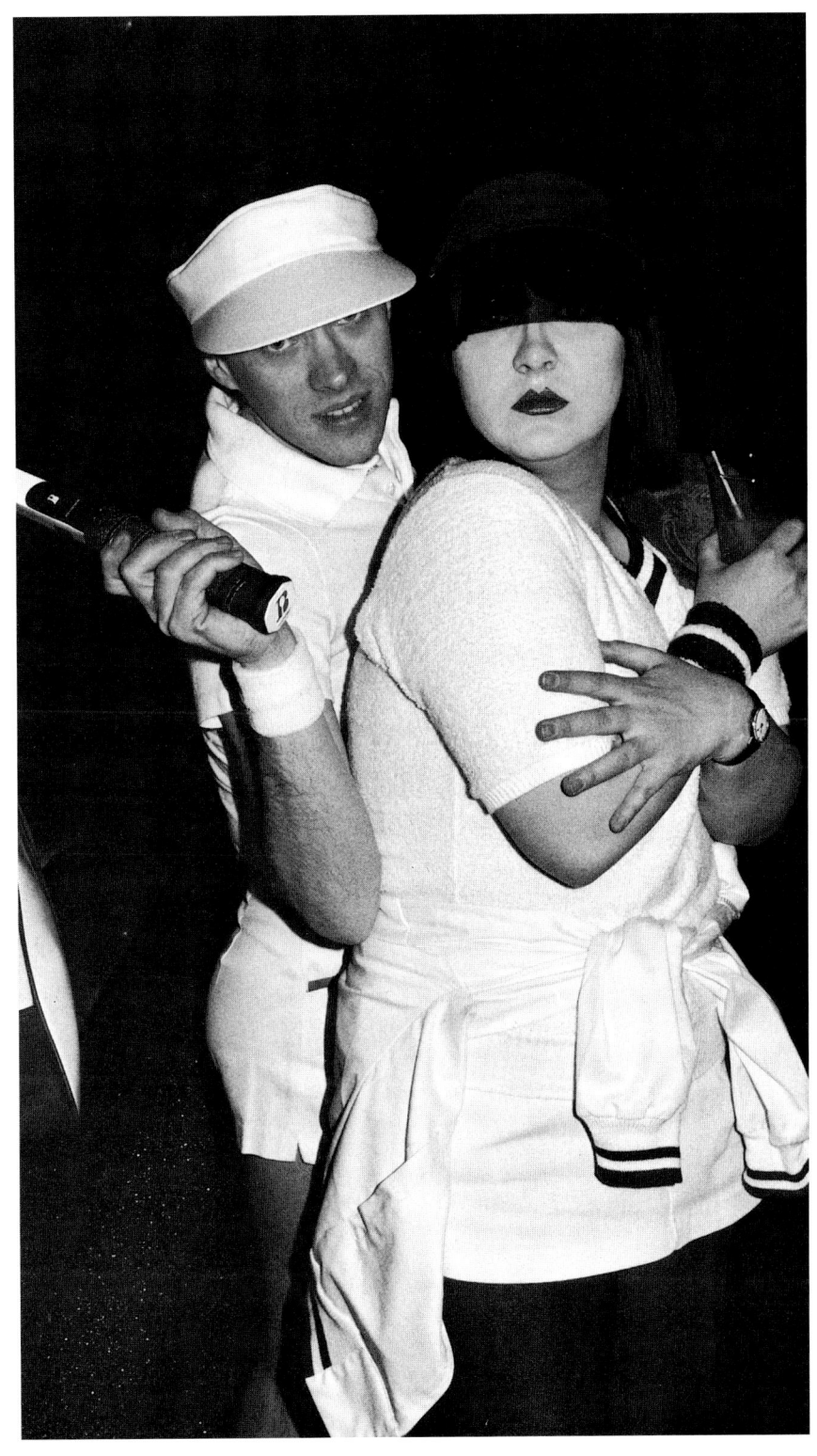

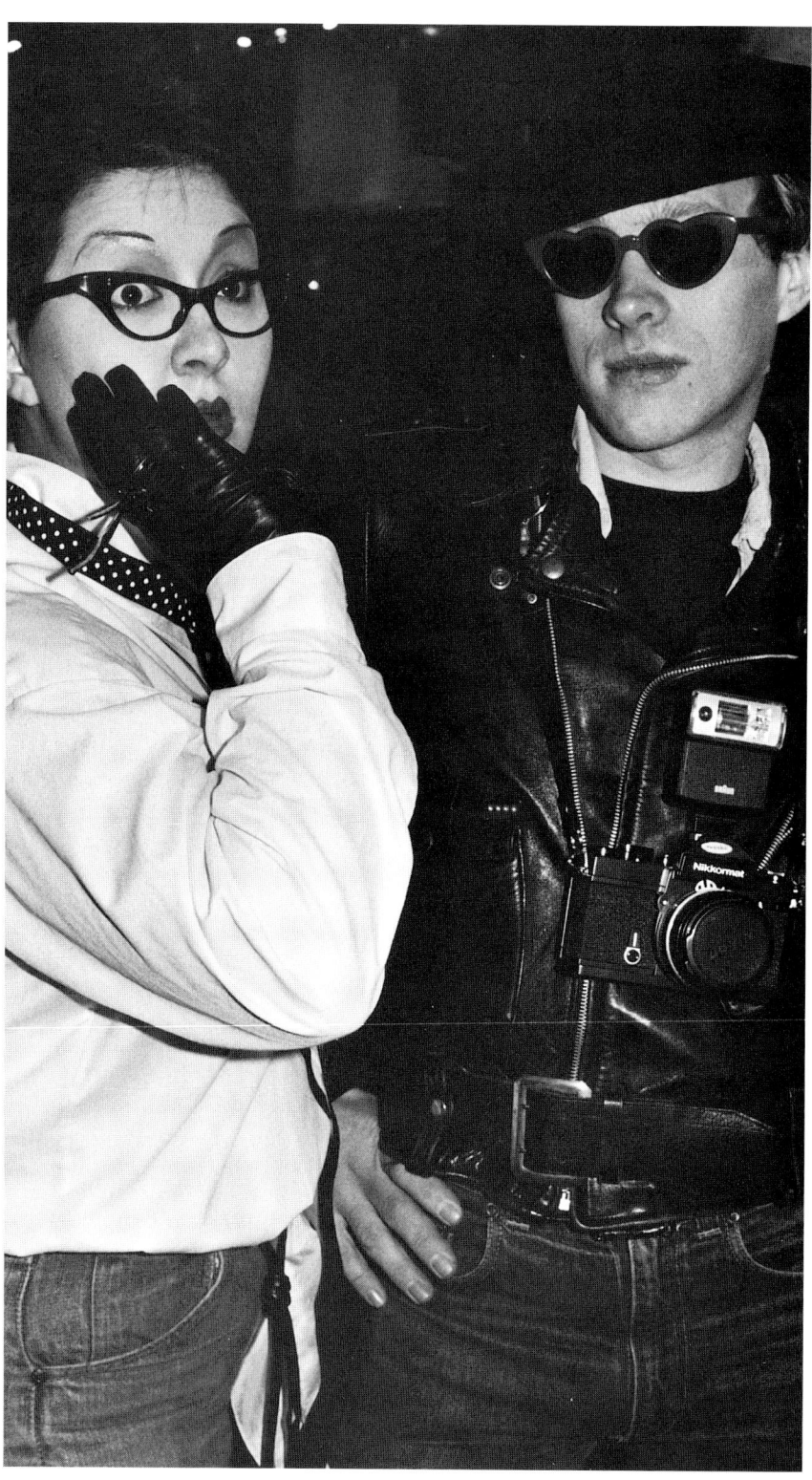

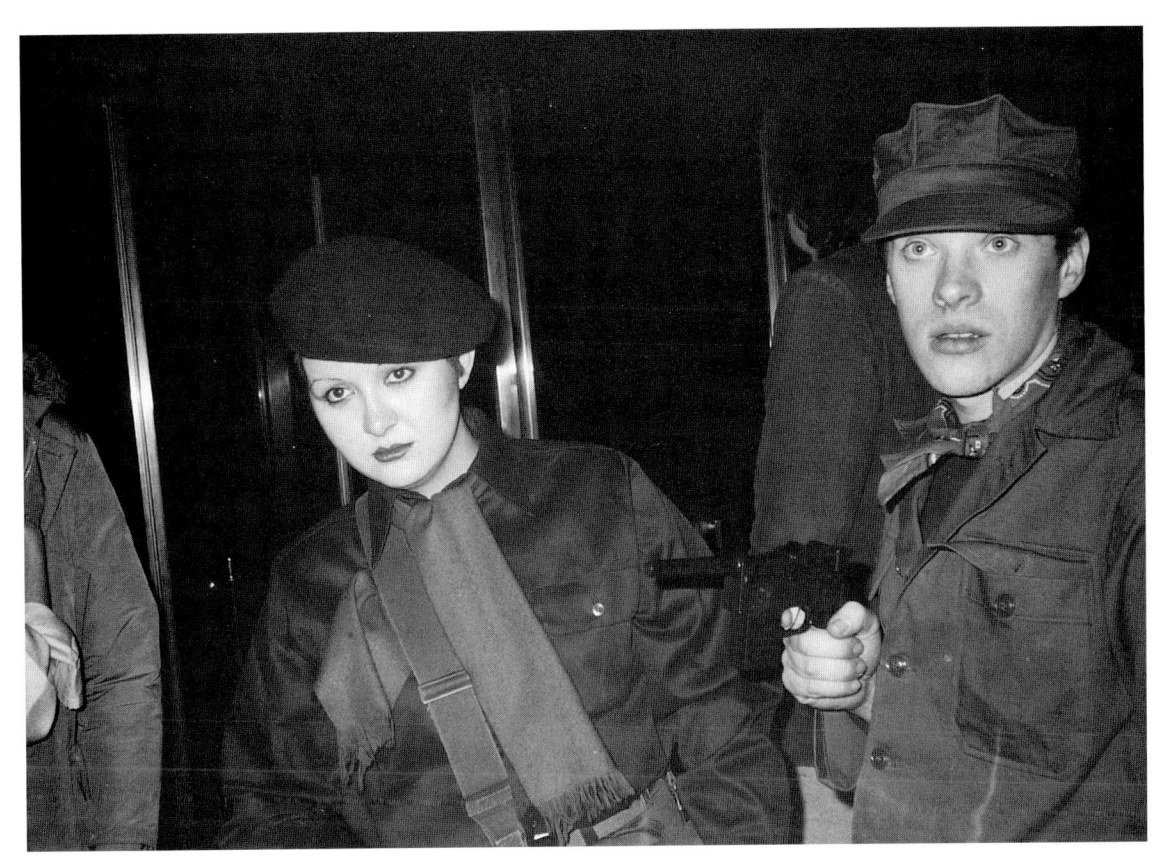

MIRA AND MATTHEW

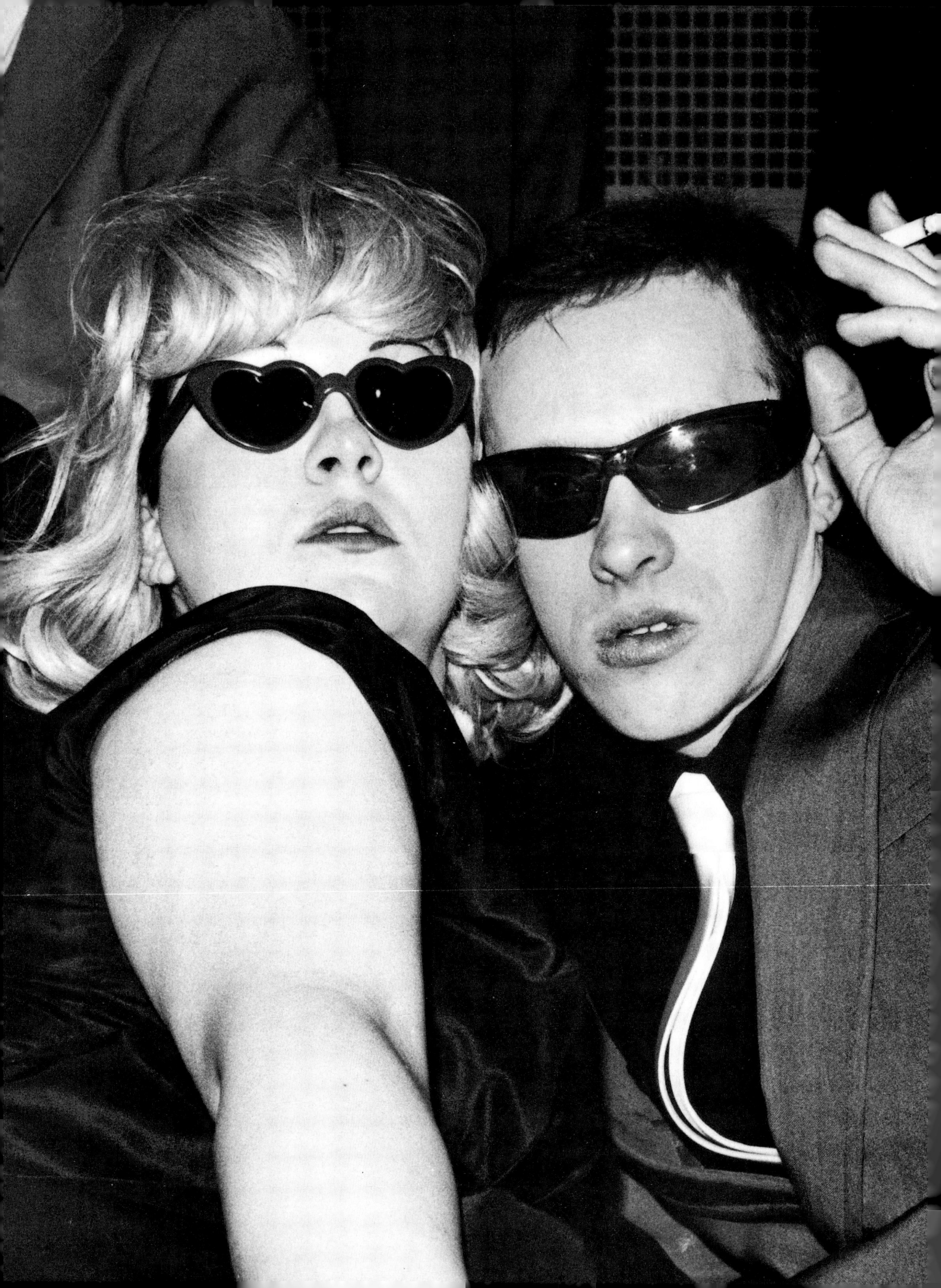

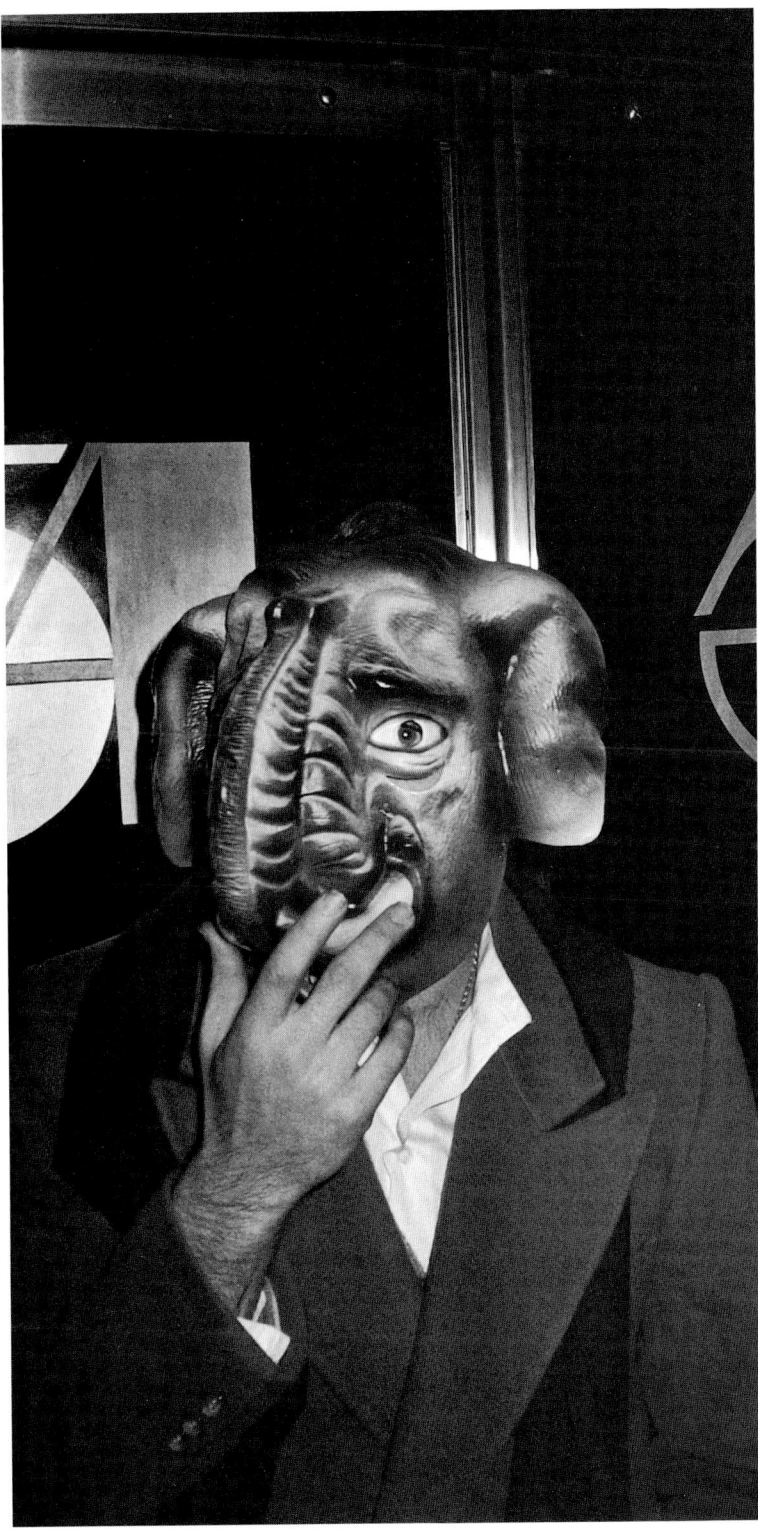

Taken after a gallery opening that featured Peter Beard's exquisite photographs of African elephants, this picture captures a special guest arriving through the Studio doors. The man behind the mask is a world-famous fashion designer who creates couture clothing for most of the world's wealthiest women. He was an icon in the Sixties, Seventies, Eighties, and is still an active force in the fashion industry. He is Italian by birth and best known for his signature evening wear and classic sophisticated suits. Do you know his name? If you guessed Valentino, you'd be correct.

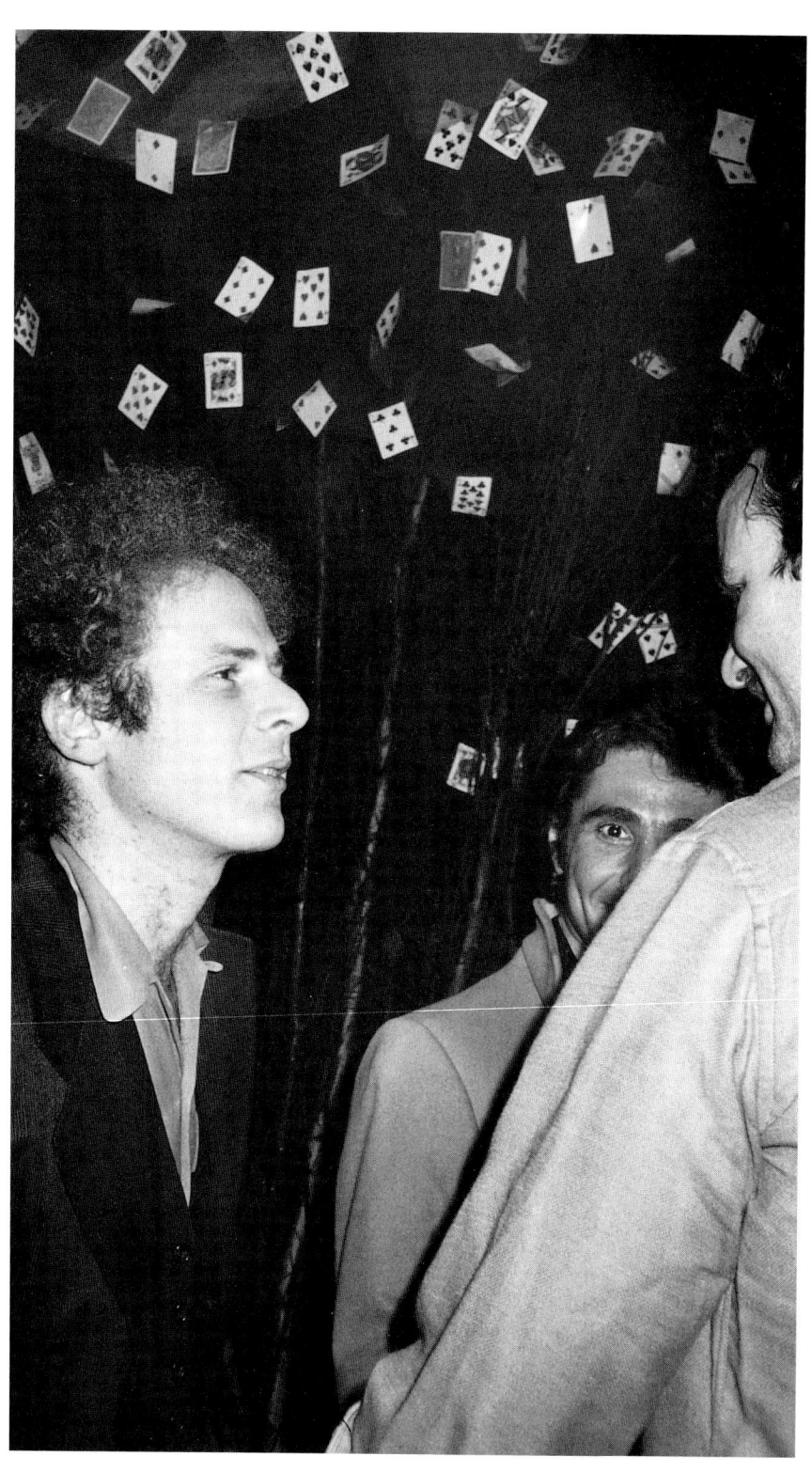

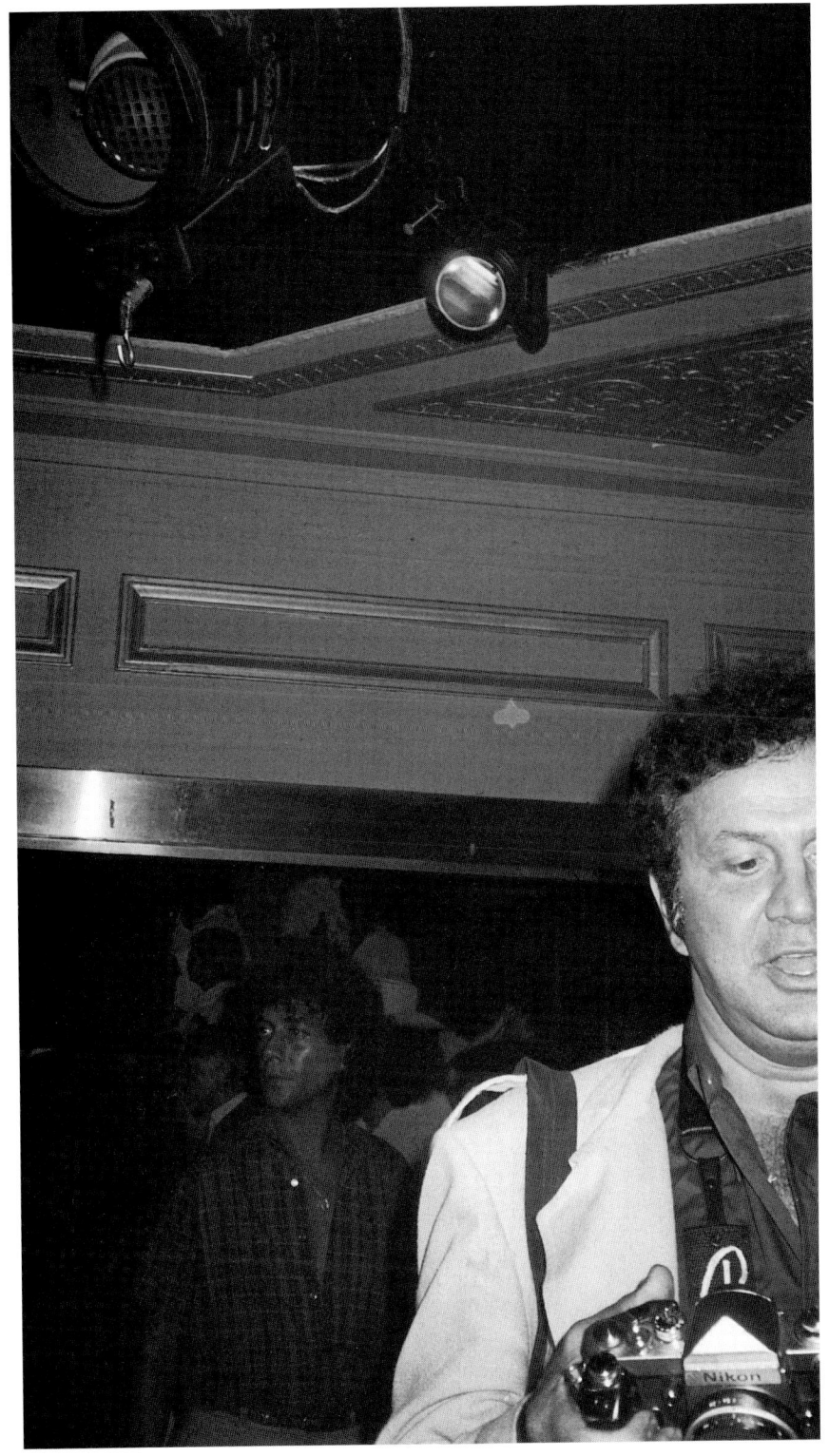

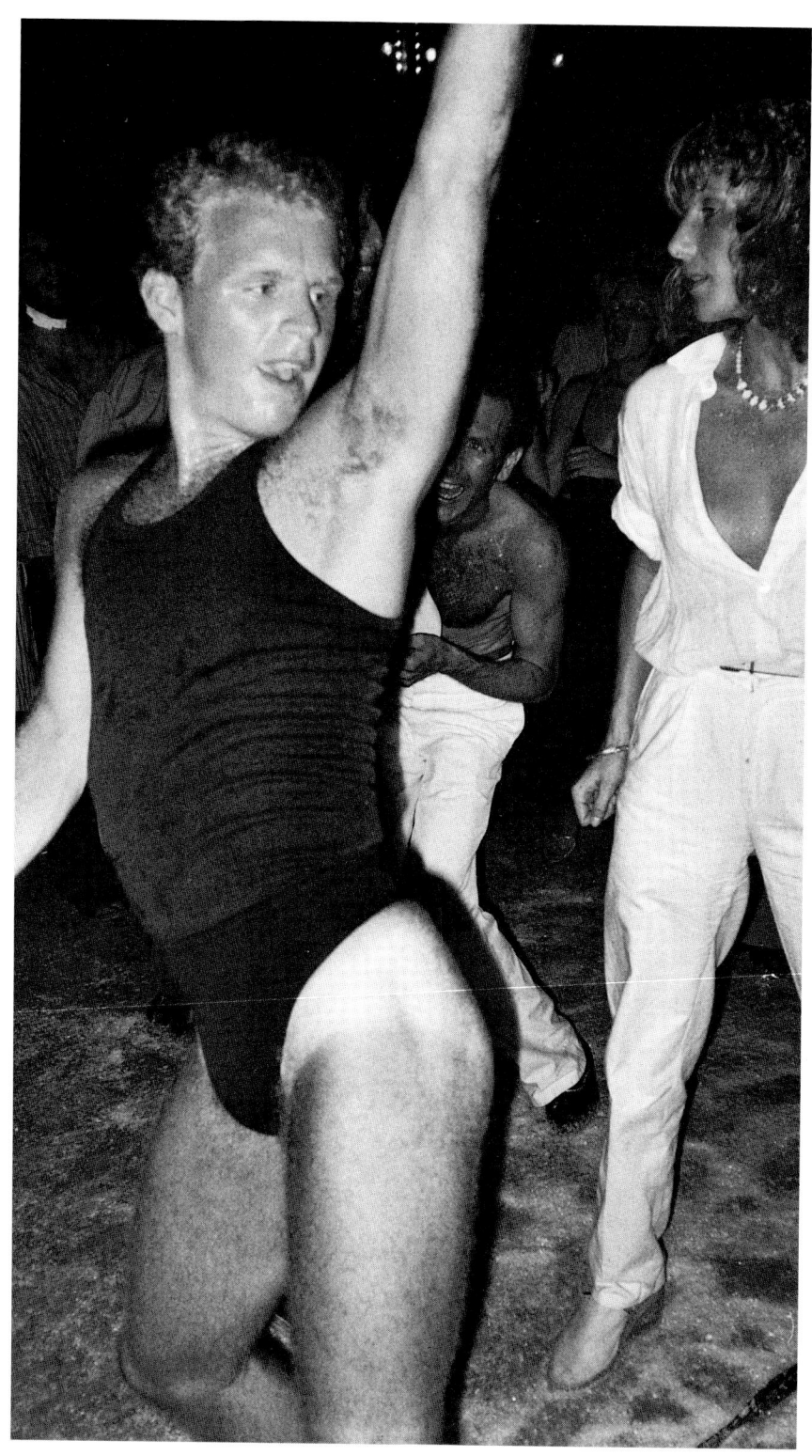

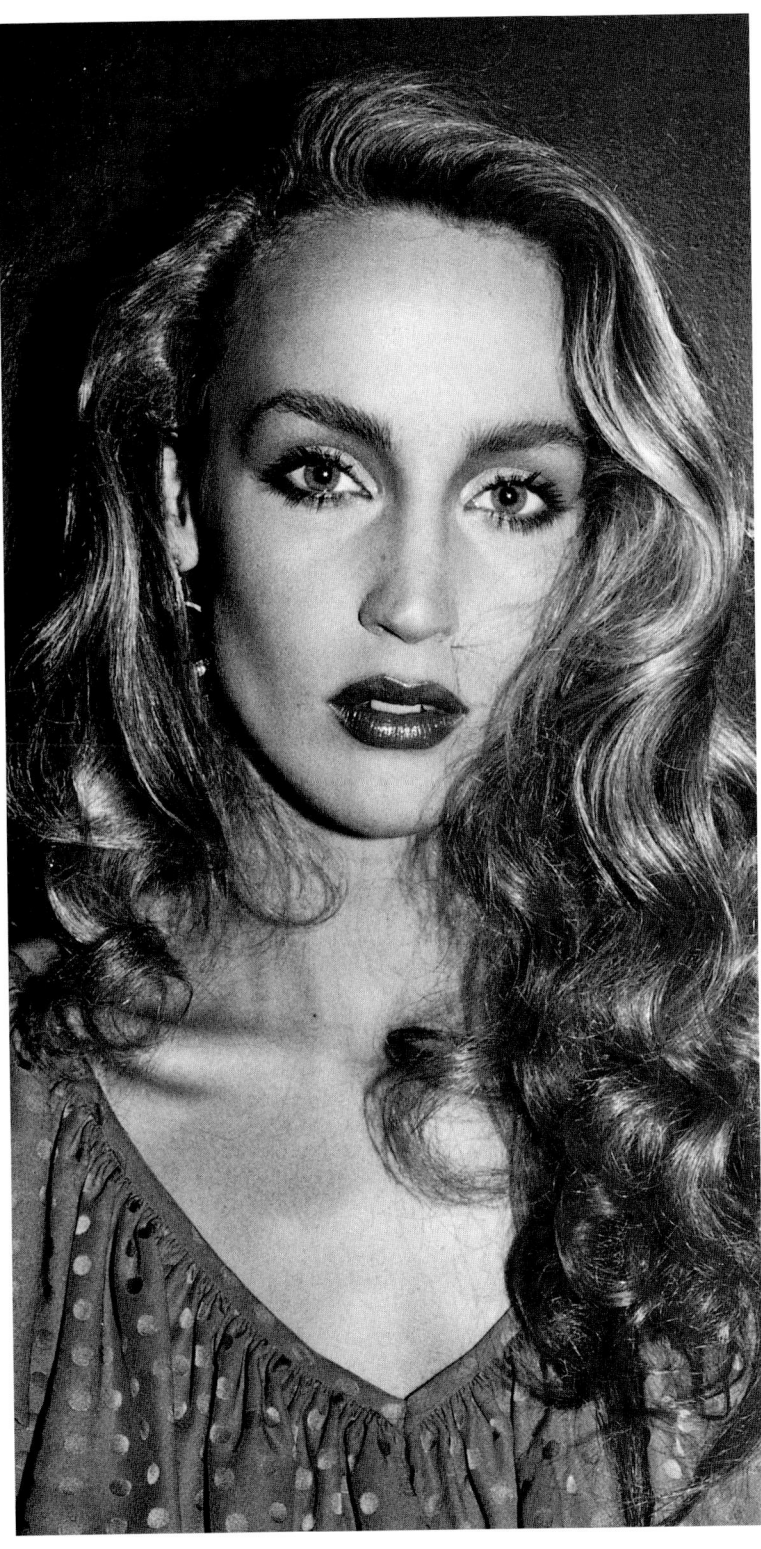

In 1977 Jerry Hall was the most beautiful woman in the world. At sixteen, she had gone to Paris to become a famous fashion model and succeeded beyond her wildest imagination. Jerry had what it took to make it in a business that chewed girls up and spit them out. I found her to be a generous and sweet-natured girl who loved a good time out and a turn on the dance floor. I met her early in her career and knew her when she was in love with singer Bryan Ferry, long before she met and fell for Mick.

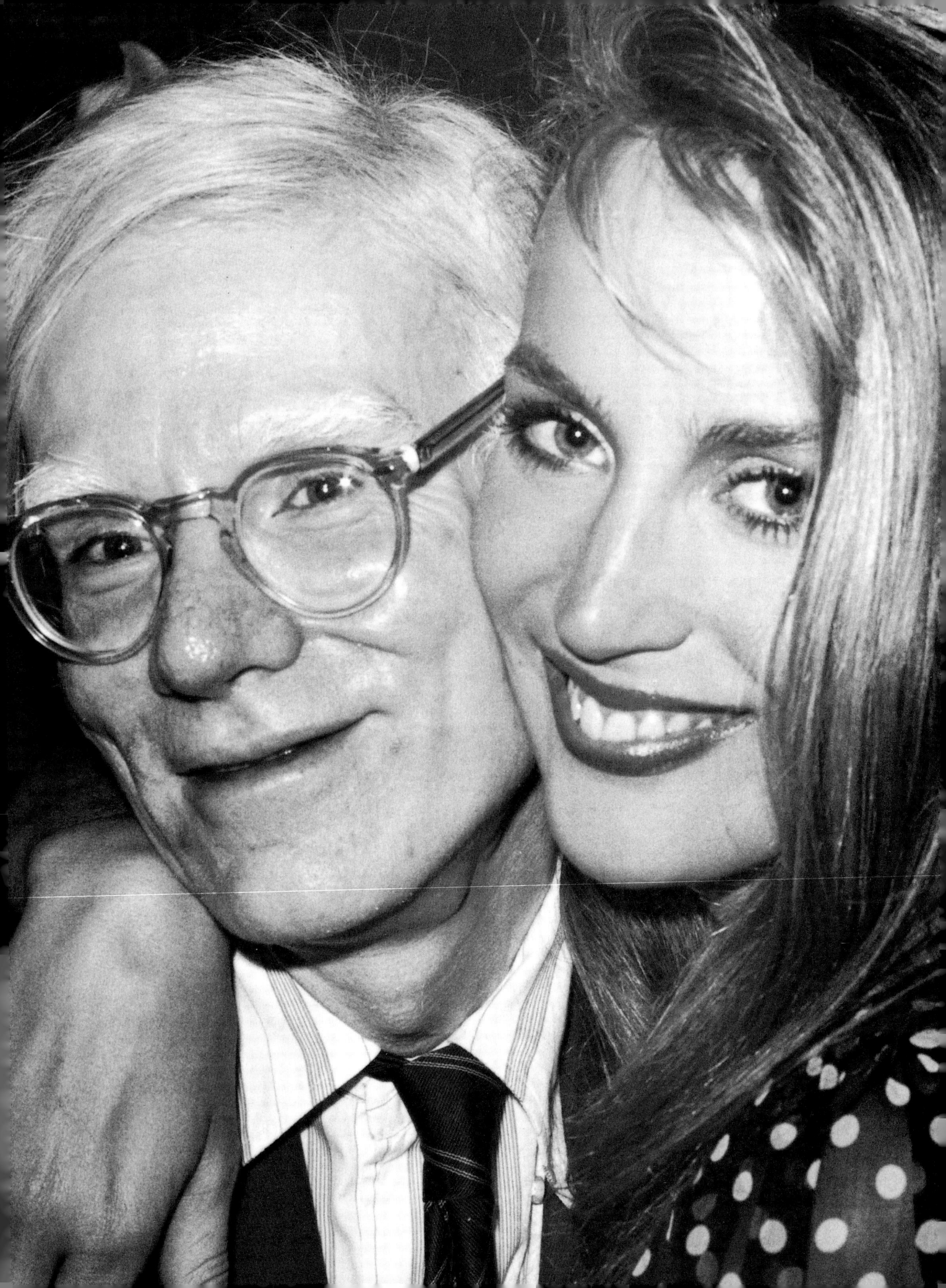

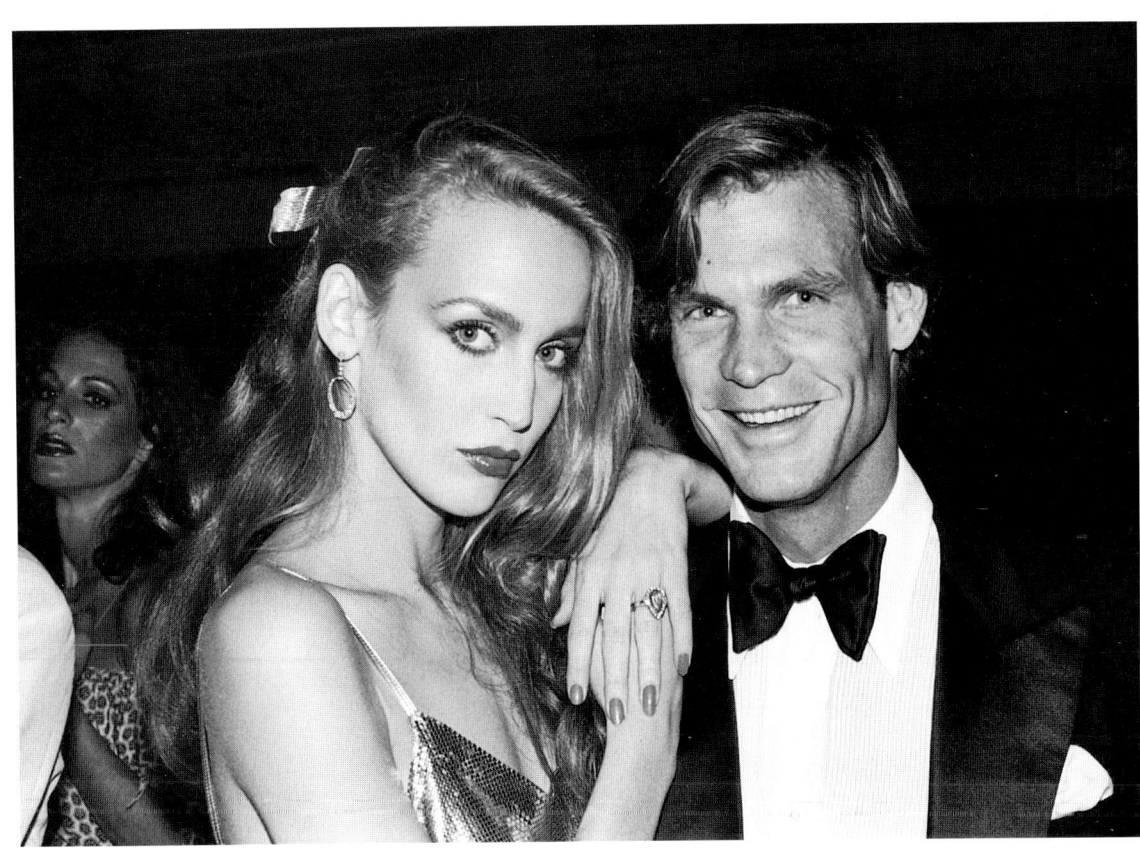

Jerry Hall and Joe McDonald were the two most famous models of the Seventies. Sadly Joe passed away in the early Eighties, but at the time of his death he was one of the highest paid and most recognized male models in the business. Together he and Jerry were the true essence and embodiment of the original supermodels.

OPPOSITE: JERRY HALL AND ANDY WARHOL

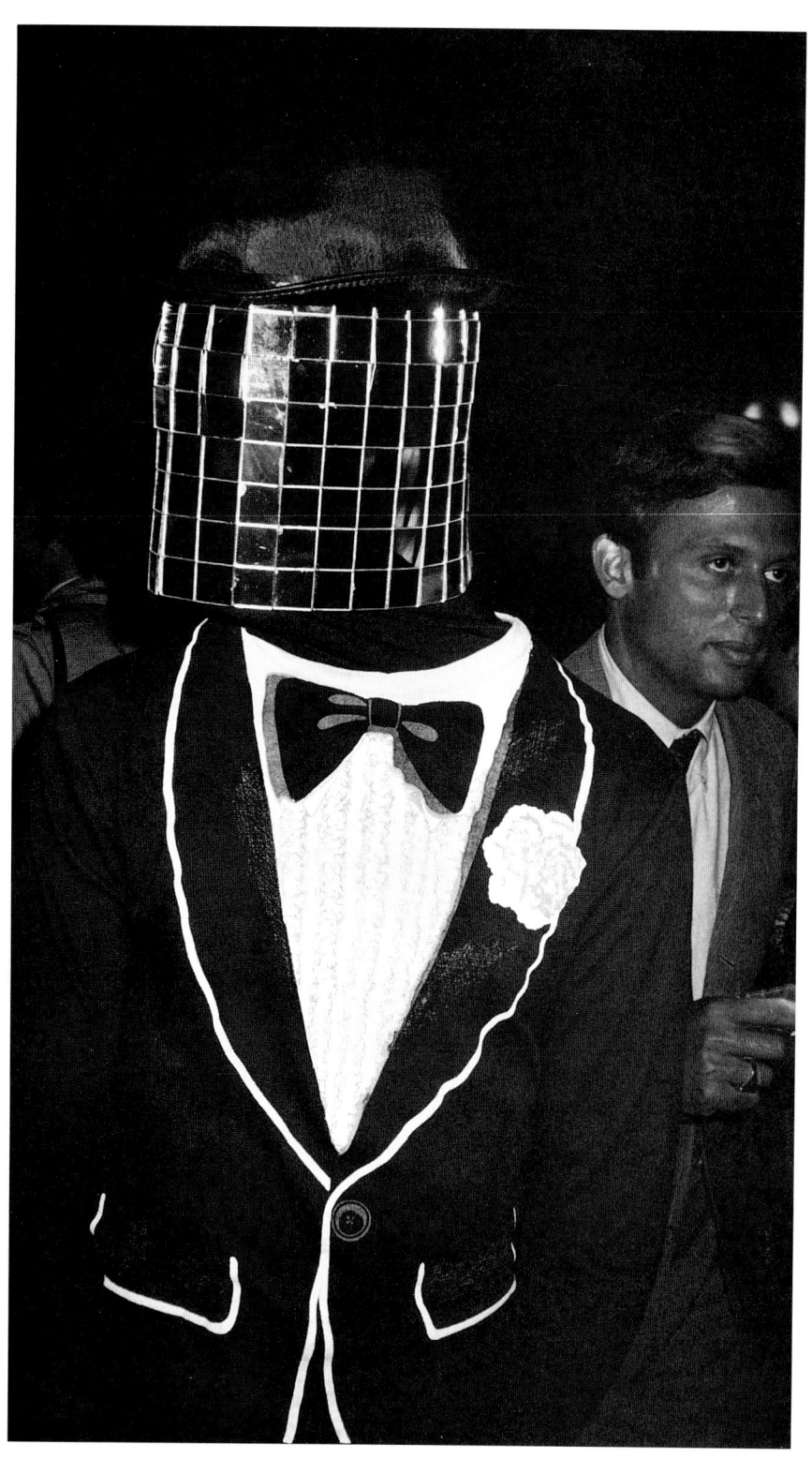

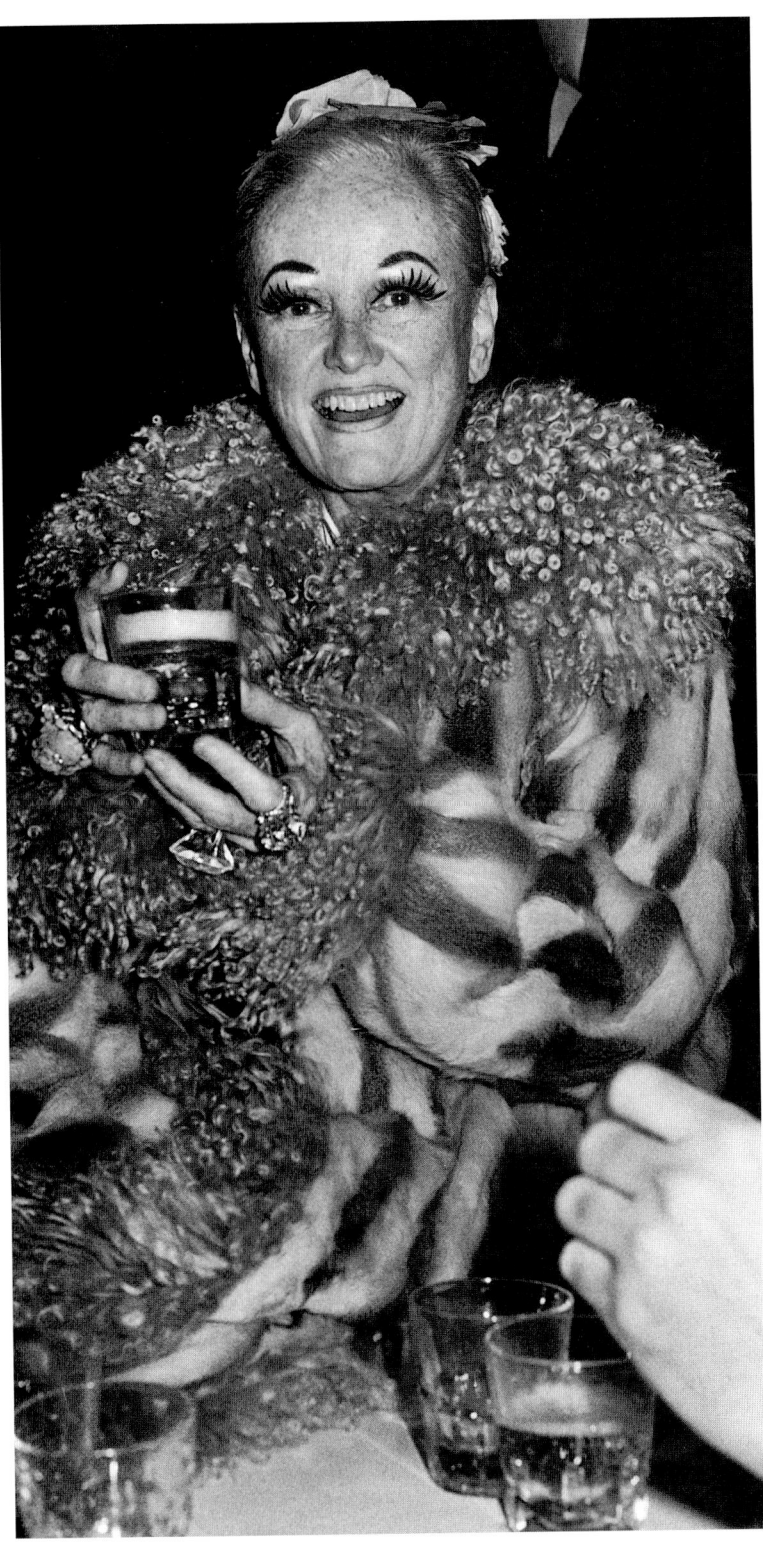

This photo was taken at the premiere party for the movie *Grease*. For effect, the promoters brought in thirty vintage Fifties automobiles, which they parked throughout the club. People dressed in period costume adorned the front and back seats, necking and making out while Phyllis sat on top of an old yellow Checker cab, drinking a beer and holding court. At the end of the evening, in true star fashion, she got into the very same cab and was driven out of the club and taken home.

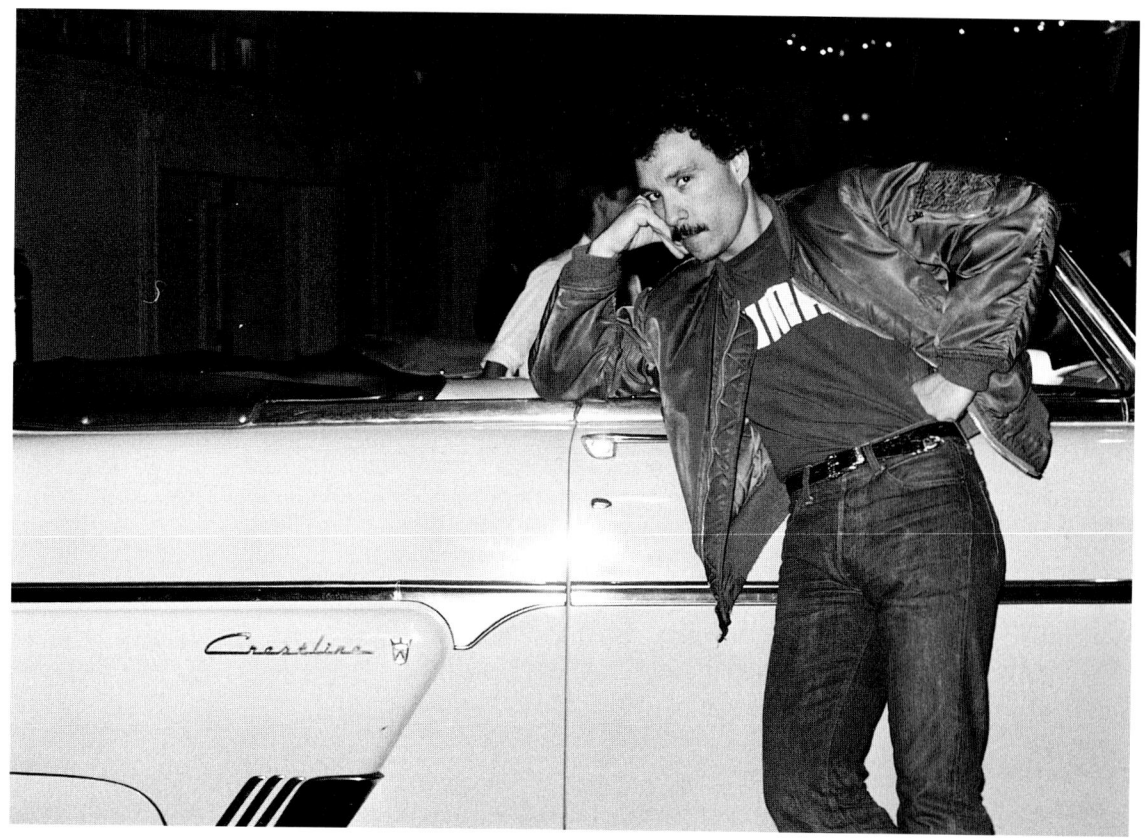

ANTONIO LOPEZ

The gifted and talented fashion illustrator Antonio Lopez's work appeared in most of the finest fashion magazines of the Seventies. Puerto Rican by birth and raised in Manhattan, Lopez moved to Paris in the early Seventies, where he met and drew Jerry Hall, Grace Jones, and Pat Cleveland, just to name a few. His beautiful drawings of these women helped them to create their unique looks, and his work contributed greatly to their success as supermodels. Sadly, Antonio passed away in the early Eighties.

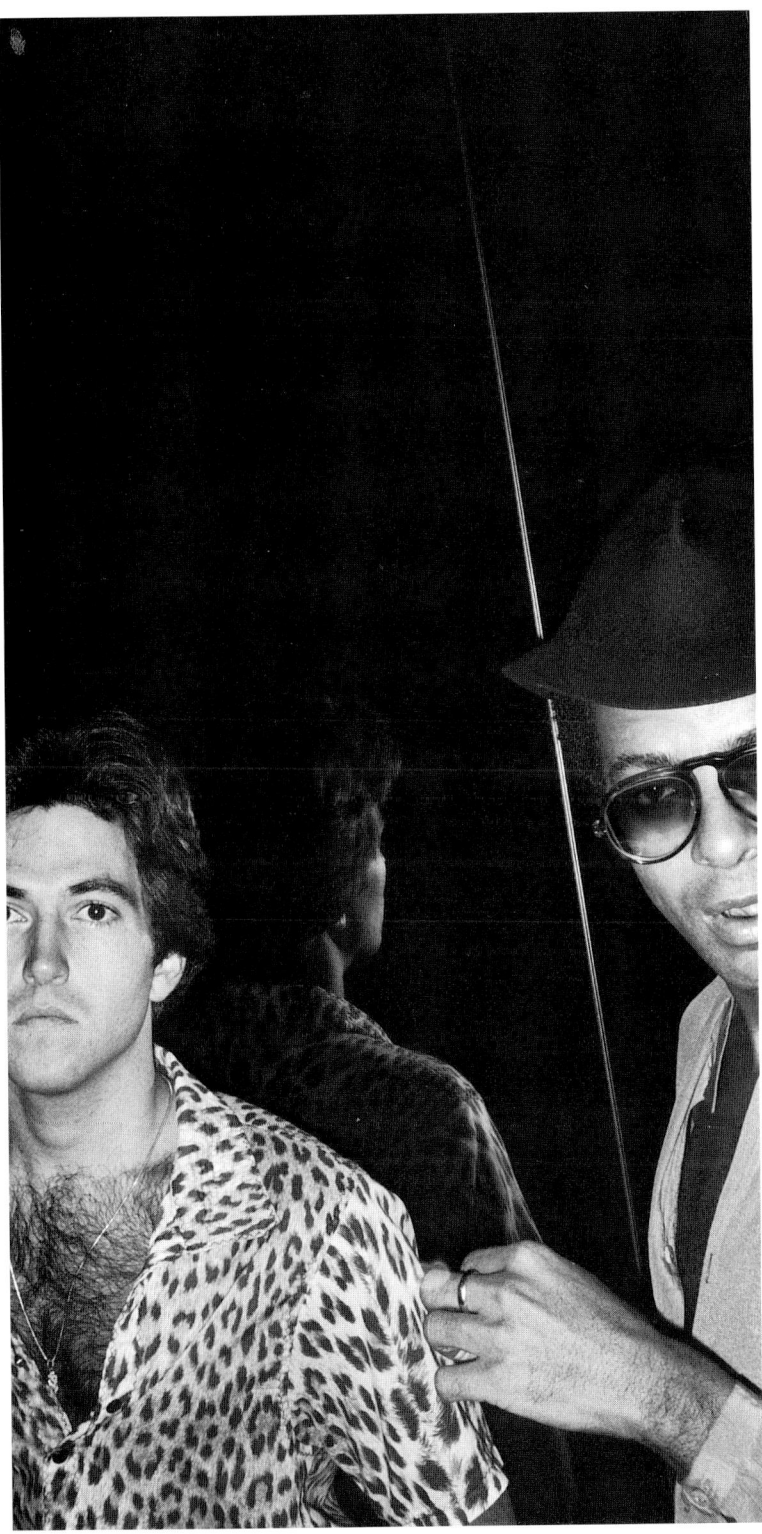

Stephen Burrows was one of the major alternative fashion designers of the Seventies who went mainstream. After success on Seventh Avenue, with his own line being sold at better department stores like Bergdorf's and Bendel's, his career simply fizzled. Still, he was an innovative artist who created and popularized certain styles that became a part of American fashion history. He disappeared from the fashion scene during the Eighties.

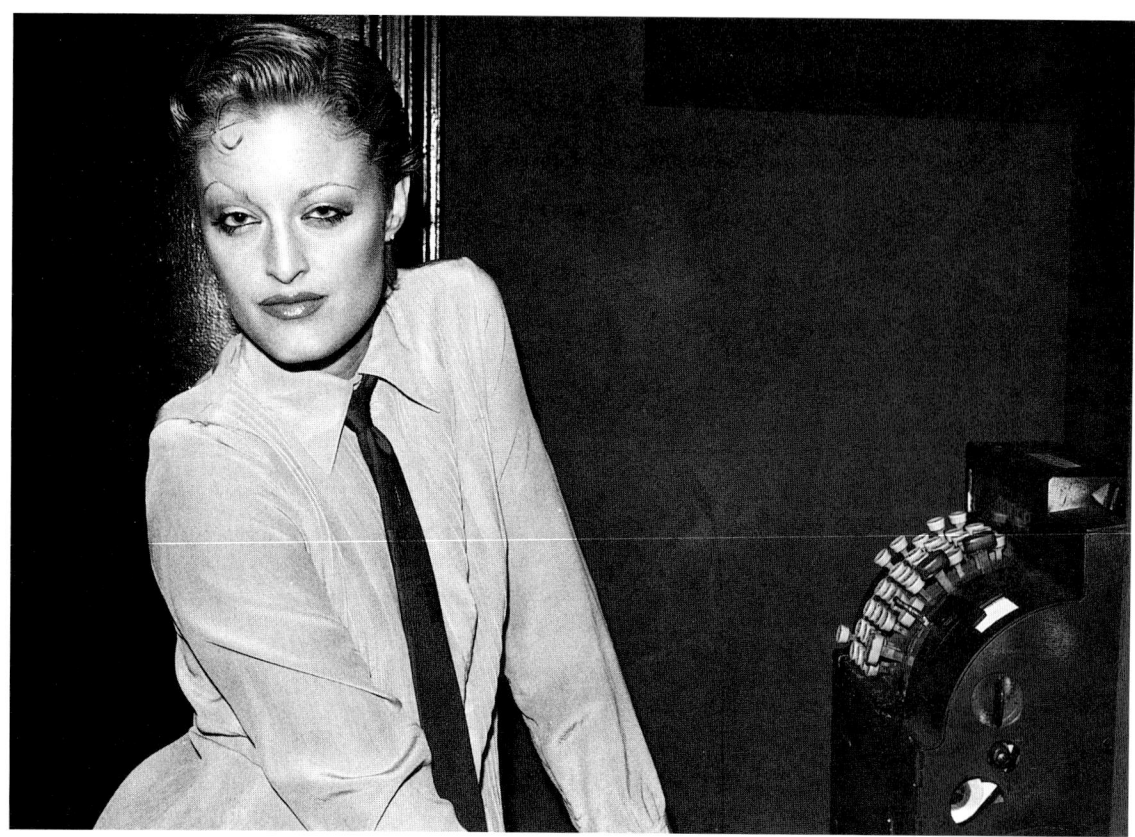

AMINA

With its many celebrities, Studio produced a host of celebrity hopefuls. Night after night young people came from all over to be "discovered." With perfect makeup and dramatic style, these would-be stars captured the eye and interest of many. This photo is of Amina, a green-eyed beauty who was a regular at the club. This was a staged photo shoot, set up in an alcove with an old cash register that was no longer in use. It wasn't unusual to see similar mock shoots going on all over the club.

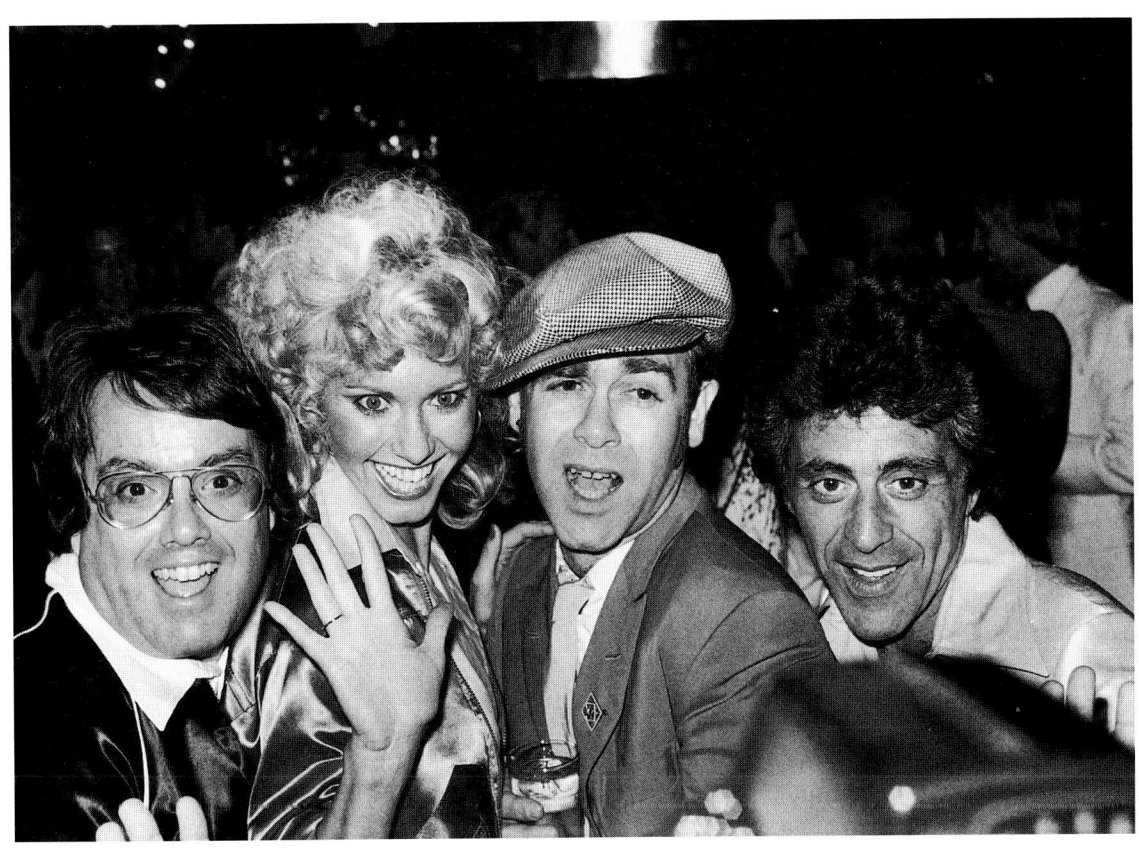

ALLAN CARR, OLIVIA NEWTON-JOHN, ELTON JOHN, AND FRANKIE VALLI

The cast party for *Grease* was one of the most colorful parties held at Studio 54. Allan Carr was one of the movie's producers, Olivia Newton-John the star, Frankie Valli sang the title song, and Elton John just came to help celebrate. This captured moment in front of another photographer's camera epitomized the fame, glamour, and diversity of a Studio party.

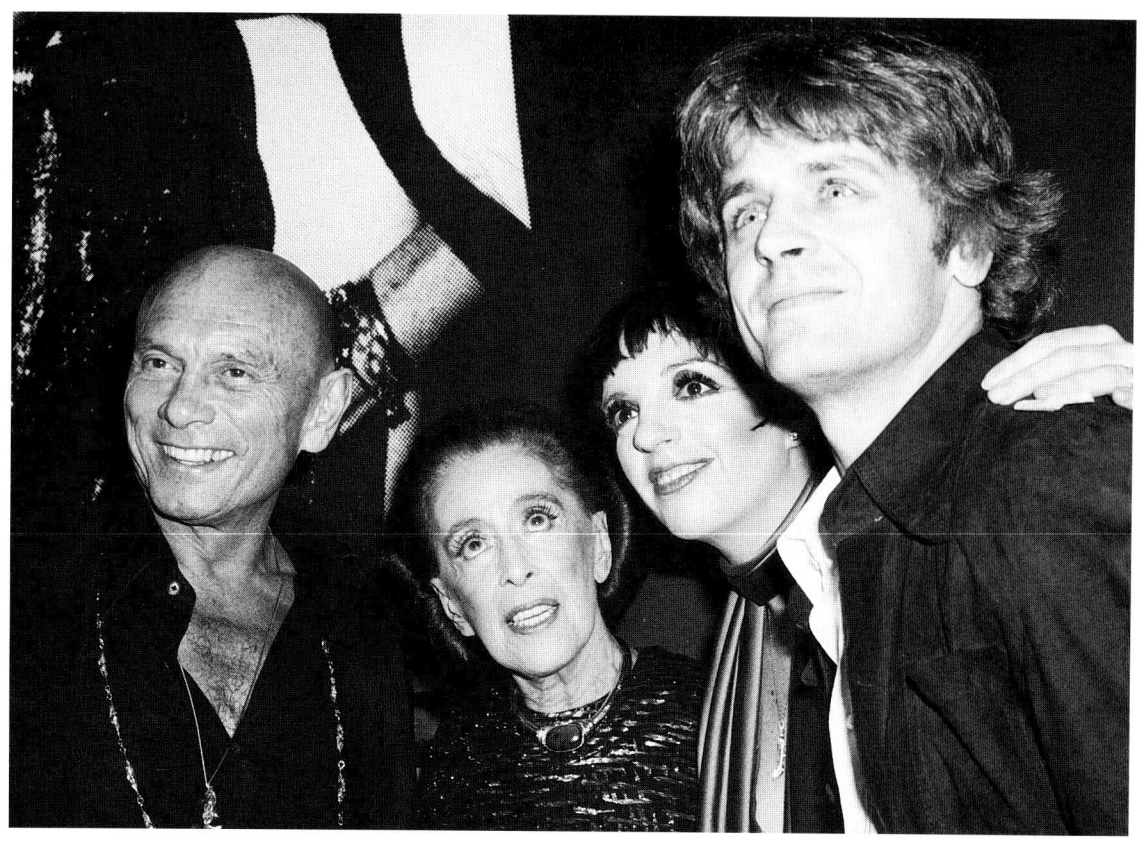

YUL, MARTHA, LIZA, AND MISHA

Studio 54 often gave parties to honor the talents of great geniuses like Martha Graham, shown here with the great actor Yul Brynner, the actress and singer Liza Minnelli, and the legendary Russian ballet dancer Mikhail Baryshnikov. This party paid homage to Martha Graham's dance company and was also a benefit to help keep her dancers on their toes.

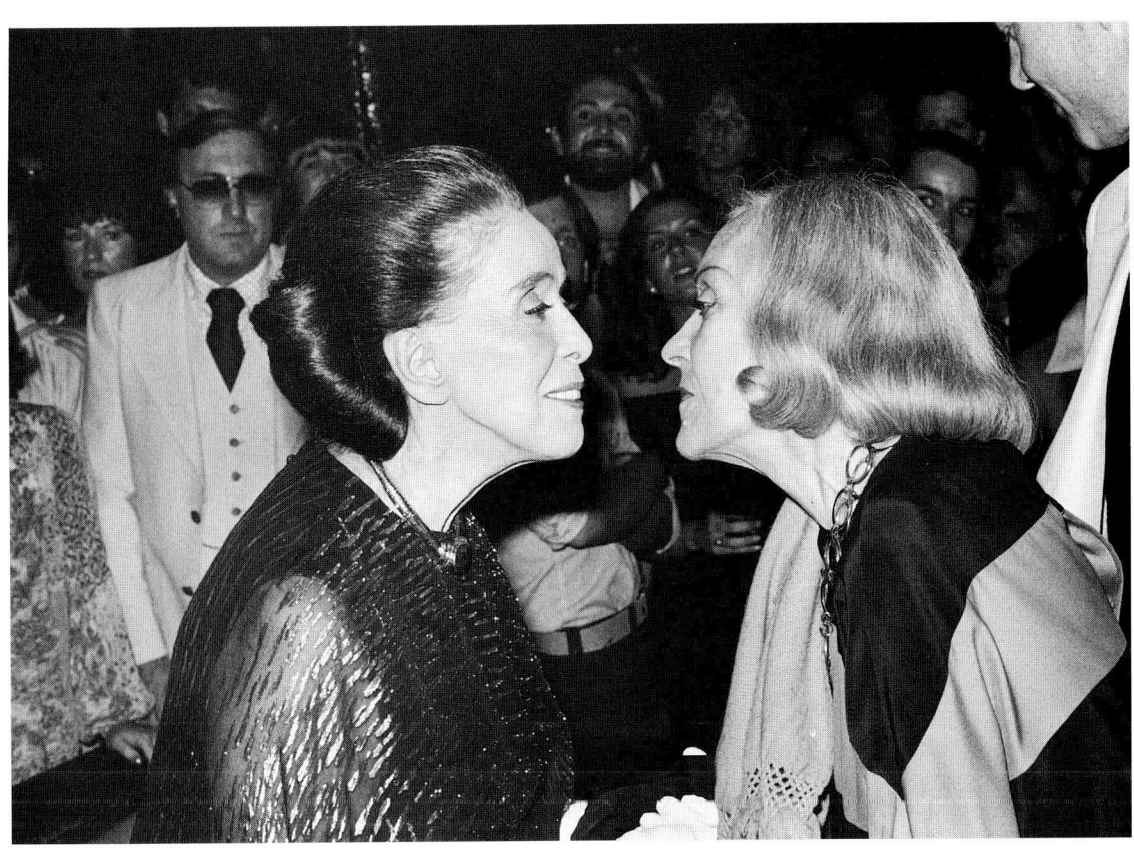

MARTHA GRAHAM AND GLORIA SWANSON

Seeing two great legends like Martha Graham and Gloria Swanson meet face to face for the first time was a thrilling sight to behold. Martha Graham was the greatest modern dancer and choreographer of the twentieth century. She had been to Studio 54 several times before the night this photo was taken, and she handled the loud music and colorful scene like the seasoned trouper that she was. Gloria Swanson, having survived the early years of Hollywood and international stardom, seemed to fit right in immediately. Seen over Gloria's shoulder is fashion designer Halston, who was responsible for bringing the two ladies together at the club.

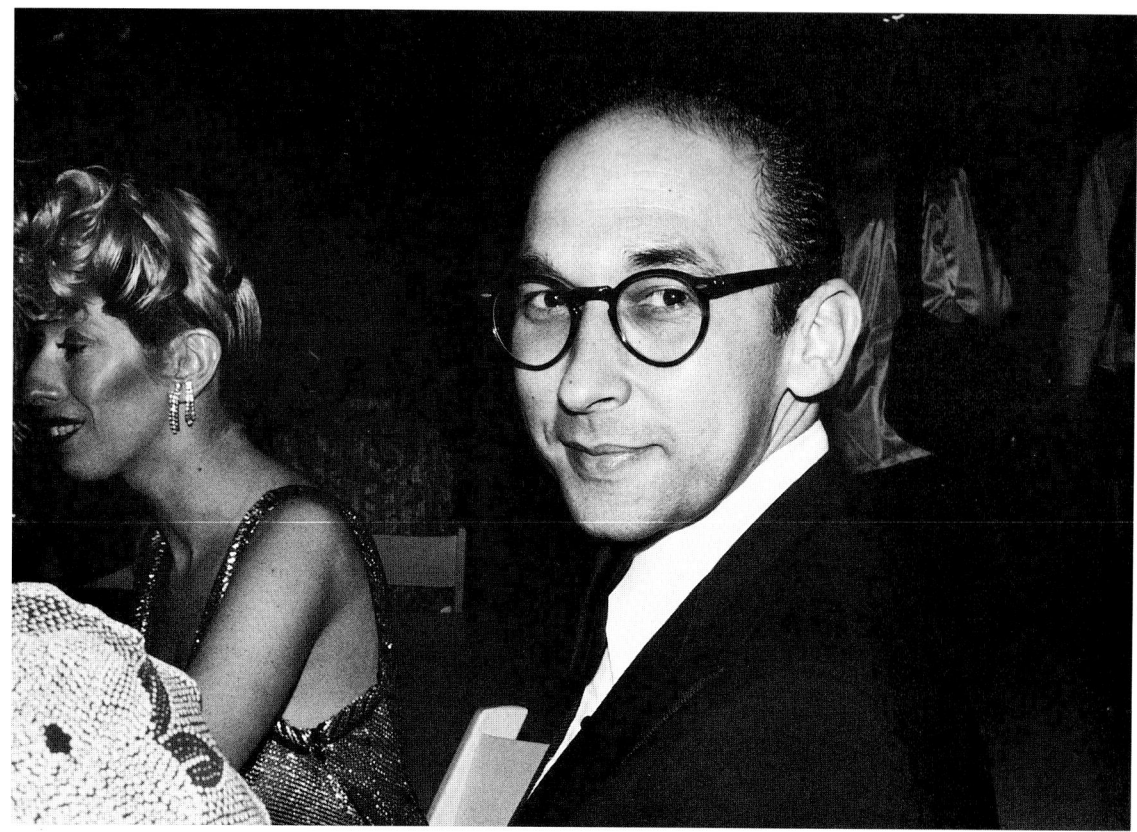

GEORGE PAUL ROZELLE

One of the greatest party planners of the decade, George Paul Rozelle produced many of Studio's more brilliant theme parties. His events were legendary for their carefully thought-out decorations and impeccable style, and he was one of the first to create parties that centered around one color. As a publicist he was able to invite the top of the "A" list, knowing full well they would all show up, and he never left them disappointed. His pink party, held on Fire Island, was attended by Studio's elite and other exclusive partyers who all wore the prescribed color. Even the beach house where the party was held was properly attired: a pink crepe-paper bean-stalk, eight feet in diameter, was wrapped snugly around the stilted house, giving it an otherworldly appearance. It was a colorful and unforgettable evening, with George Paul himself making a dramatic entrance during the evening's peak: he was lowered from a skylight into the main room on a swing. The next day it was discovered that so many people had attended the party that the house's foundation had sunk more than a foot into the sand under their weight.

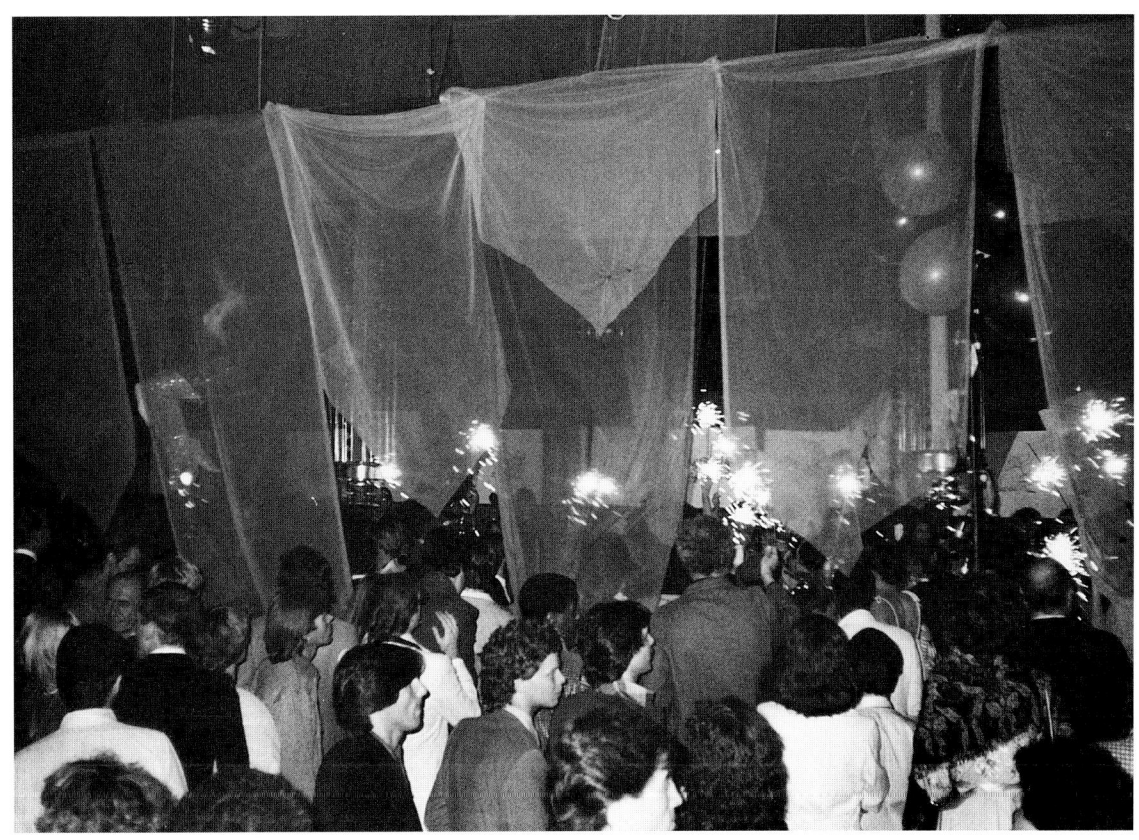

DANCE FLOOR

Regardless of the action going on in the basement, the balcony, the bathrooms, or at the bar, it was the dance floor that was the center of activity. There, among the sweaty bodies pulsating and prancing, all things were equalized. Rich danced next to poor, straight next to gay. It was the one place in the club where everyone could just let loose and be themselves. People who wouldn't normally speak to you off the dance floor would sidle up next to you and be your new best friend if only for a song or two. The magic of Studio sprung to life here—at the push of the deejay's button it would snow or a thousand lights and colors would suddenly surround you and whisk you away to a netherworld. The man in the moon and the coke spoon were only the tip of the iceberg when it came to the dance floor and its many illusions.

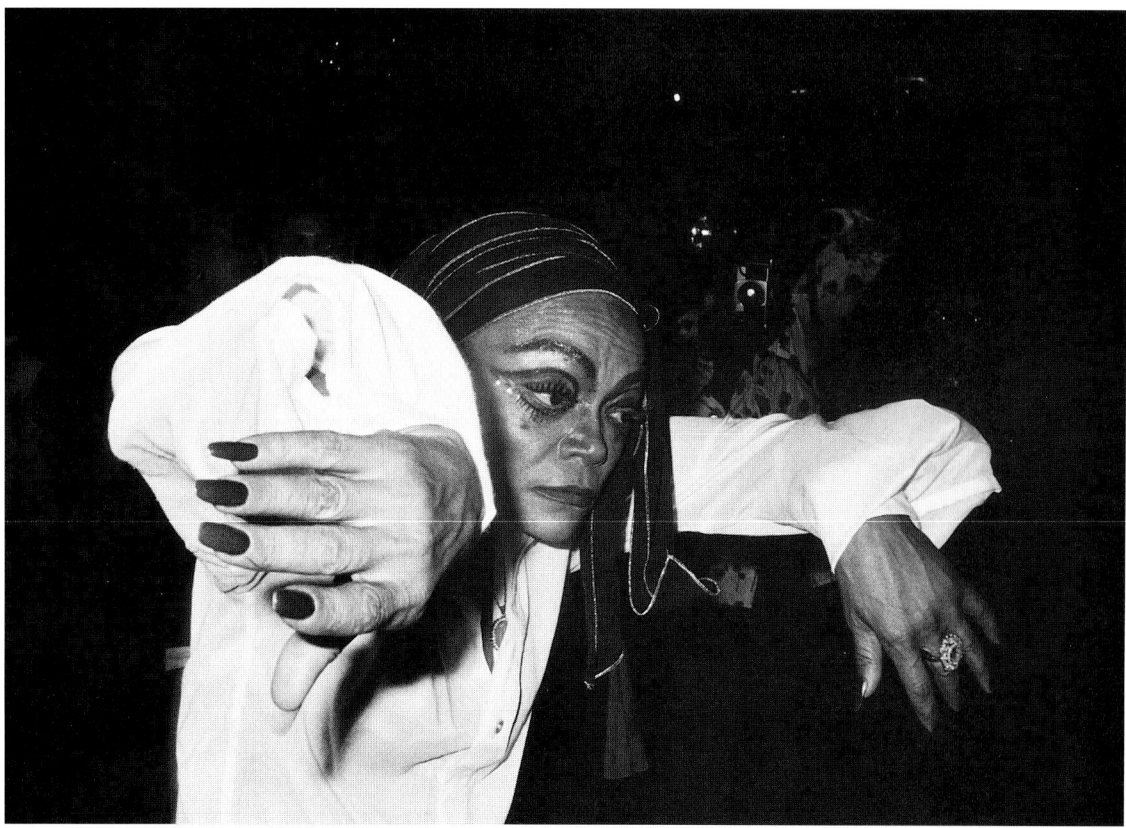

EARTHA KITT

The great Orson Welles once called Eartha Kitt "the most exciting woman on Earth," and after seeing her on so many occasions at Studio I came to agree. She was always vivacious and exhilarating and could invariably be found on the dance floor doing an exotic samba or interpretive move for the cameras.

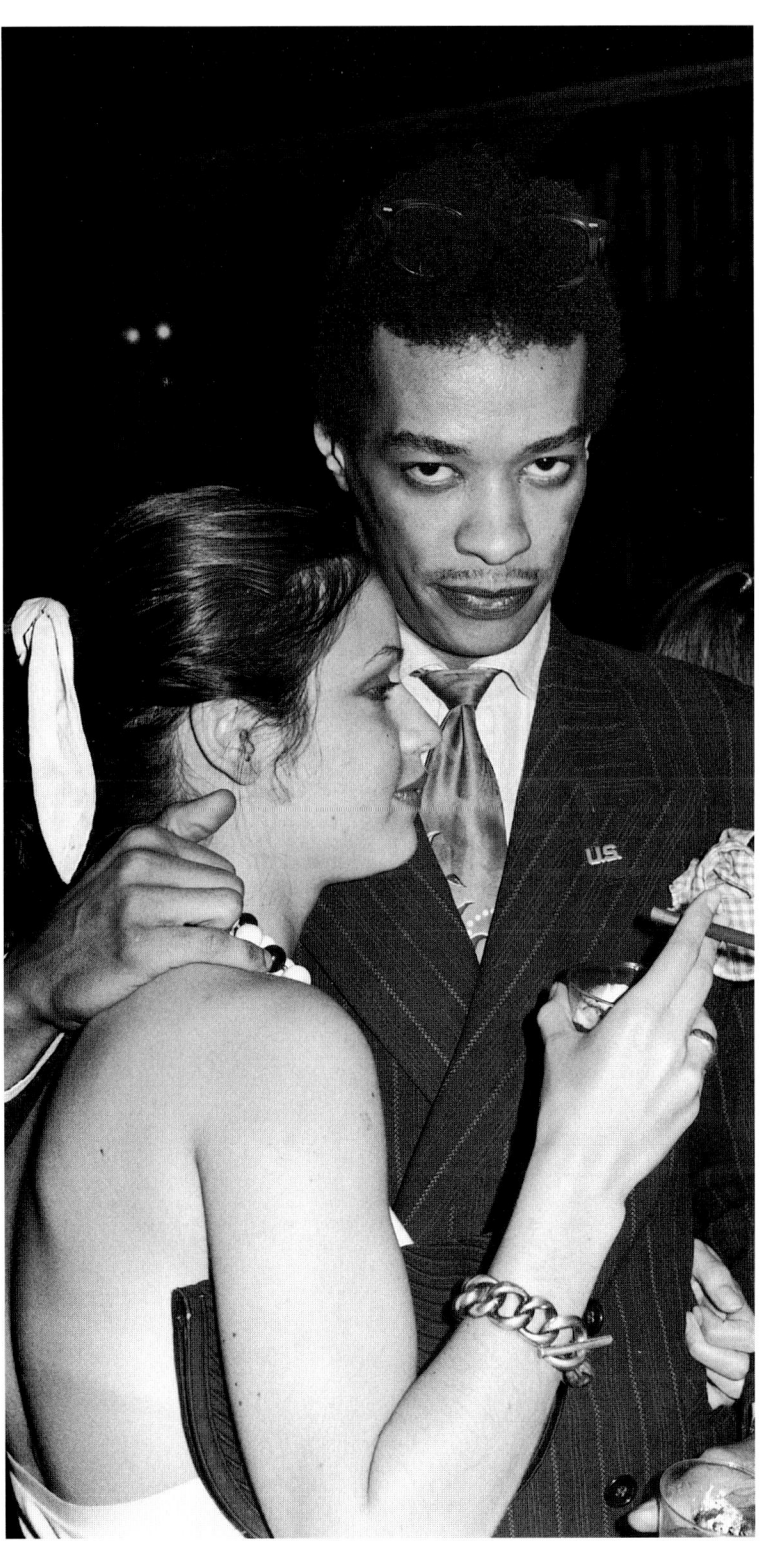

Dr. Buzzard's Original Savannah Band was one of the best dance albums of the Seventies. Bronx-born Haitian Stony Browder Jr. together with his brother August Darnell and the legendary voice of Cory Daye were a recipe for success, and the band had hit after hit, including "Cherchez la Femme" and "I'll Play the Fool." If you listen carefully to that album you can also hear the majestic Patti Austin singing backup vocals.

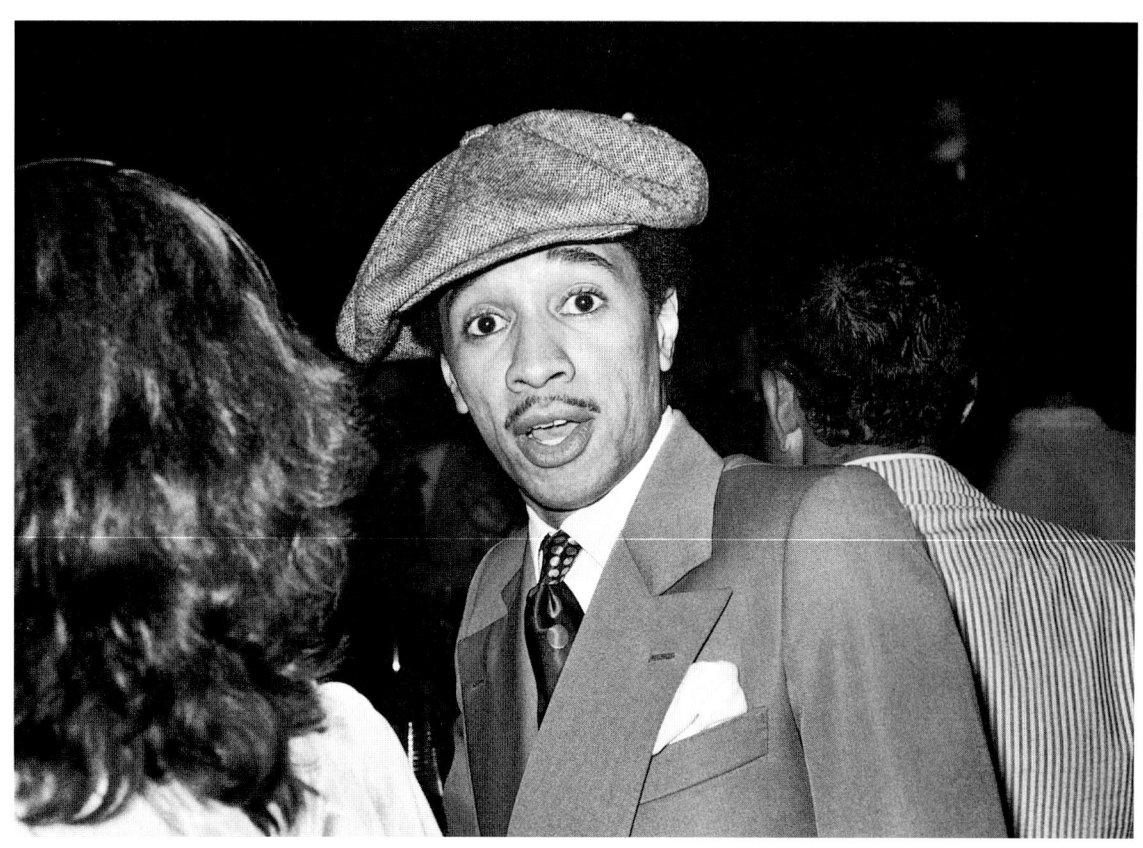

AUGUST DARNELL

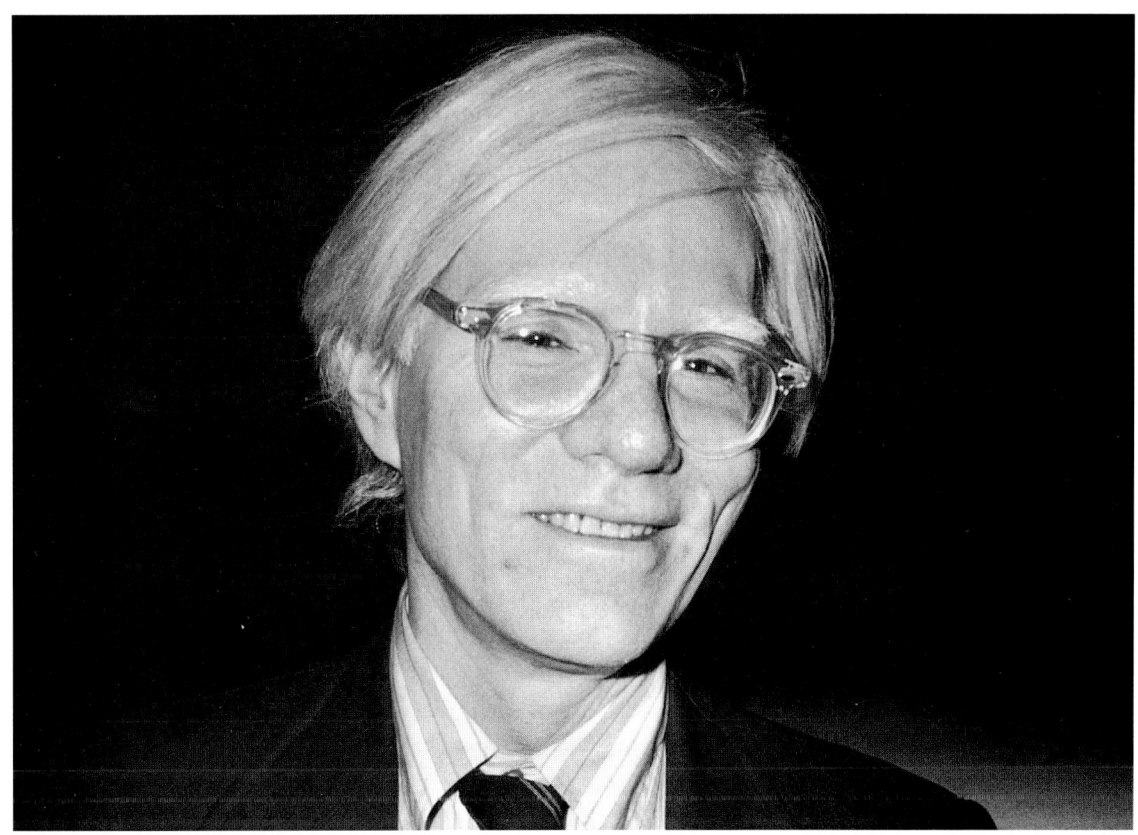

ANDY WARHOL

I met Andy Warhol in 1976 at a tea party at the Plaza Hotel and found him funny and childlike. This photo was taken as he was surrounded by movie stars and cute boys, all vying for his attention. His look of self-assurance and satisfaction was a rare thing to see. Most of the time he seemed anxious and worried. I think a real sweetness is present in his smile.

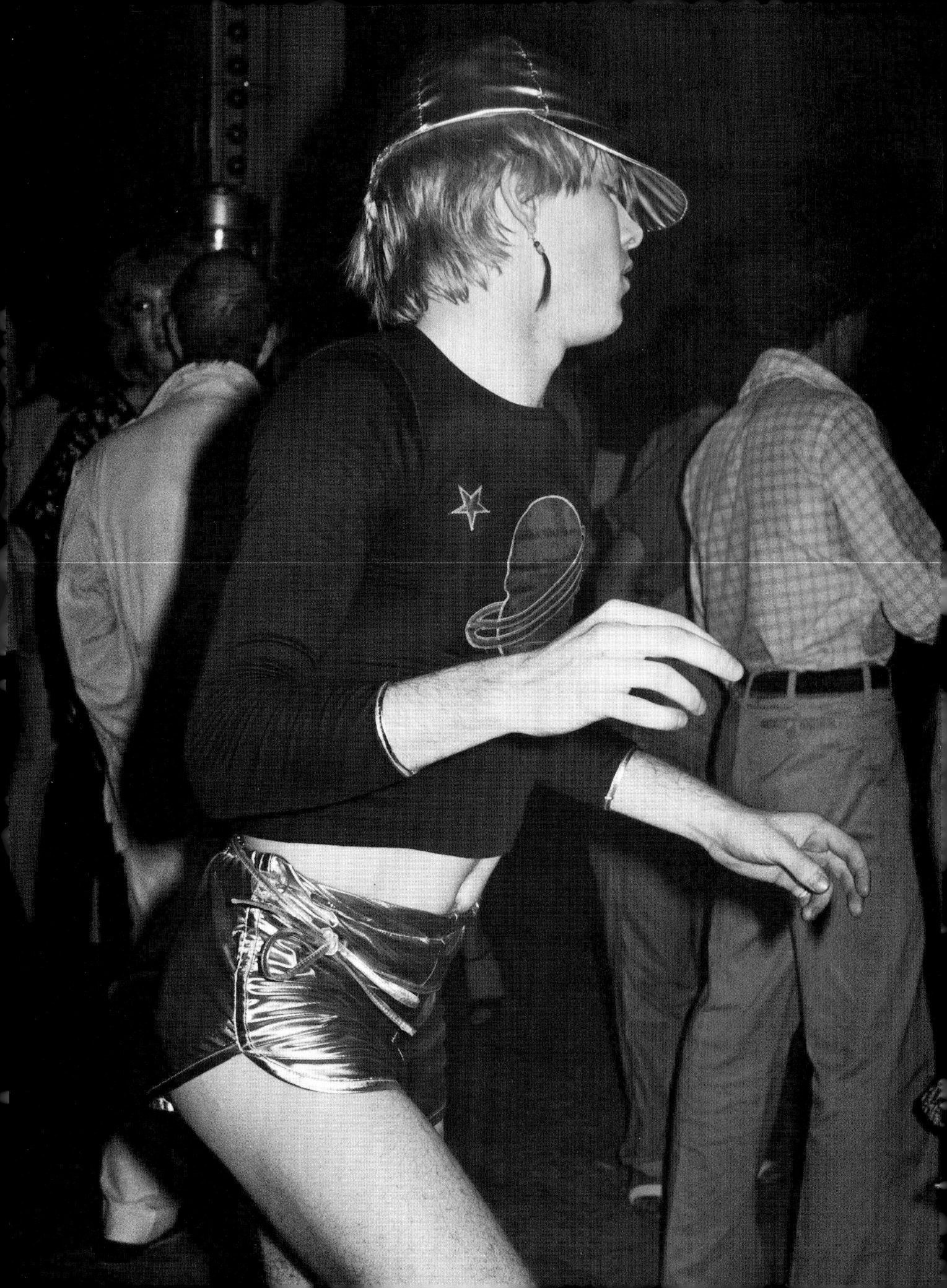

OPPOSITE: BOY IN GOLD HOT PANTS

CHERYL TIEGS

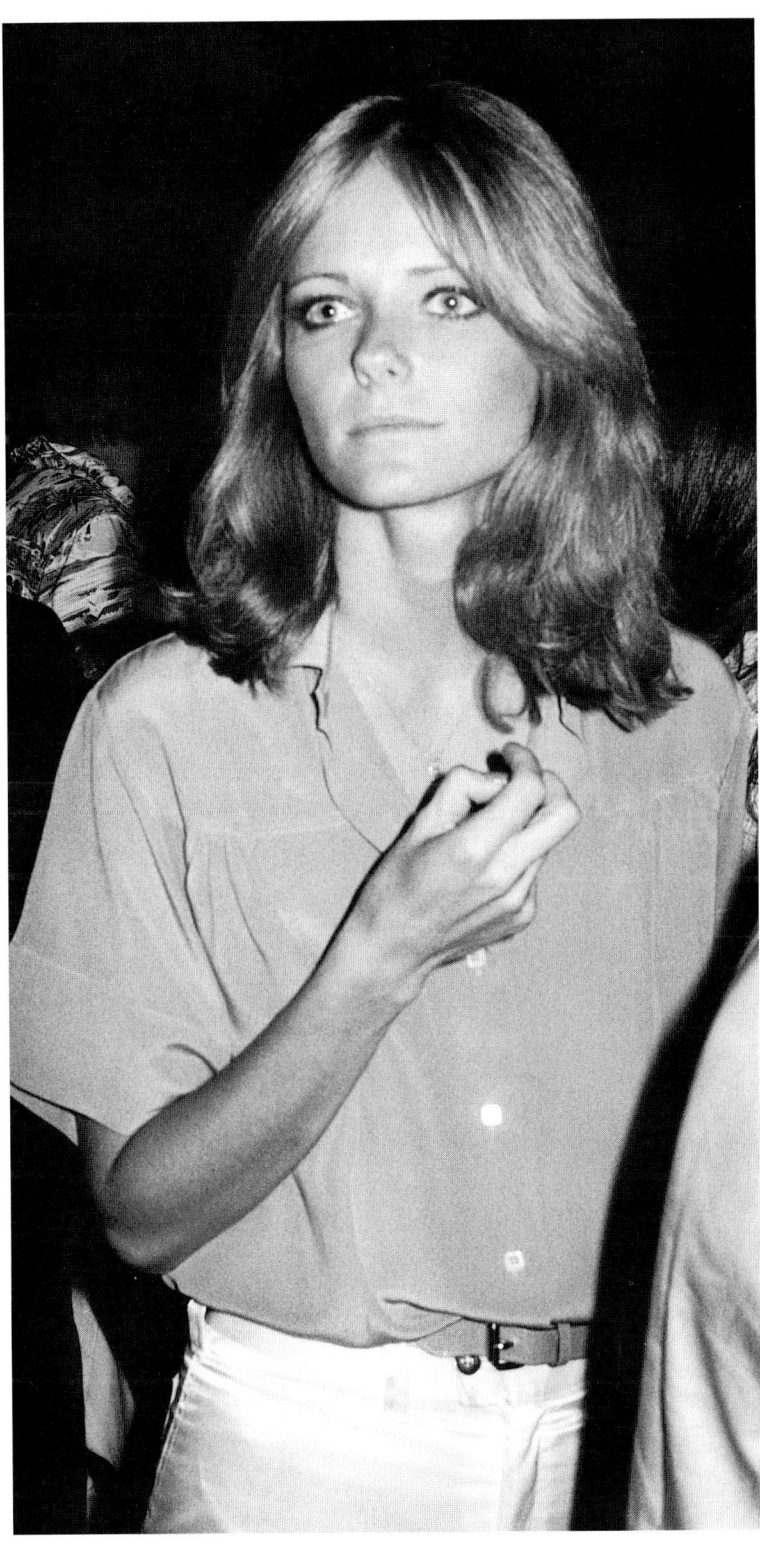

Cheryl Tiegs was one of the biggest models of the Seventies and was a regular on the party circuit and at Studio. She would often arrive with the same group of friends, including photographer Peter Beard, who was her boyfriend at the time, and make her way to a relatively quiet spot. Despite her fame and beauty, Cheryl seemed shy and withdrawn in person and always made an effort to remain in the background rather than posing for the many cameras at the club.

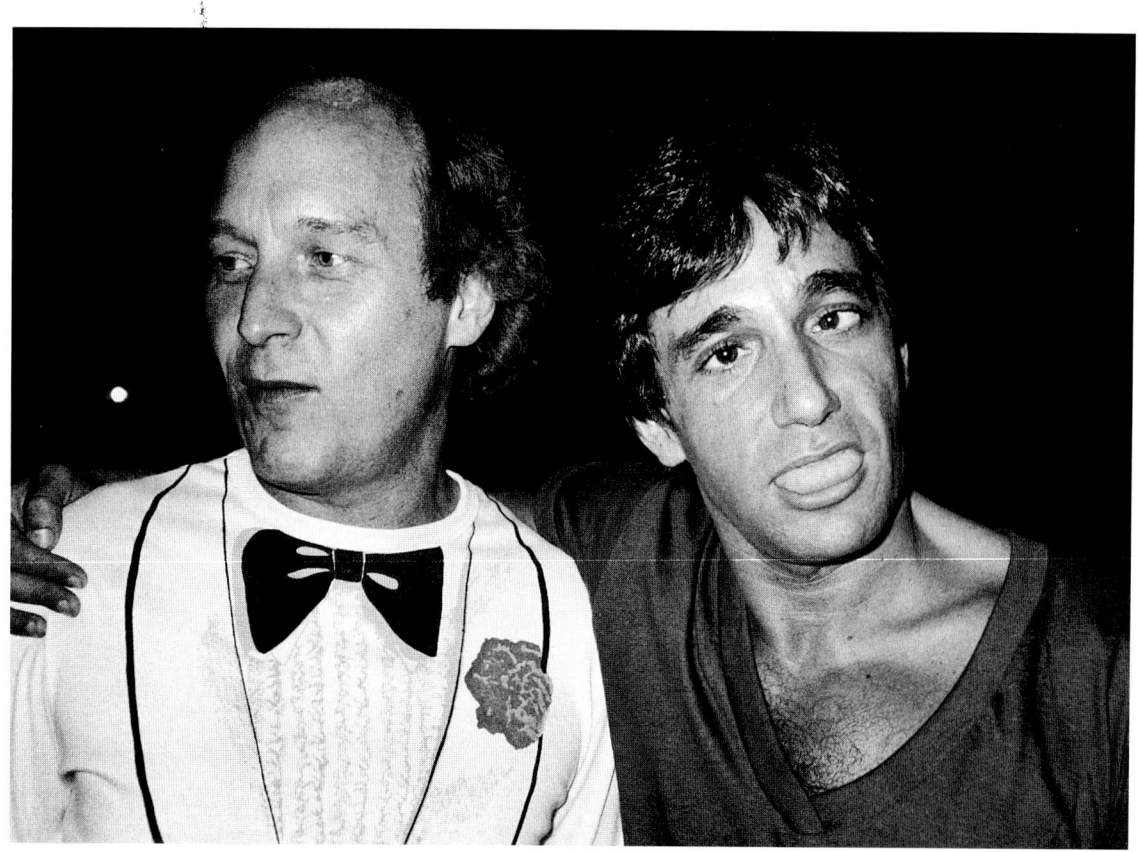

JAMES RADO AND ROBERT EYE

Robert Eye (right) was an actor and performance artist in the Seventies and Eighties. James Rado and Gerry Ragni were the creators and composers of the Sixties musical *Hair*. Jimmy and Gerry were regulars at Studio and were both funny, quick-witted, and enjoyable to be with. Jimmy directed a 1994 national tour of *Hair* for which I designed the wigs. Sadly, Gerry passed away in the Eighties.

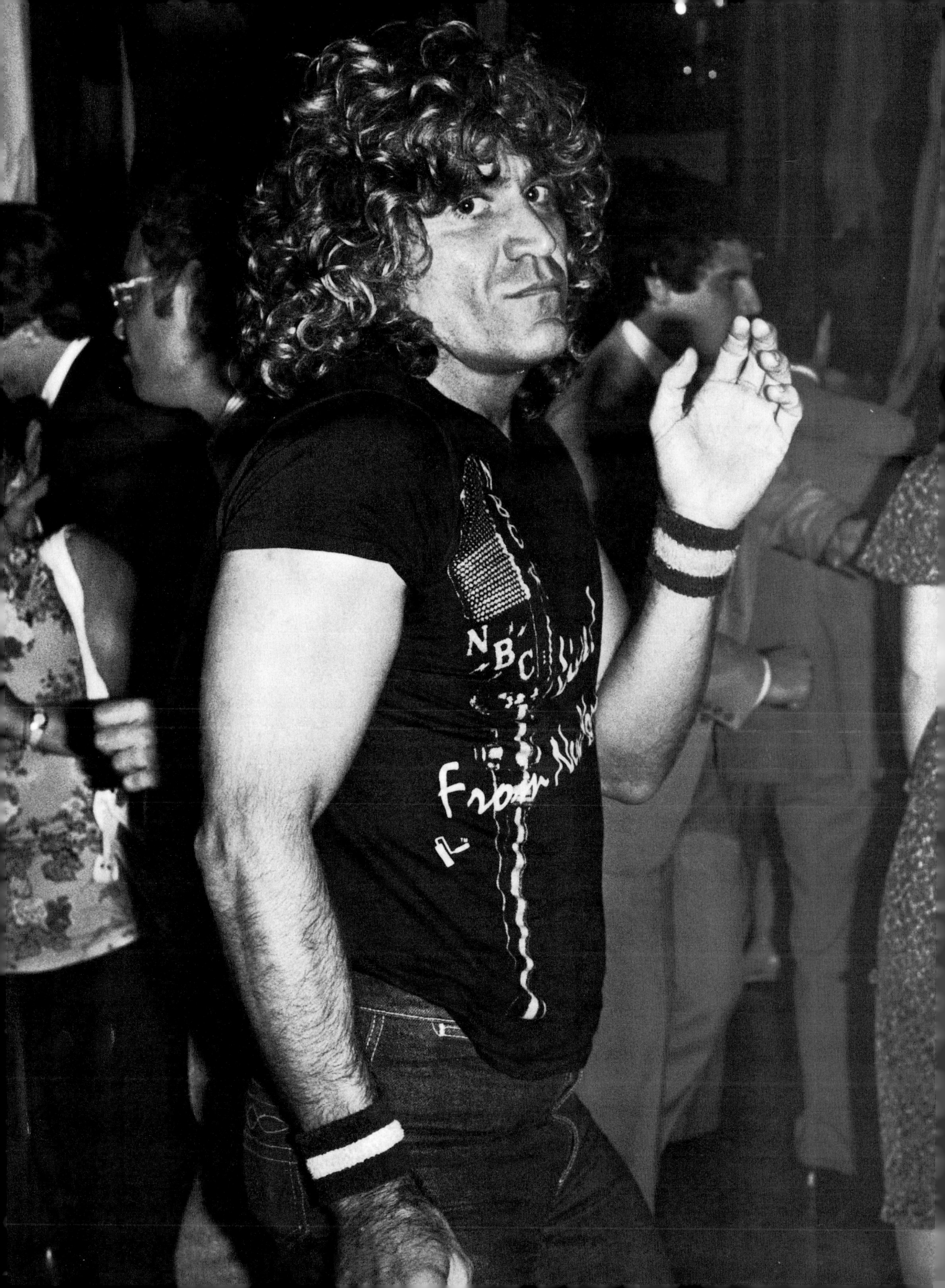

CALVIN KLEIN

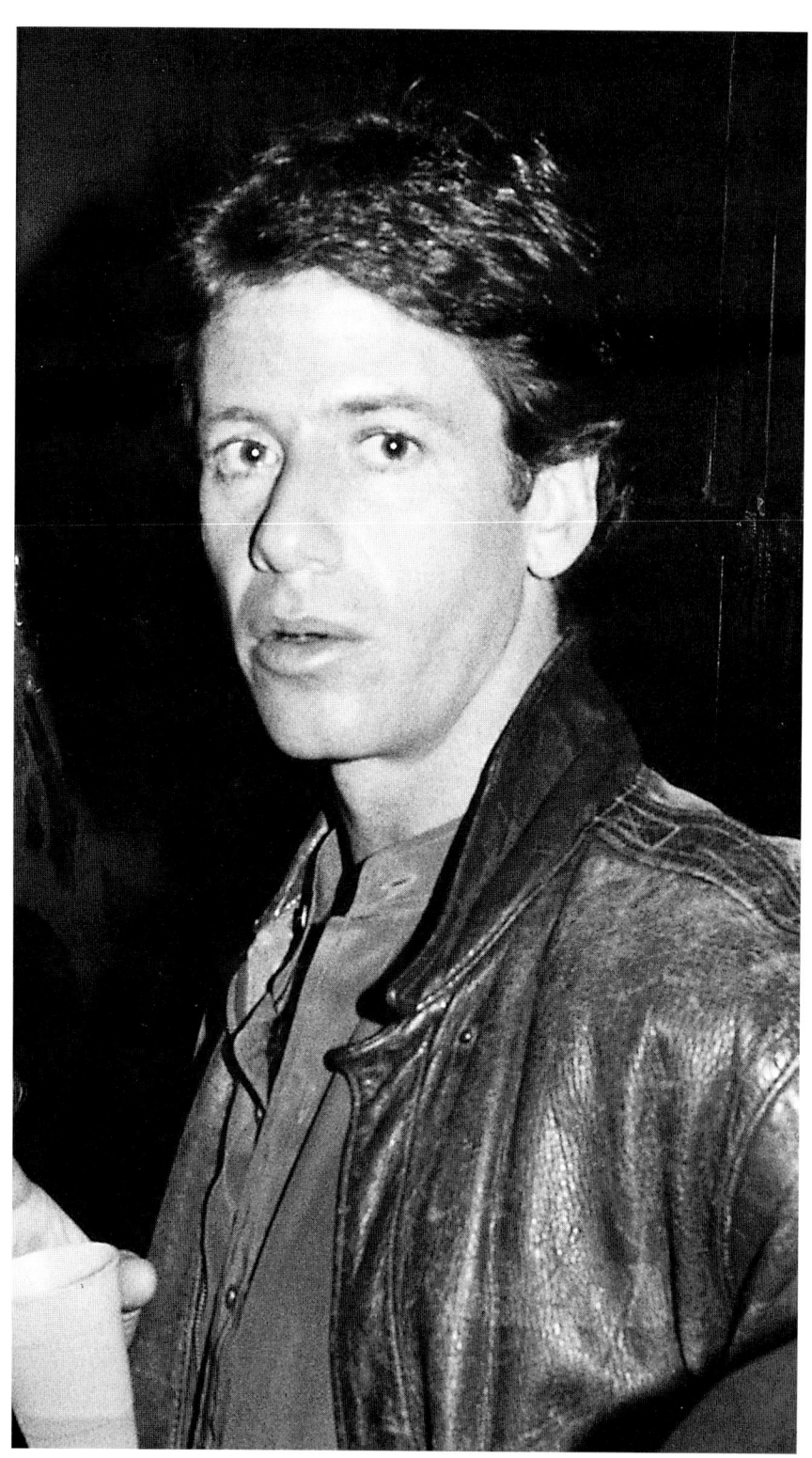

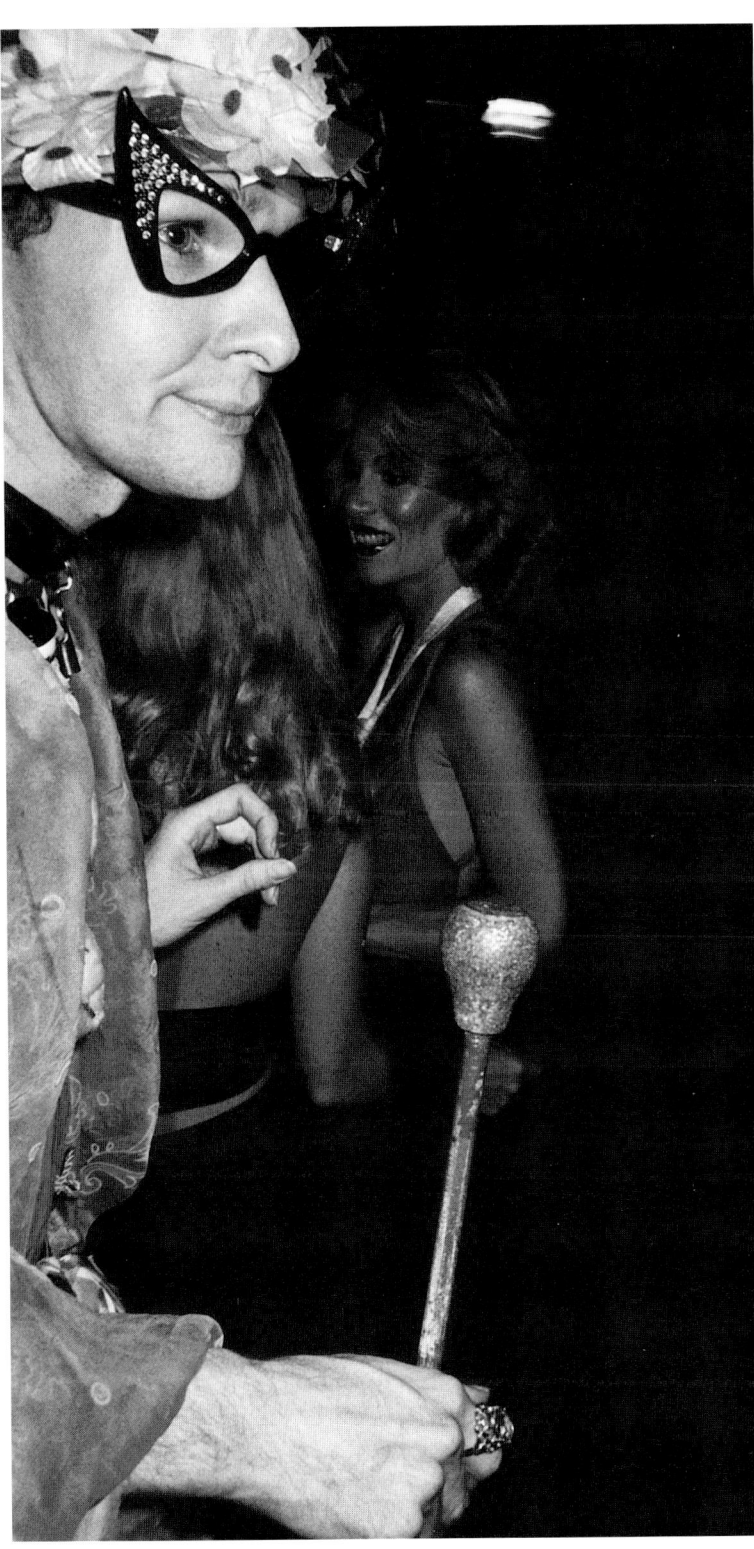

Rollerena was the *fairy* godmother of the Seventies. A Wall Street broker by day, at night he would don a wedding dress, colorful hat with lace flowers, festive decorative eyeglasses, roller skates, and of course the magic wand shown here. Rollerena showed up at every grand opening of every great nightclub and at every Gay Pride Parade, too. At Studio she would roll around the dance floor, waving her magic wand over the revelers, occasionally sprinkling some glitter fairy dust over their heads. On one rare night, I saw a fight about to break out when suddenly, appearing out of nowhere, came Rollerena. A sprinkle of glitter, a wave of the wand, and presto, peace was restored.

STEVE RUBELL

This is a photo of Studio 54 owner Steve Rubell, kneeling on the floor looking for a lost Quaalude. I know this to be true because I was the one who handed it to him right before he dropped it, and Steve's love for Quaaludes was no secret—after cocaine, Quaaludes were the drug of choice for most partyers in the Seventies. Steve never found the lost Quaalude that evening, and although I made several passes around the dance floor hunting for it myself, I never recovered it either.

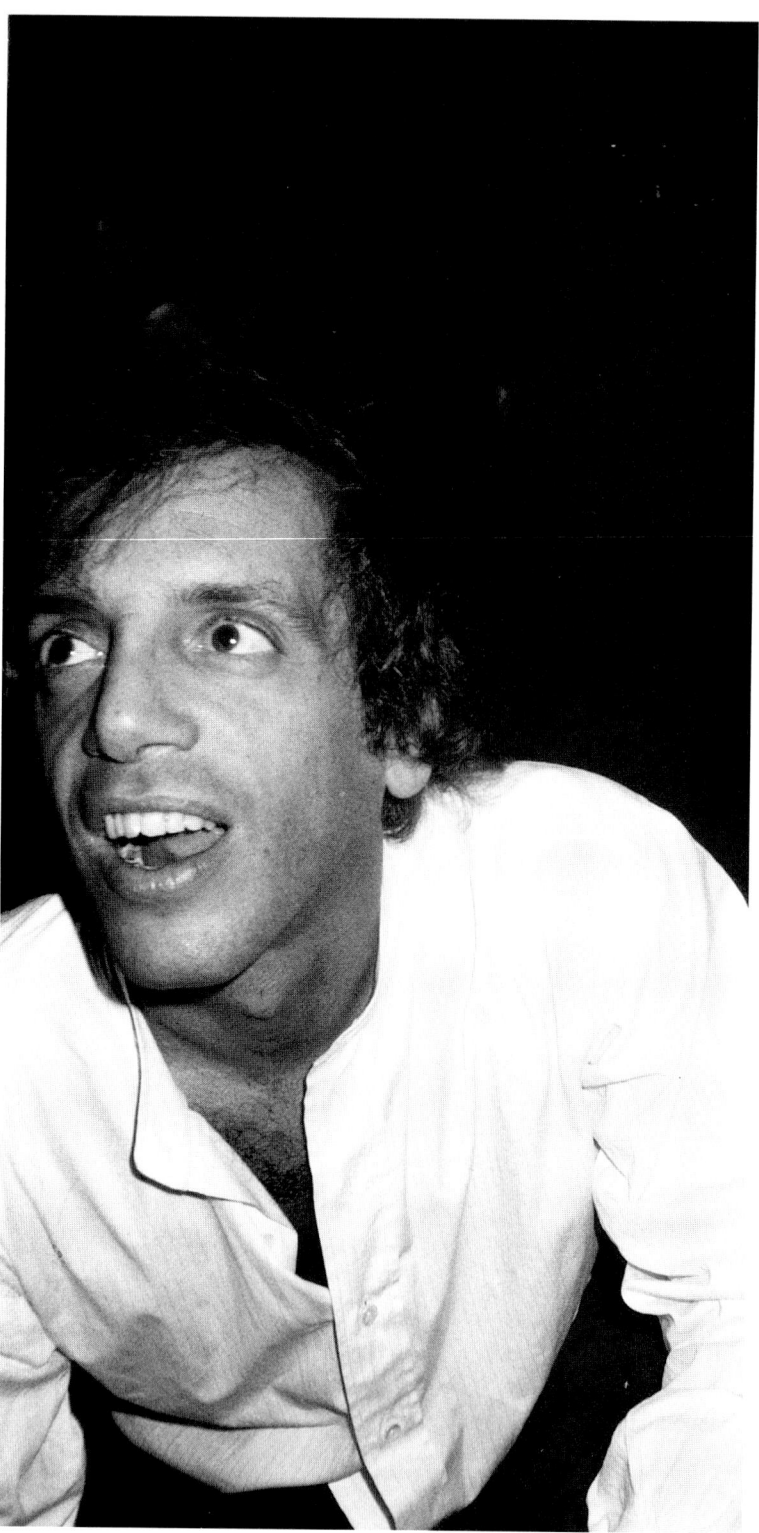

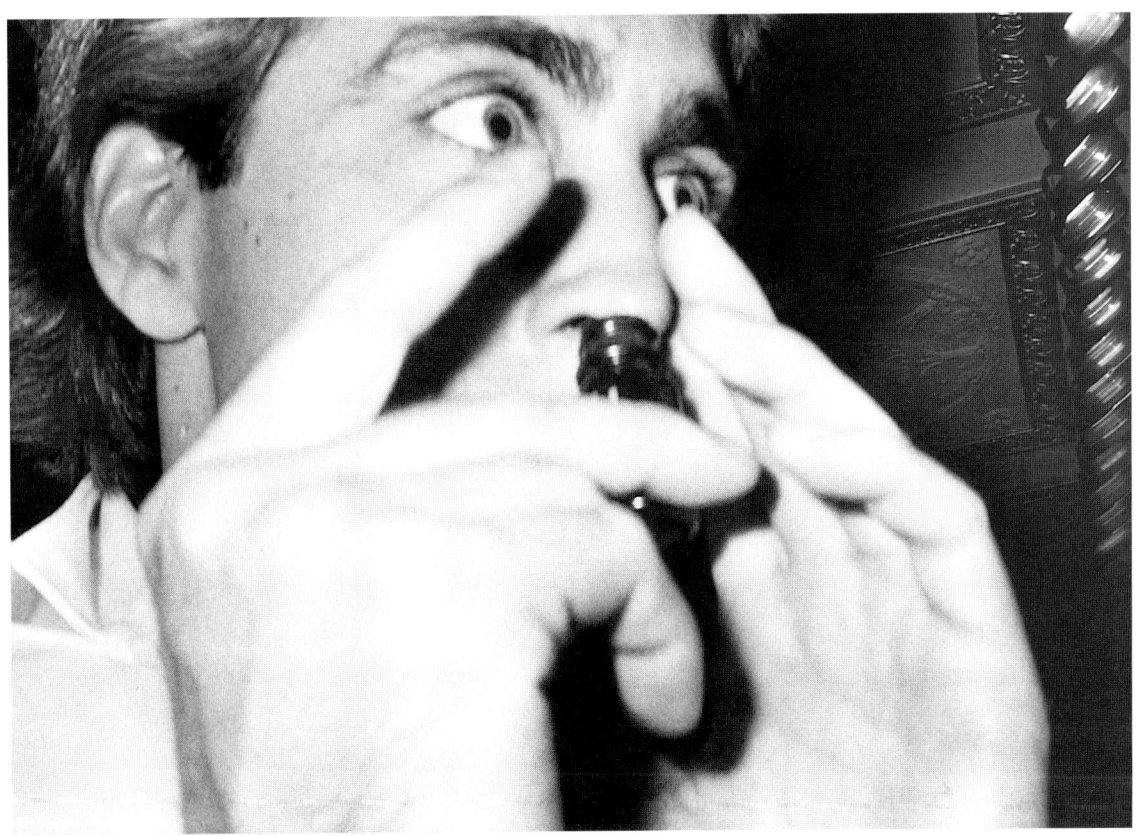

AMYL AND ETHYL

Amyl nitrate was a common disco drug used on the dance floor by many, along with its sister drug ethyl chloride. The high these drugs induced increased the intensity of the music, and dancing became a religious experience. Also called poppers, amyl nitrate was taken simply by removing the cap from a little brown bottle and inhaling the fumes; it was also available in small, breakable capsules. Ethyl chloride, on the other hand, was a bit more complicated. You had to squirt the liquid onto a handkerchief and then quickly inhale it before it evaporated. It was a comic sight to see people on the dance floor, their little brown bottles in one hand and a handkerchief in the other, trying to time things just right.

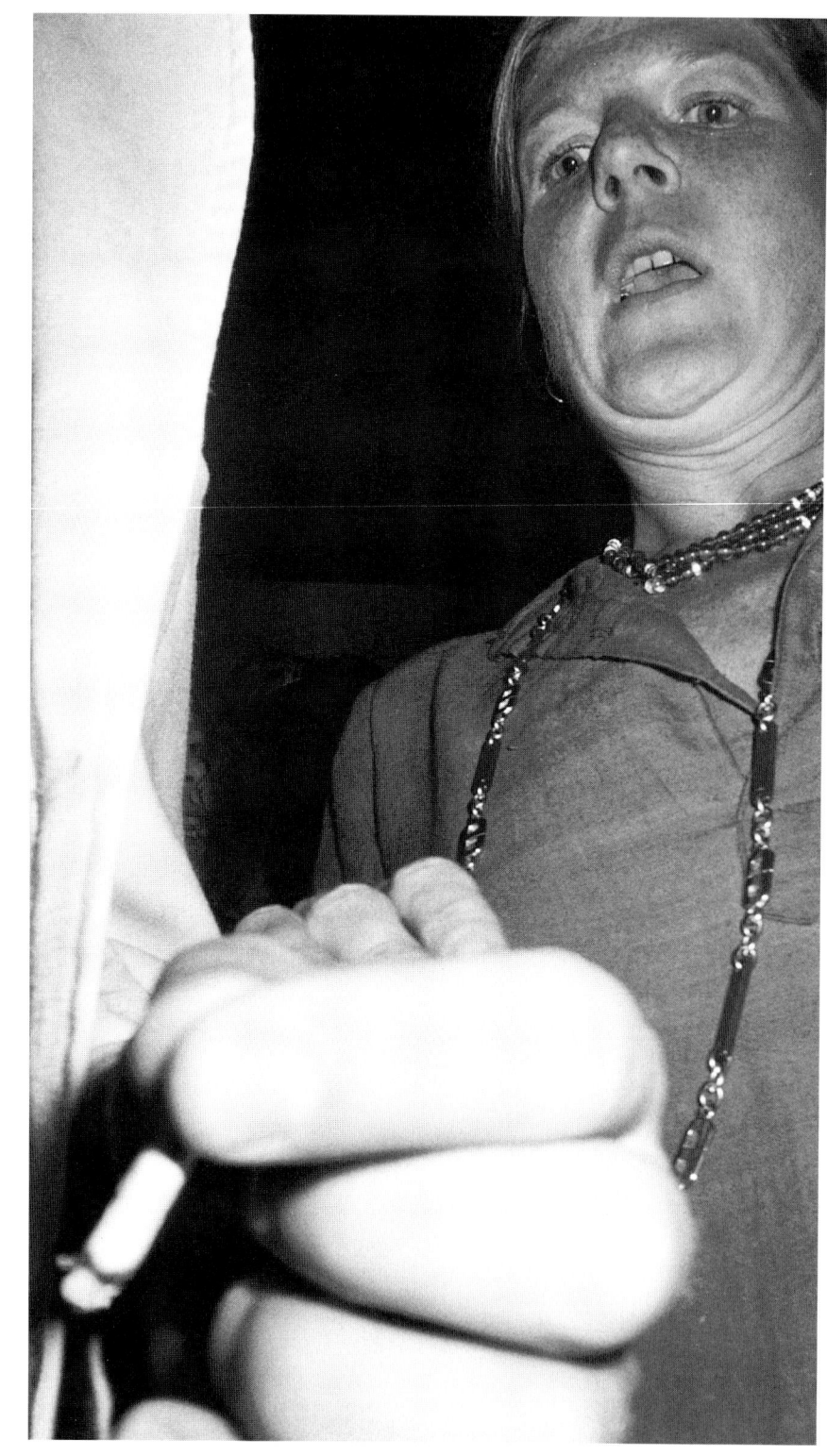

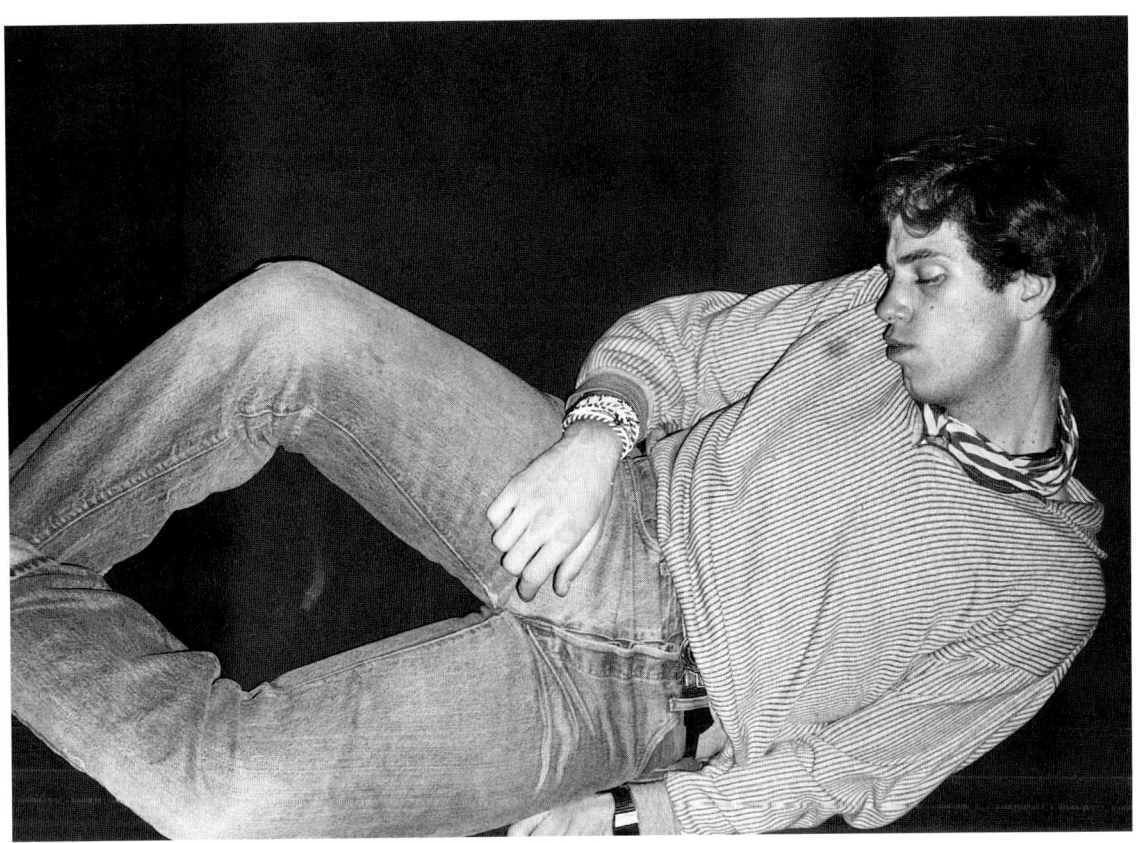

RIP VAN WINKLE

In the Seventies, drug use gained enormous popularity, and nowhere was the precedent for its use more firmly established than at Studio. I can recall people snorting cocaine on the dance floor right out in the open—not a common sight before the advent of disco. People would walk around with coke rings around their noses and nobody seemed to care. But no matter how many drugs some people took, others went the natural route and would simply take a brief disco nap in order to last till dawn.

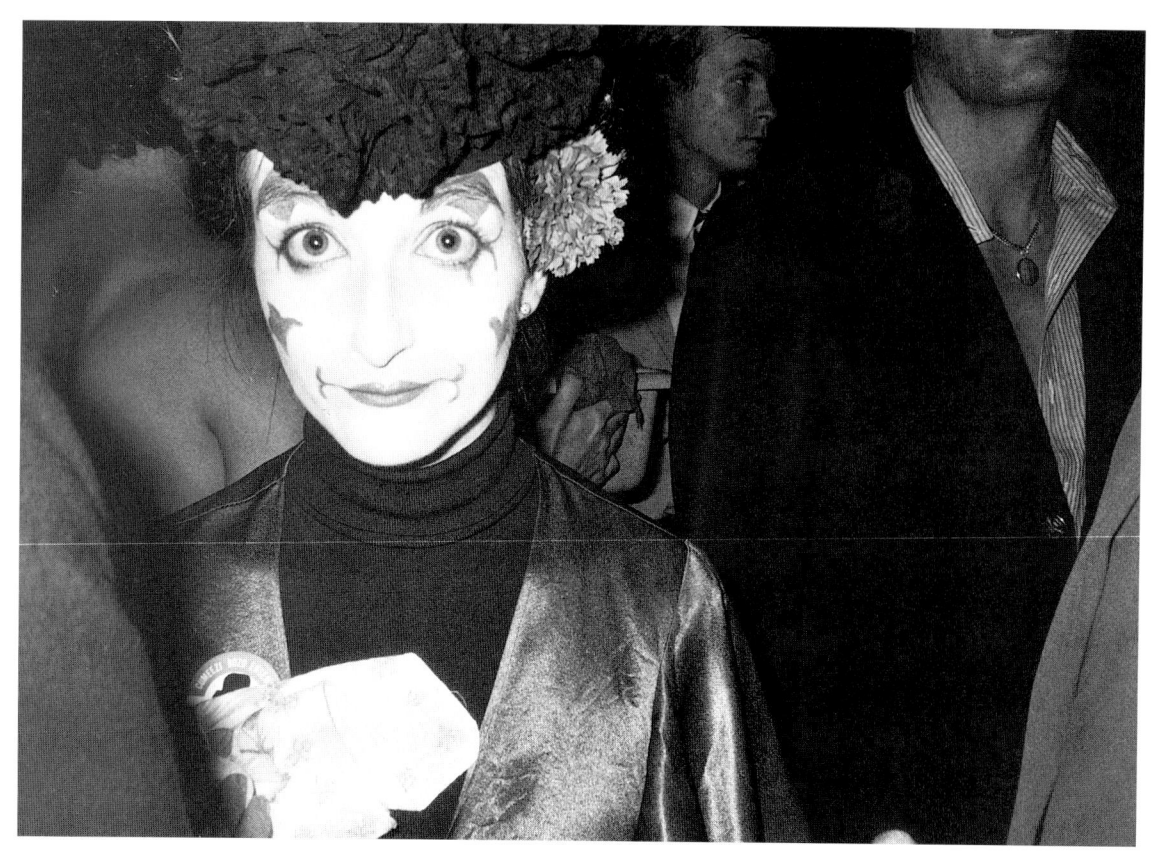

CAMEEZI BOZO CLOWN

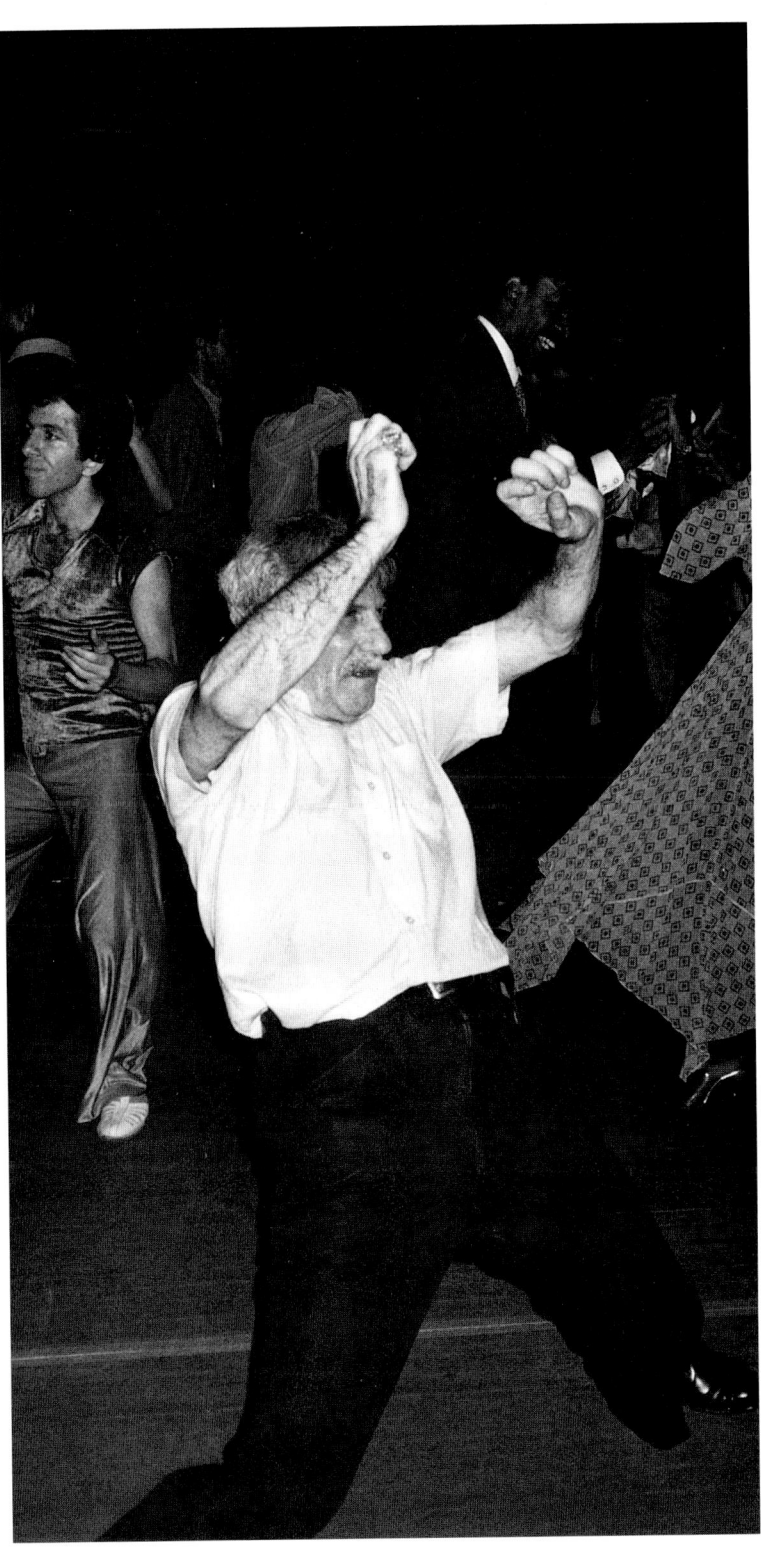

This grandfatherly figure shattered all previously held stereotypes for me. I watched him dance till dawn and walk out into the morning sunlight with a beautiful young woman. The smile on his face proved that dreams did come true for many who entered the magic kingdom of Studio 54.

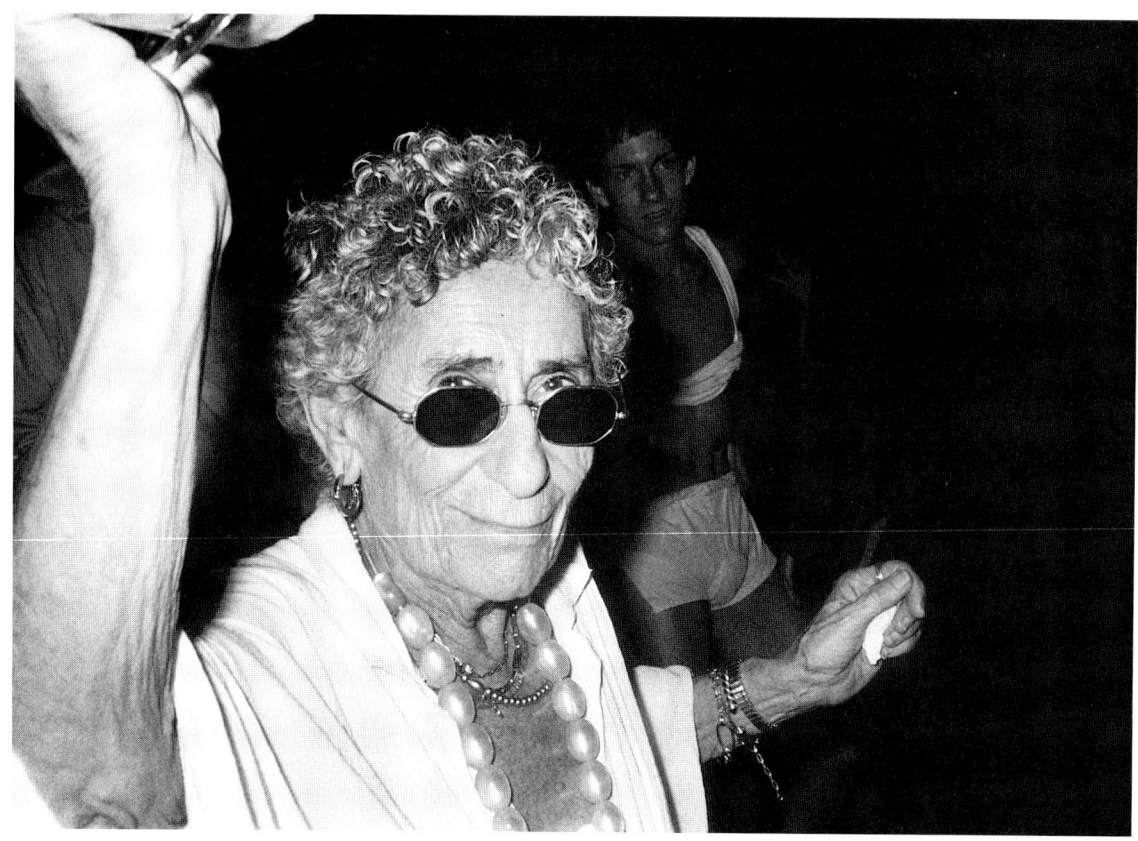

DISCO SALLY

Disco Sally was an eighty-five-year-old lawyer who came to Studio every night and literally danced until dawn. In true studio fashion, she always arrived tambourine in hand, on the shoulder of her dashing twenty-three-year-old Greek boyfriend, whom she later married. I heard she passed away in the late Eighties from a heart attack.

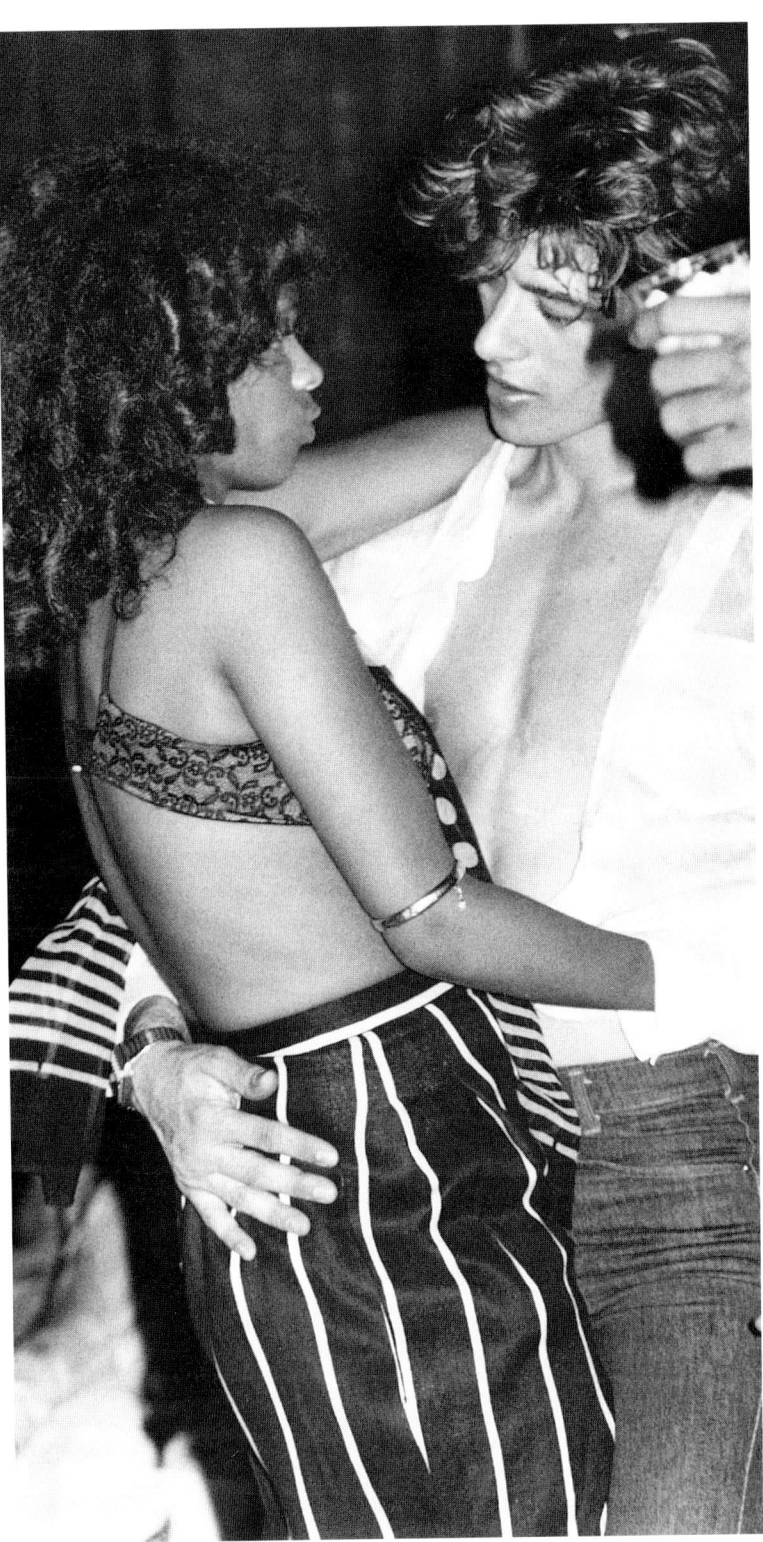

These two lovers captured the wild abandon that was so prevalent at Studio. Before the advent of Madonna, dancing blouseless in a bra was behavior frowned upon in other nightclubs. Still, this woman carries it off naturally. Her partner seems preppy with an early alternative edge in his French-cut jeans—so popular in that era.

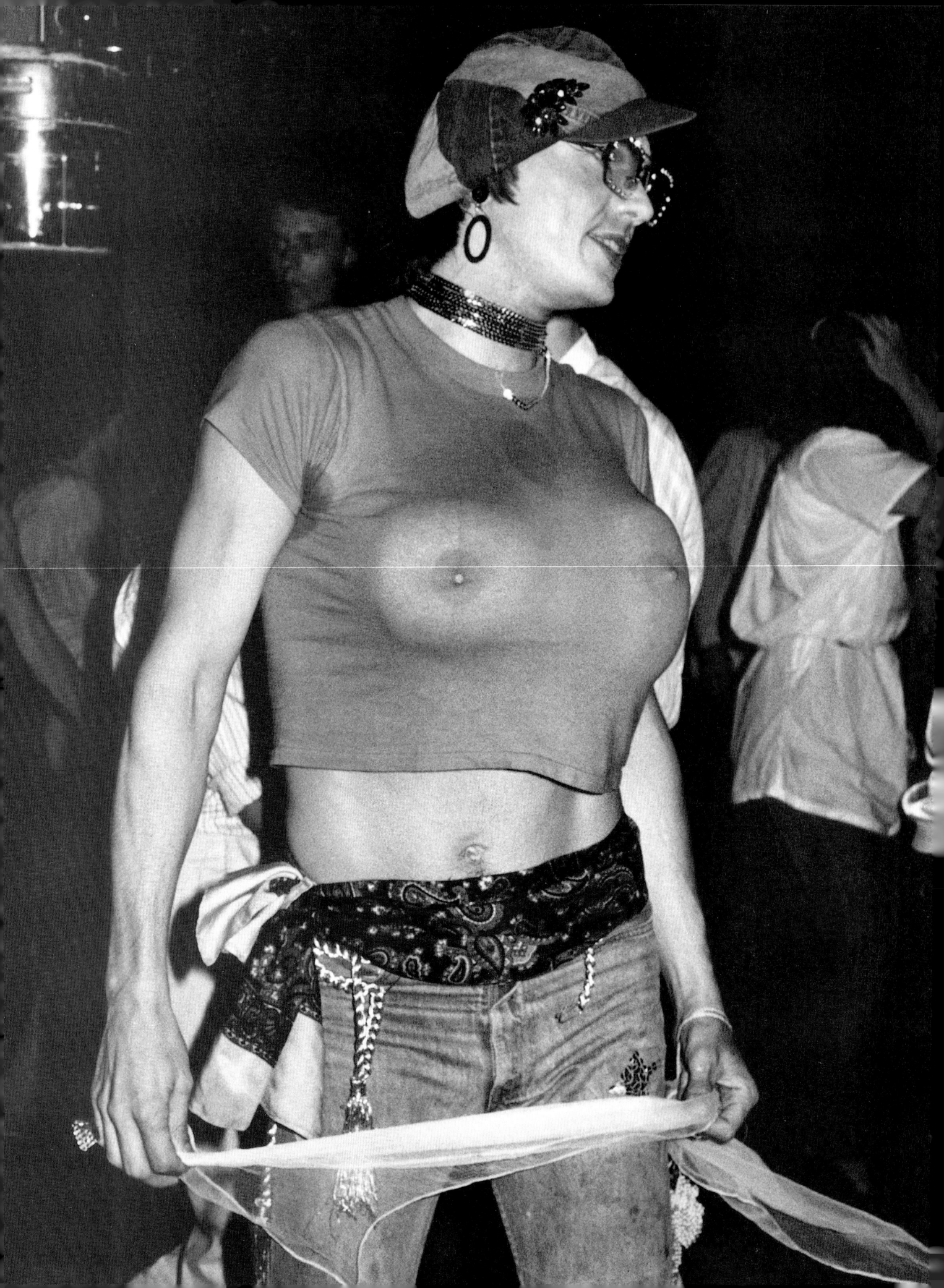

One hot July evening I was on my way to the club when I stopped at a deli on Broadway to get cigarettes. Coming out of the deli was a plain-looking boy in jeans and a T-shirt carrying a paper bag. He stopped me and asked how to get to Studio 54. Rather than tell him that he probably wouldn't get past the front door dressed so casually, I merely gave him directions. After buying my smokes and turning onto Fifty-fourth Street I spotted him standing in a doorway and emptying his paper bag. Out came a few scarves, which he wrapped around his waist, some cheap costume jewelry, a pair of decorative eyeglasses, an old denim hat, and a tube of lipstick. I watched him apply all of these accessories, still thinking he didn't have a chance at the door, when suddenly he pulled two balloons out of his pocket. Without skipping a beat, he blew them up, placed them gently under his T-shirt, and headed toward the front entrance. Mark, the main doorman, spotted him right away and whisked him into the club. Who said it was impossible to get into Studio 54?

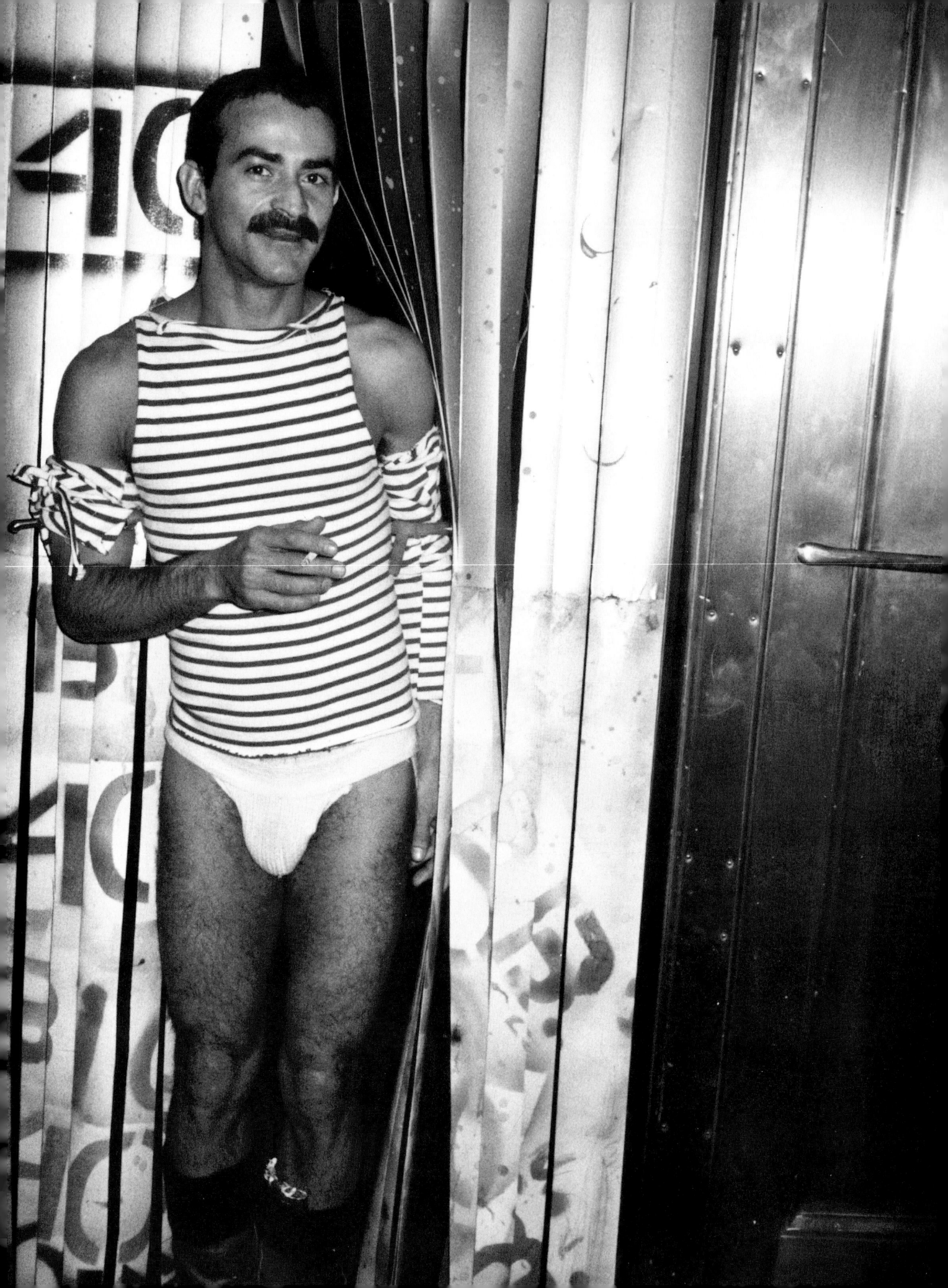

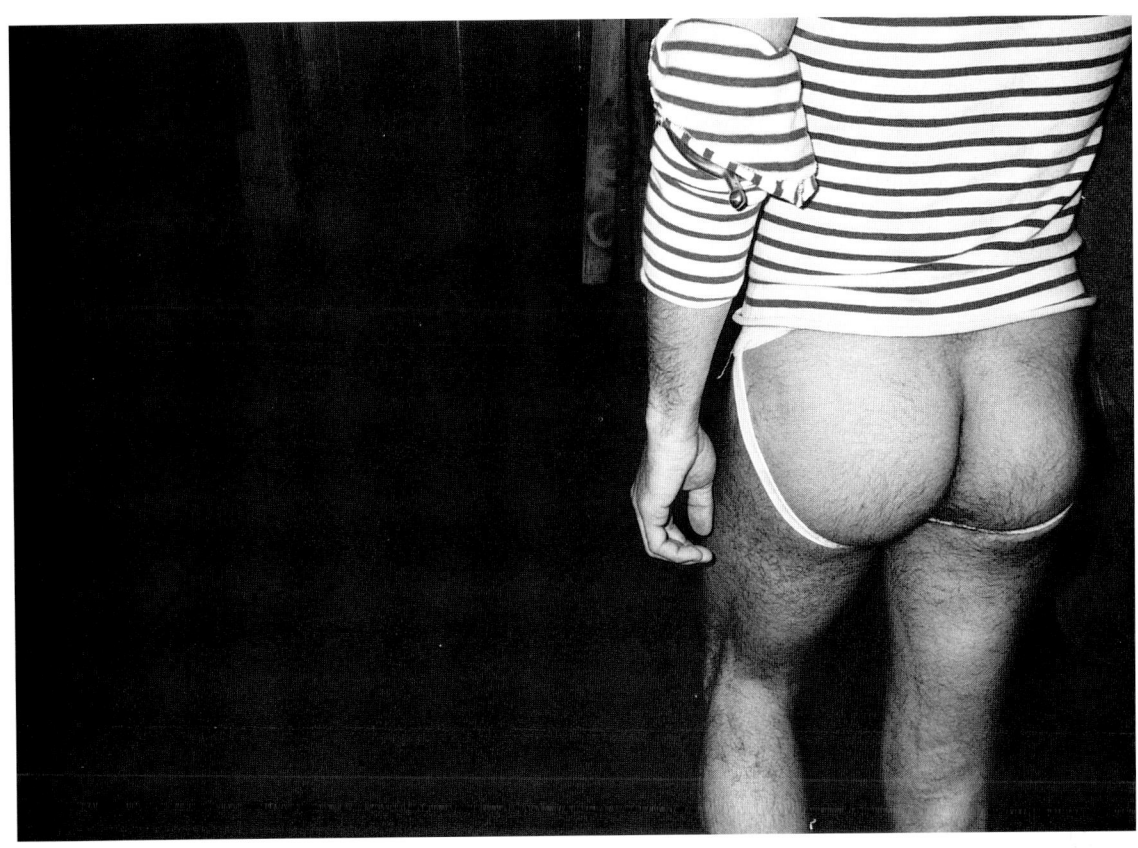

OPPOSITE: VICTOR HUGO (FRONT)   VICTOR HUGO (BACK)

Venezuelan artist Victor Hugo came to New York, met Halston, and quickly became his
boyfriend/art adviser and the window dresser for his Madison Avenue store. Victor was a
wild one who could often be seen at Studio in an outrageous outfit, carrying on a conver-
sation with the in crowd that he had so swiftly become part of. His friendships with Andy
Warhol and Halston gave him carte blanche with the inner circle that included Liz Taylor,
Liza Minnelli, and Bianca Jagger. Unfortunately, Victor passed away in the early Nineties
while living at the Chelsea Hotel. I miss him and his wonderful, exuberant laugh.

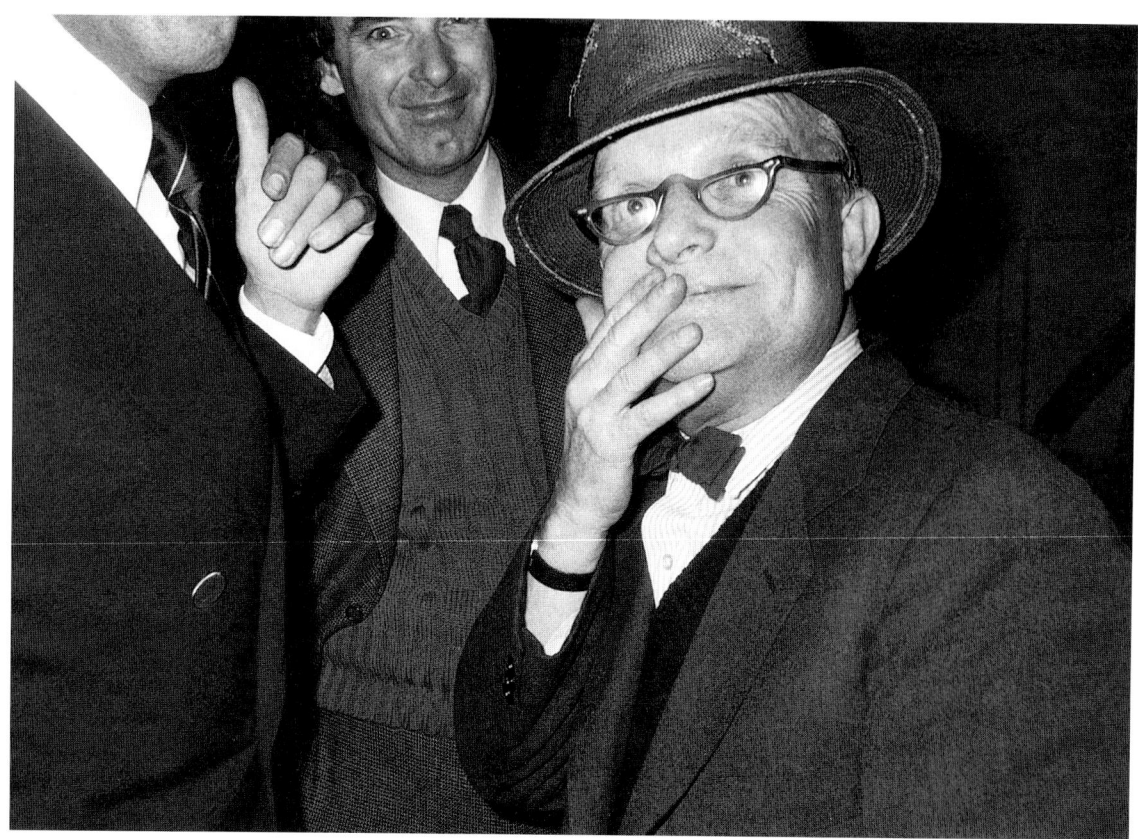

TRUMAN CAPOTE

Truman Capote discovered Studio 54 for the first time just a week before this photo was taken—as a dare Andy Warhol had brought him to Studio wearing only his silk bathrobe and embroidered slippers. I approached Mr. Capote the following week and took this photograph. Afterward, I asked him to dance. He politely declined.

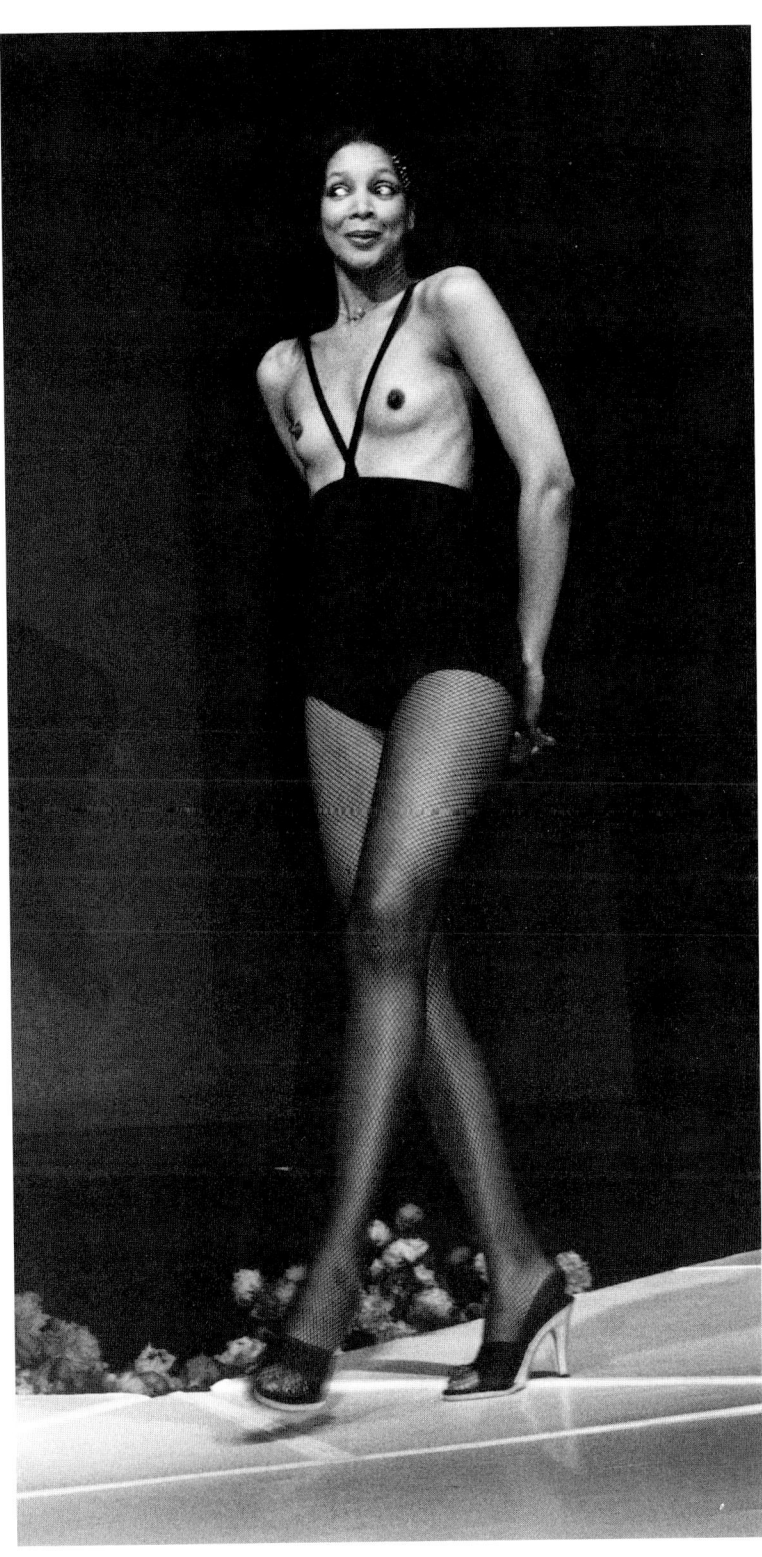

This is June Murphy, a model from the Sixties and Seventies, wearing the original topless bathing suit designed by Rudi Gernreich. Rudi was a brilliant fashion designer from the early Sixties who was also the first designer to make unisex fashions and makeup for men. We also have him to thank for the thong.

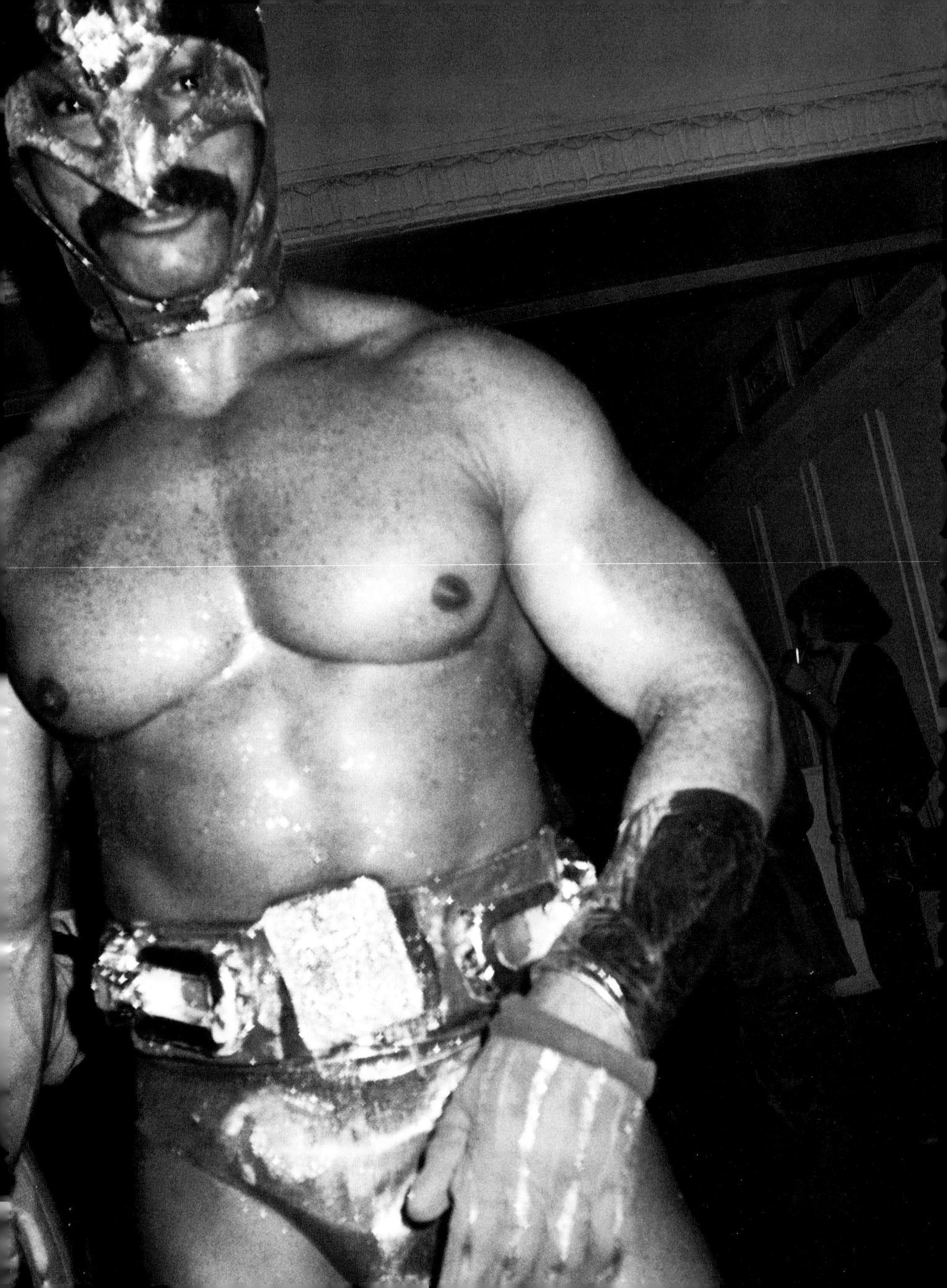

This massive gladiator was in a troupe of twelve men who scattered in different directions as soon as they entered the club's main room, making it impossible to photograph them as a group. They were dressed identically and were all roughly this fellow's size and scale. Note his proportion compared to the large entrance doorway.

MUHAMMAD ALI

As a rule there was a comfort zone at Studio that allowed celebrities to move about fairly freely, unhindered by fans. But occasionally a star would arrive that caused even seasoned groupies to lose their sophisticated cool and act like any other fan. Muhammad Ali was one such star—a legend so loved that people simply couldn't control themselves. On this night, Ali was surrounded by bodyguards sheltering him from a sea of people trying to get close enough to speak to him and shake his hand. After attempting to approach him several times, I finally gave up and went to wait by the exit. An hour or so later, too suffocated to enjoy himself, he headed for the door. I finally took his picture as he escaped from a mob of loving fans.

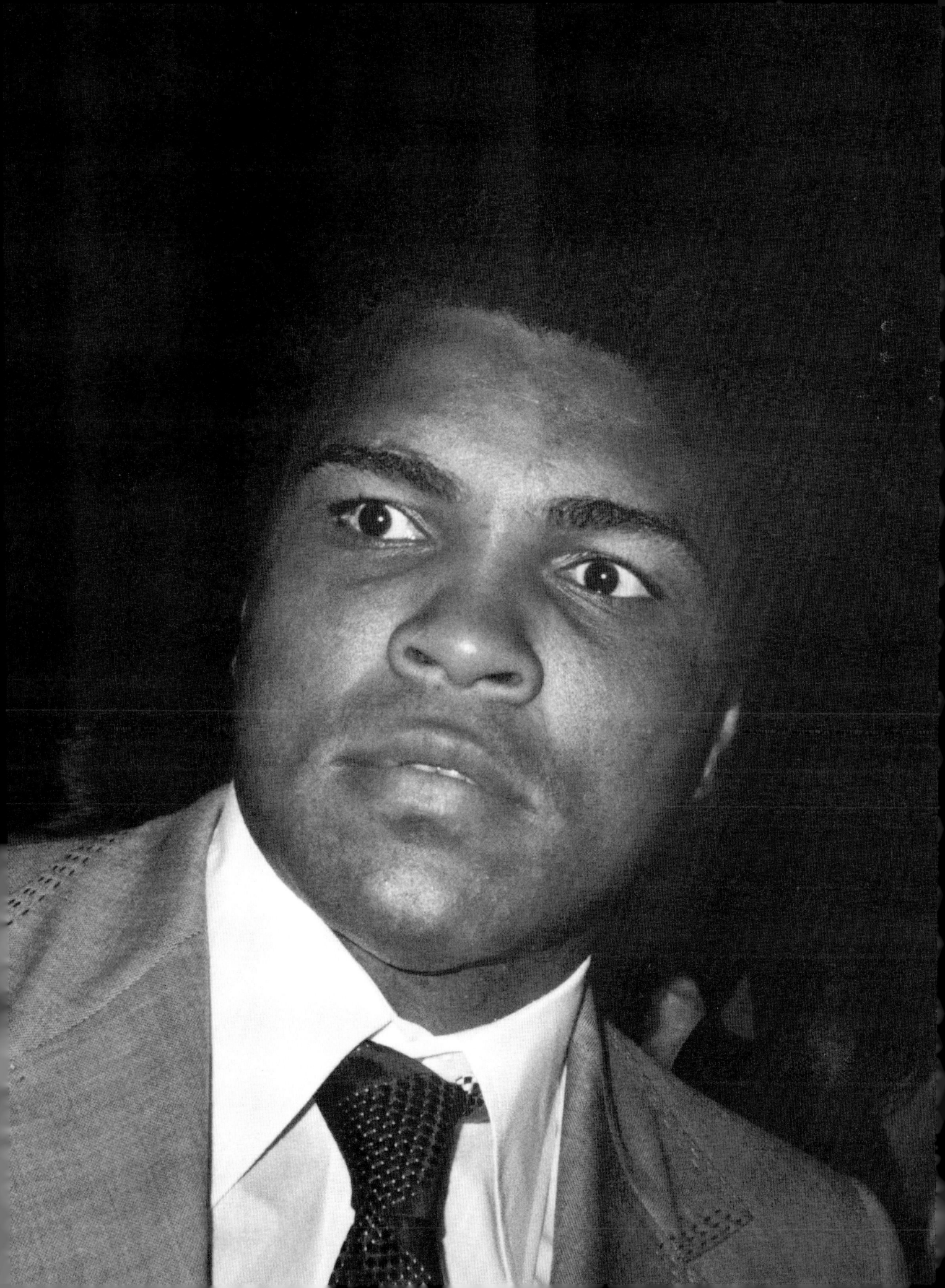

EDITH BEALE

The reclusive cousin of Jacqueline Bouvier Kennedy Onassis, Edith Beale lived in a ramshackle old house in East Hampton throughout the seventies with her eighty-year-old mother, also named Edith, and their thirty cats. Little Edie, as she was called by her mother, had come to Studio 54 after a screening of *Grey Gardens*, a documentary film by the Maysles brothers that premiered in 1976 at the New York Film Festival. Edie loved to wear her dresses and skirts backwards or upside down, along with festive headwraps that she usually made from sweaters.

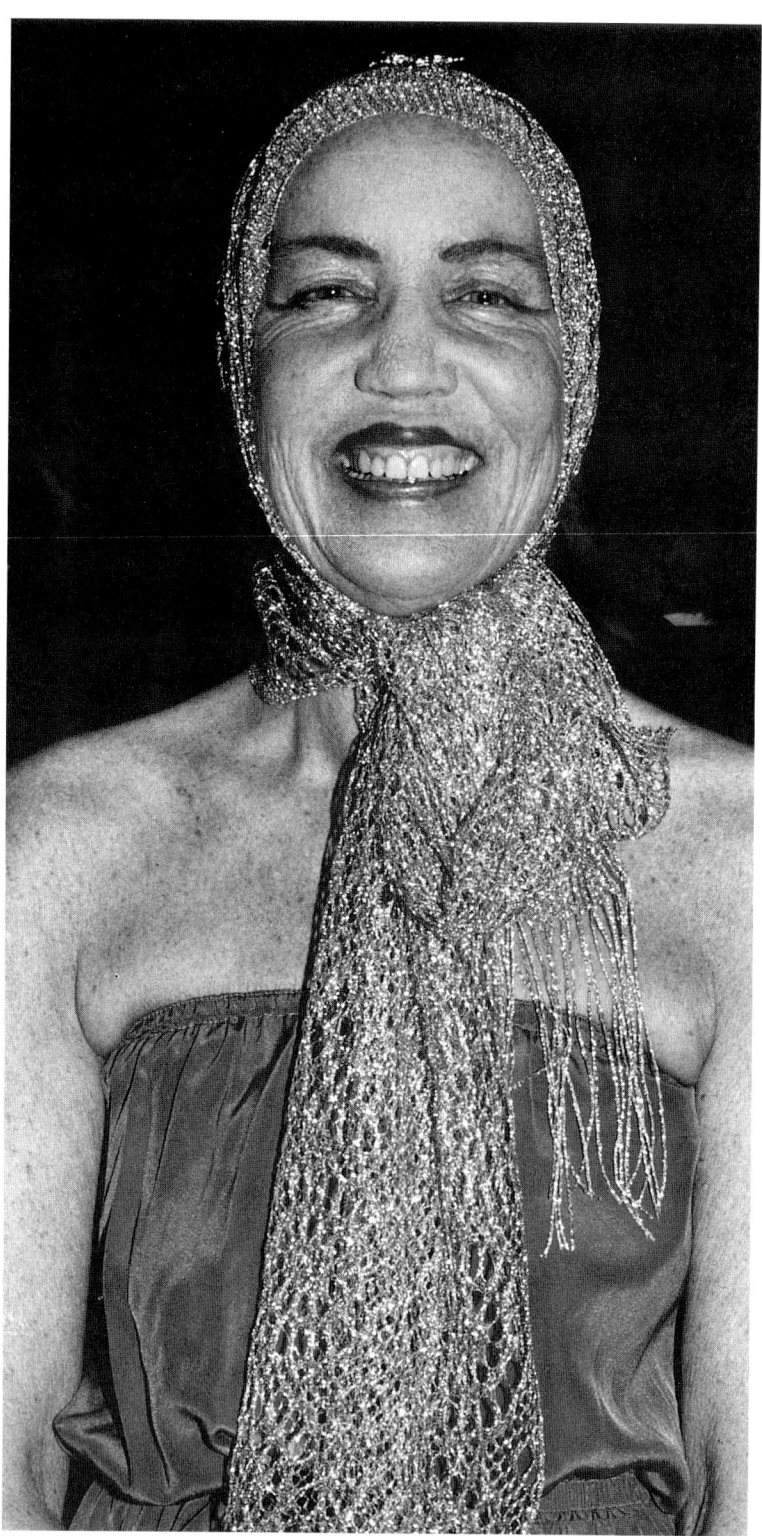

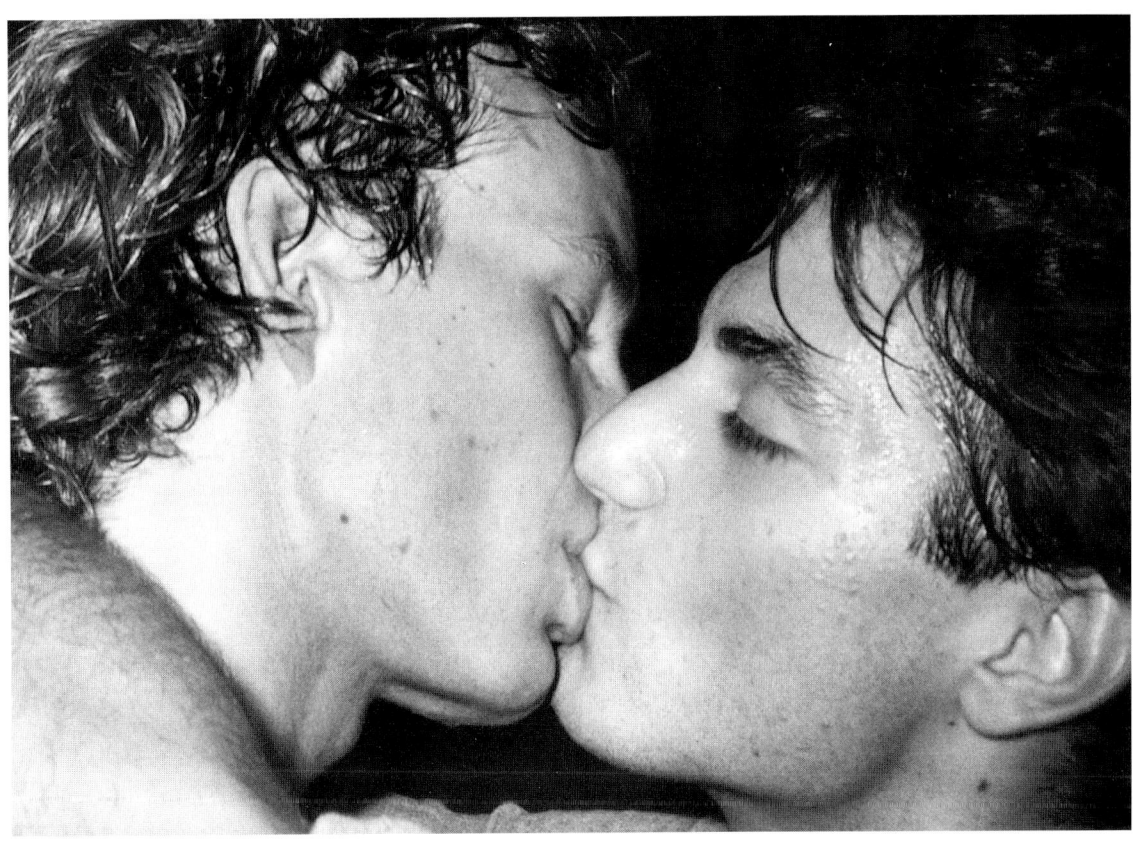

It wasn't long after the drug explosion of the late Sixties and early Seventies that more and more people could be found doing drugs in public. As soon as drugs hit the social arena, people became a lot friendlier toward each other. Barriers to physical encounters in public began to break down, and it quickly became the norm to see people of all sexual persuasions expressing their feelings for each other openly, for all to see. In its second year the Studio balcony became an active den of erotic interaction. It wasn't unusual to find couples and triples in a heated exchange in the rafters of the upper balcony. This kiss between two boys seemed innocent compared to most of the action going on around them.

EDGAR WINTER

The Winter brothers, Johnny and Edgar, were rarely seen together in public, and there always seemed to be some confusion over which one was which. The other photographers in the press pool, all convinced that this was Johnny, were calling out "Johnny, look over here." I, on the other hand, was pretty sure it was Edgar, even though he had his back to me. As I called out his name, Edgar turned around into my camera and flipped his hair at the other photographers, giving me this shot.

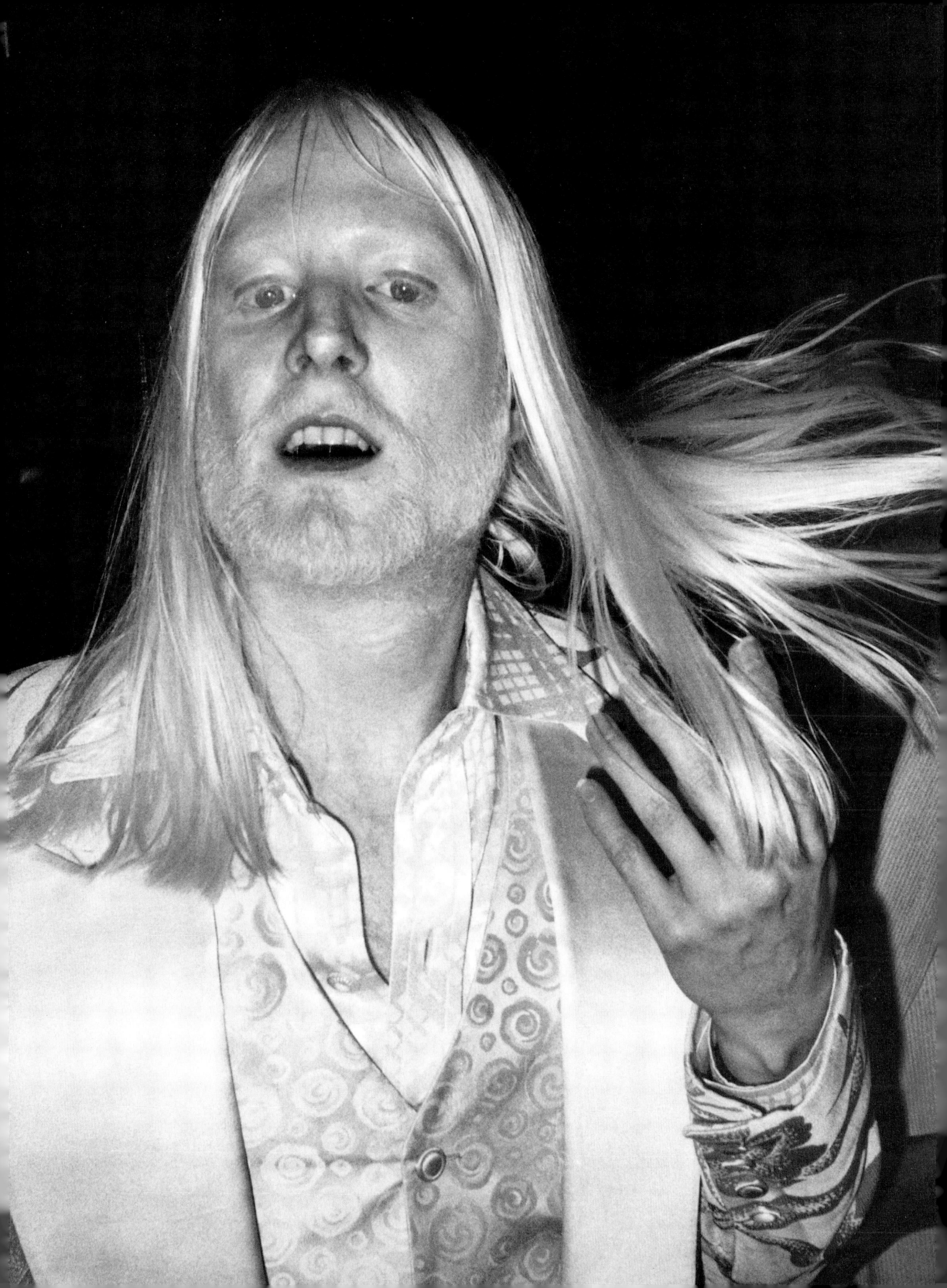

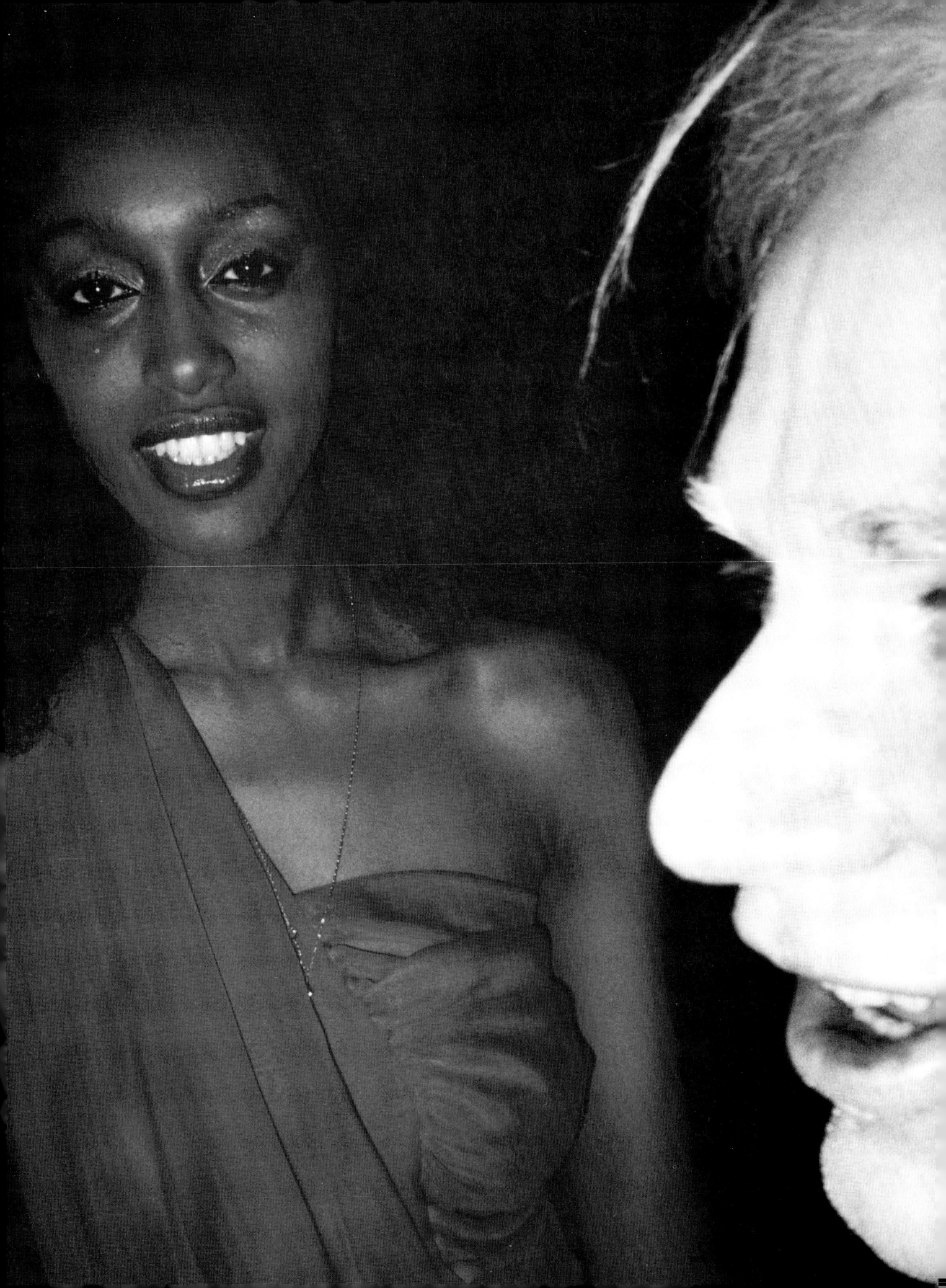

Fresh on the scene from Somalia, Iman had been brought to America and Studio by photographer Peter Beard. Upon her arrival, Andy Warhol welcomed her into the flash of bright lights and parties. Iman went on to create her own special look, making herself over into the exquisite beauty you see today. She is married to David Bowie.

MARK (10½) STEVENS AND SHARON MITCHELL

On this night at Studio, Mark (10½) Stevens and Sharon Mitchell weren't just famous porn stars, they were a work of art. They arrived at the club glittering, painted silver by the aptly named New York artist Michael Silver, who often covered people in body paint and then took them from party to party on display. And yes, the 10½ is indeed a reference to the size of Mr. Stevens's manhood.

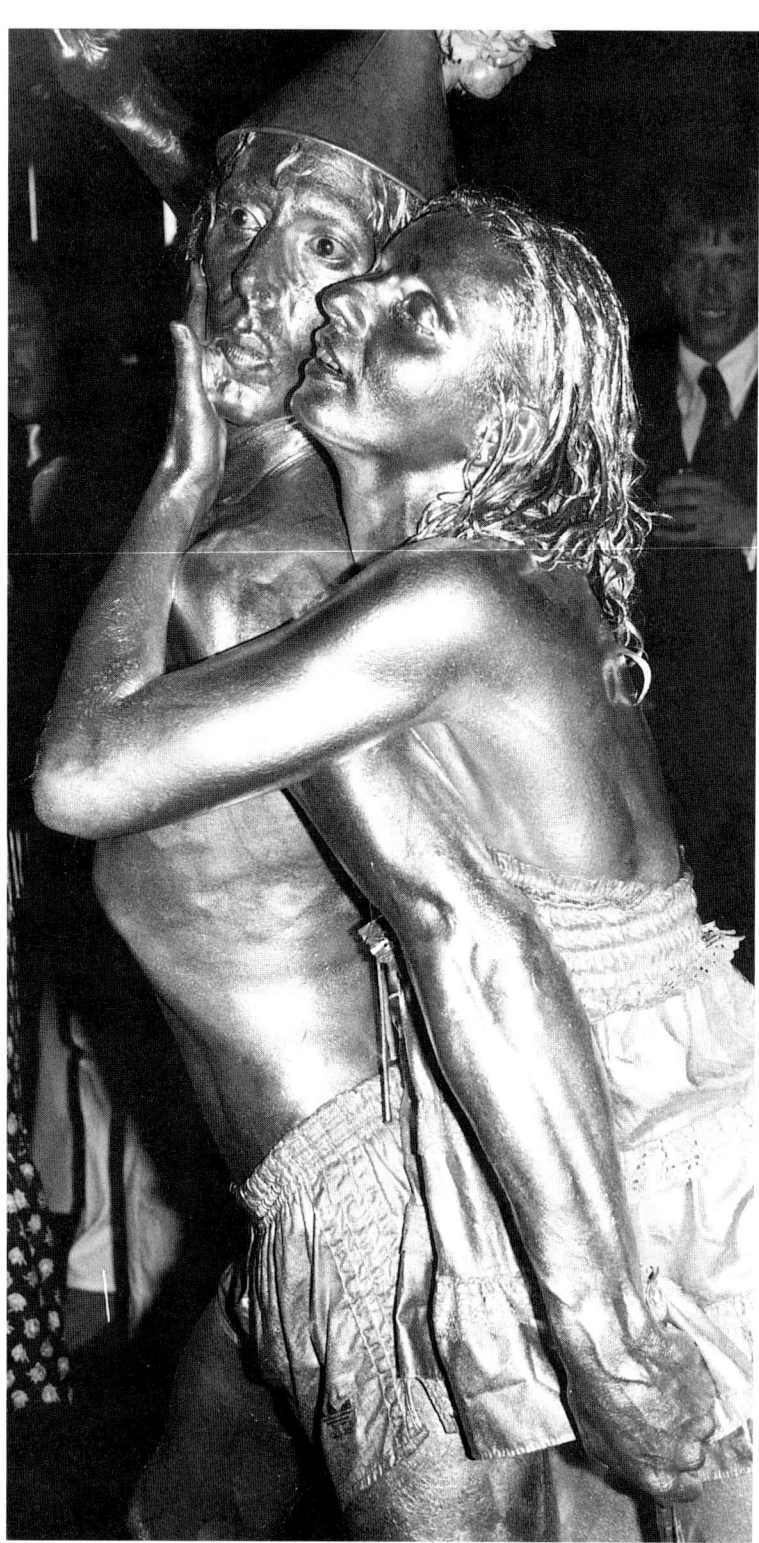

OPPOSITE: DIVINE

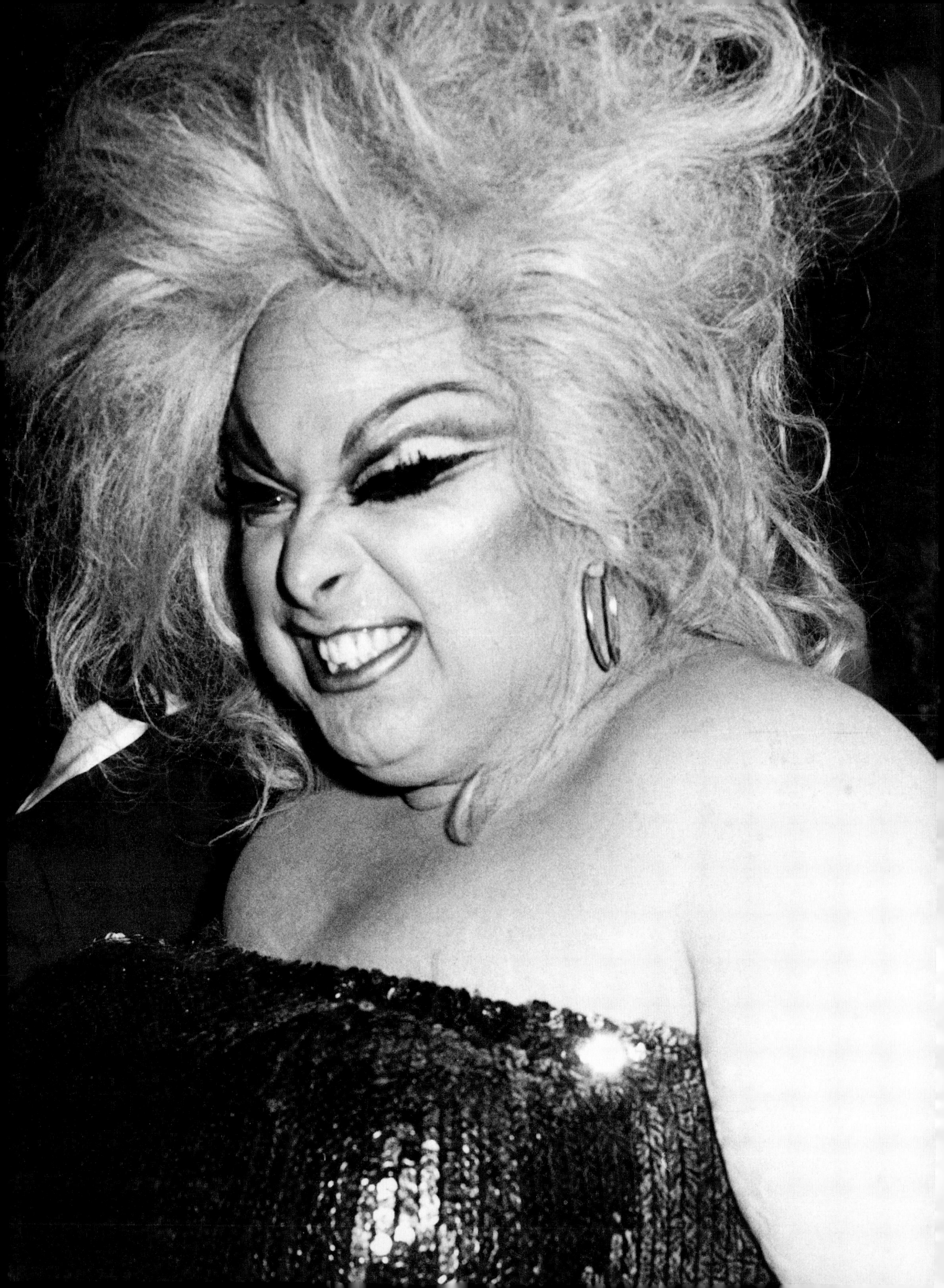

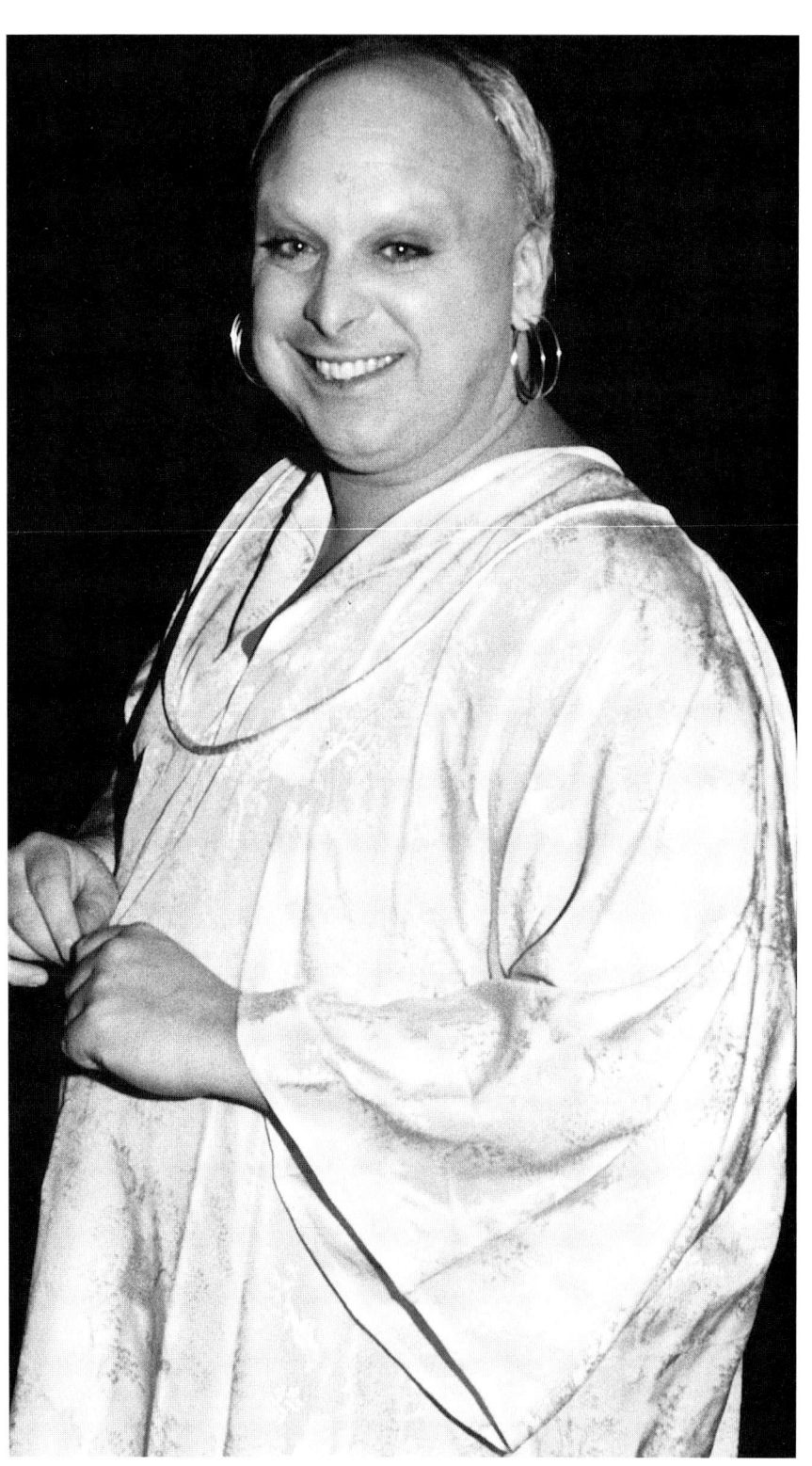

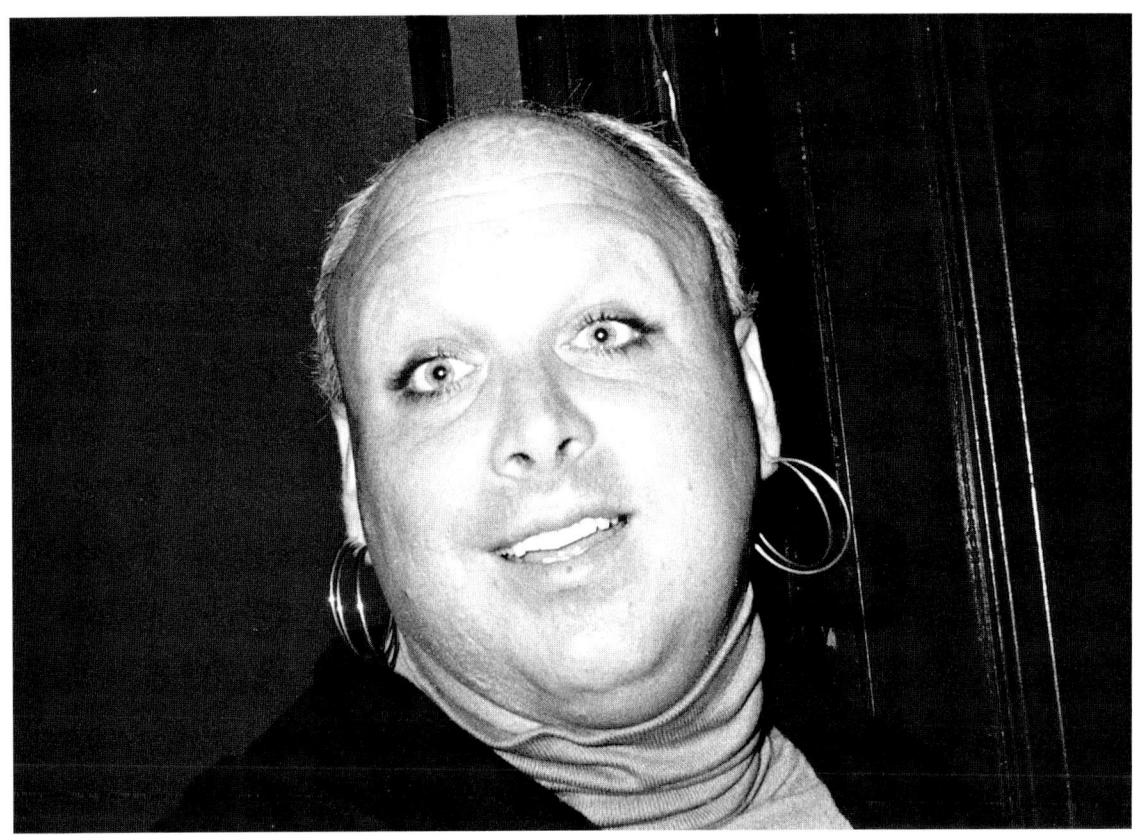

John Waters film star Divine, Divi to her friends, was a fixture at the club from the day it opened its doors. After her legendary appearances in *Neon Woman* and *Women Behind Bars*, directed by Ron Link and staged in New York in the Seventies, she unwound nightly at Studio 54. Ever the life of the party, she was an important part of the Studio mix and was often seen talking with just about anyone who wasn't intimidated by her larger-than-life presence.

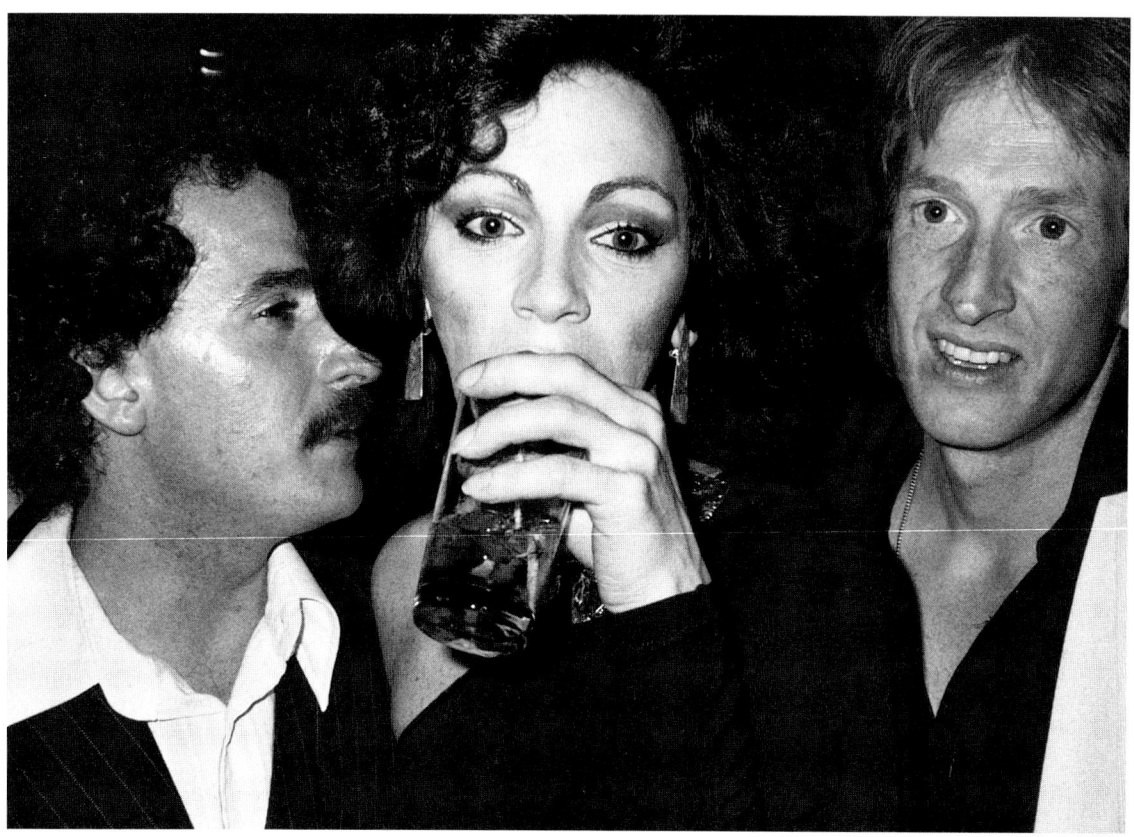

HOLLY WOODLAWN

Another from Andy Warhol's stable of underground stars, Holly Woodlawn was a Puerto Rican drag queen who made several hit films with Andy and director Paul Morrissey, among them *Trash* and *Women in Revolt*. Holly also wrote a book called *A Low Life in High Heels*, which is soon to be released as a feature film.

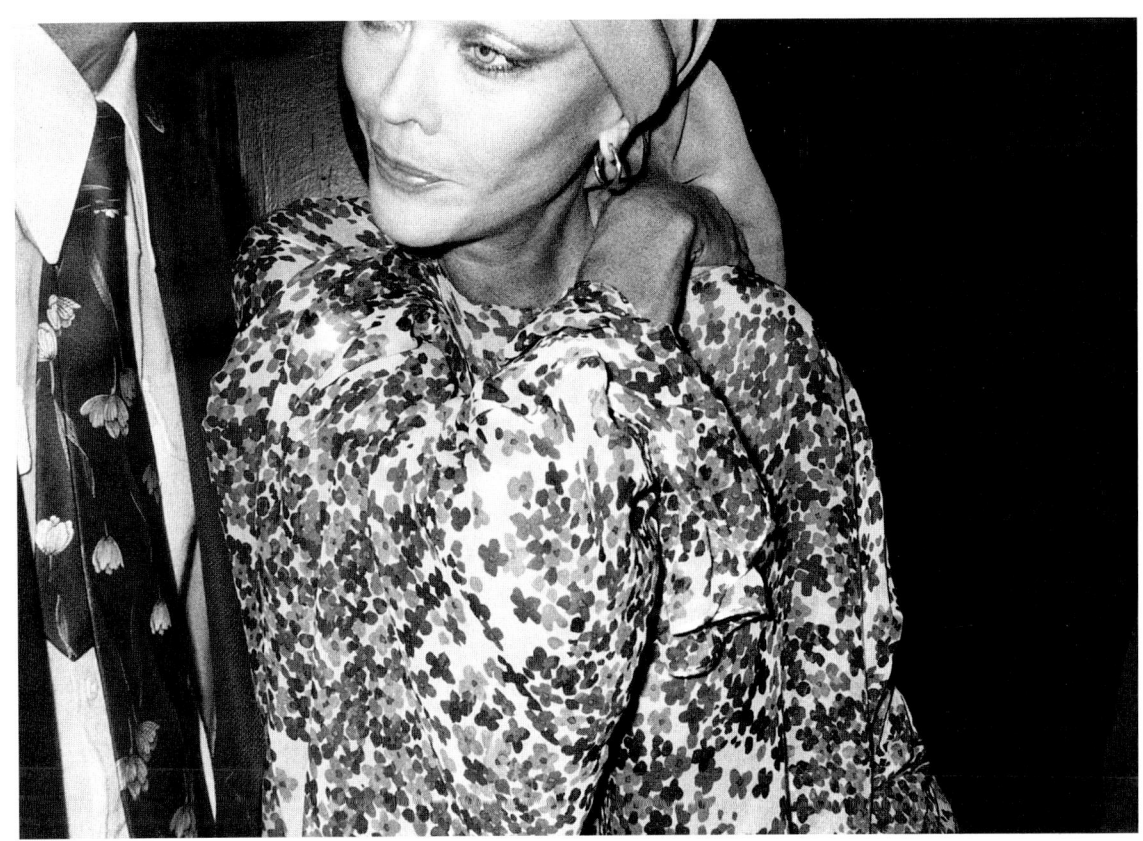

MONIQUE VAN VOOREN

An actress and cabaret singer, Ms. Van Vooren had an early career in the Fifties and was rediscovered in the Sixties by Andy Warhol, who gave her a starring role in his version of *Dracula*. Monique is still living in New York City and performs her cabaret show at upscale hotels in the city and abroad.

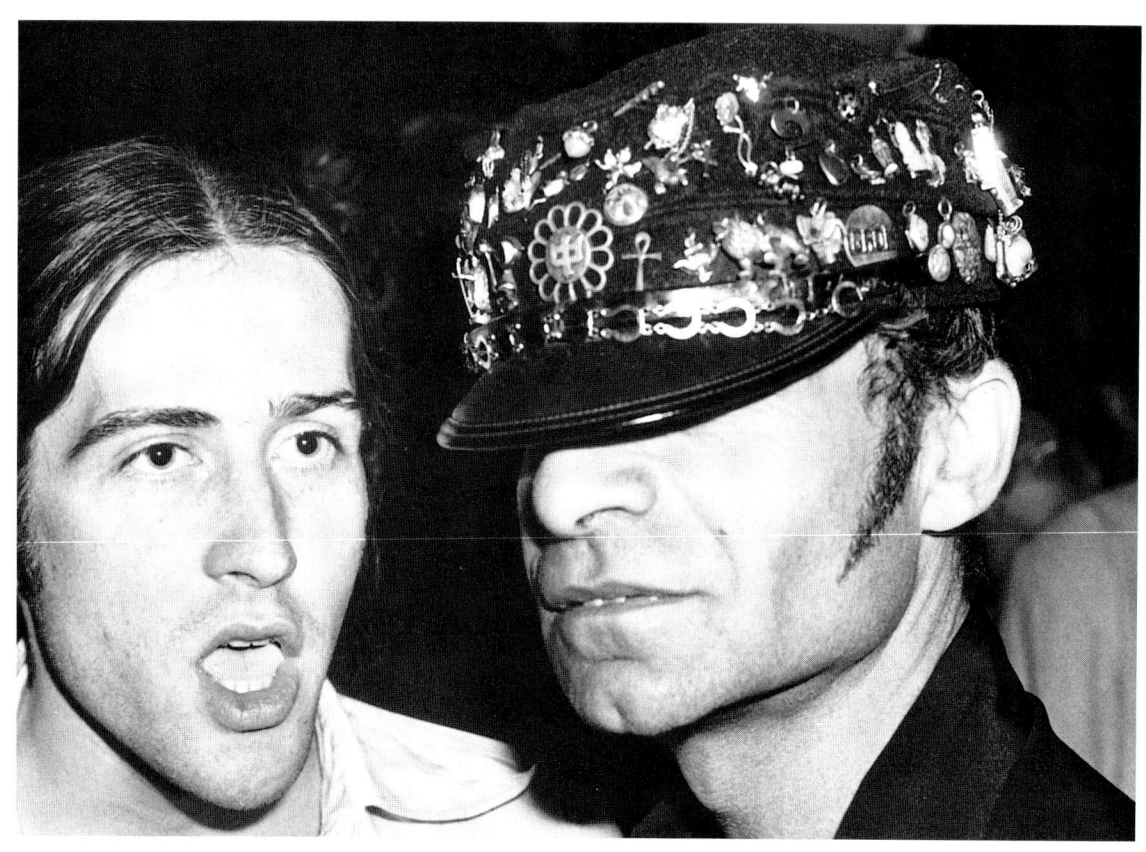

ARA GALLANT

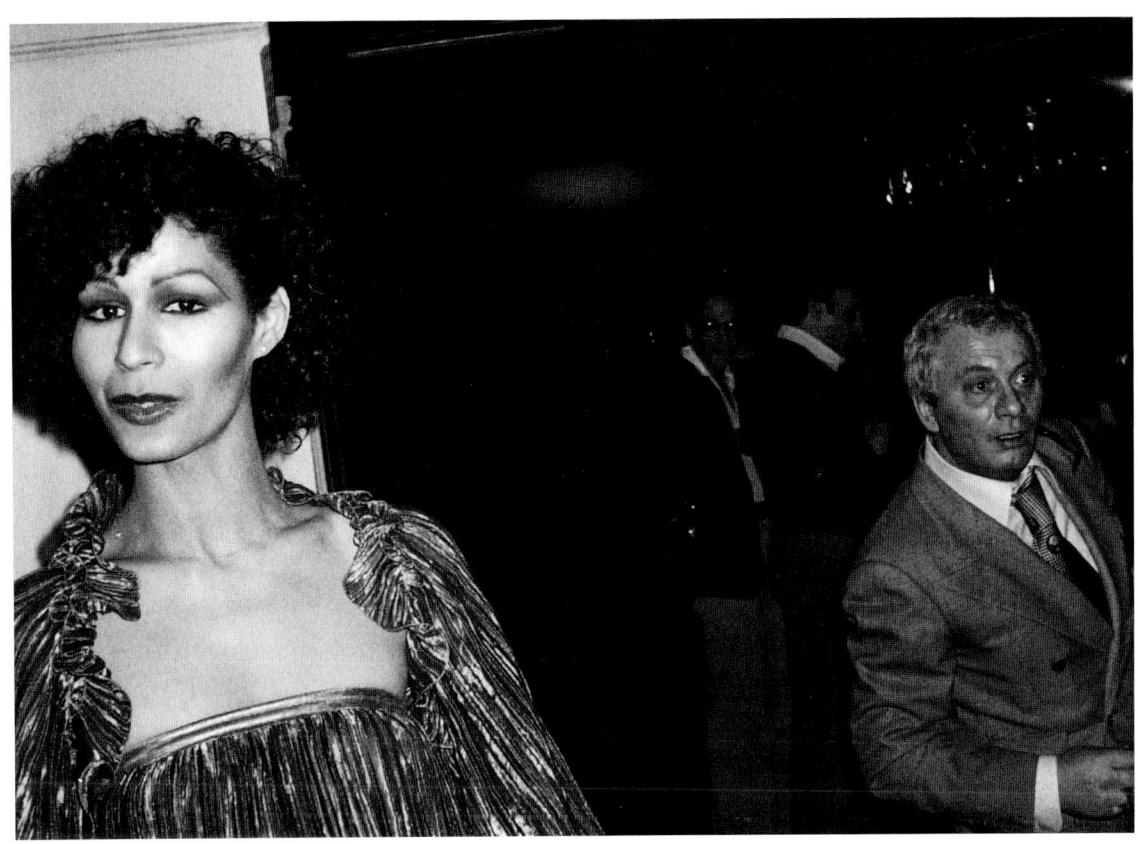

Potassa was the quintessential queen of the day. Passing as a real woman, she was the darling of the fashion set. Young up-and-coming designers often gave her clothes to wear to the club because she carried herself with such verve and style that both she and the clothing she wore always got noticed. Felice Quinto was the renowned paparazzo whose celebrity photographs were so well known that he himself became famous. His classic photograph of Anita Ekberg fighting with the paparazzi in Rome is just one example of his cunning eye at work. Oddly, he is pictured here without his cameras—a rare sight indeed.

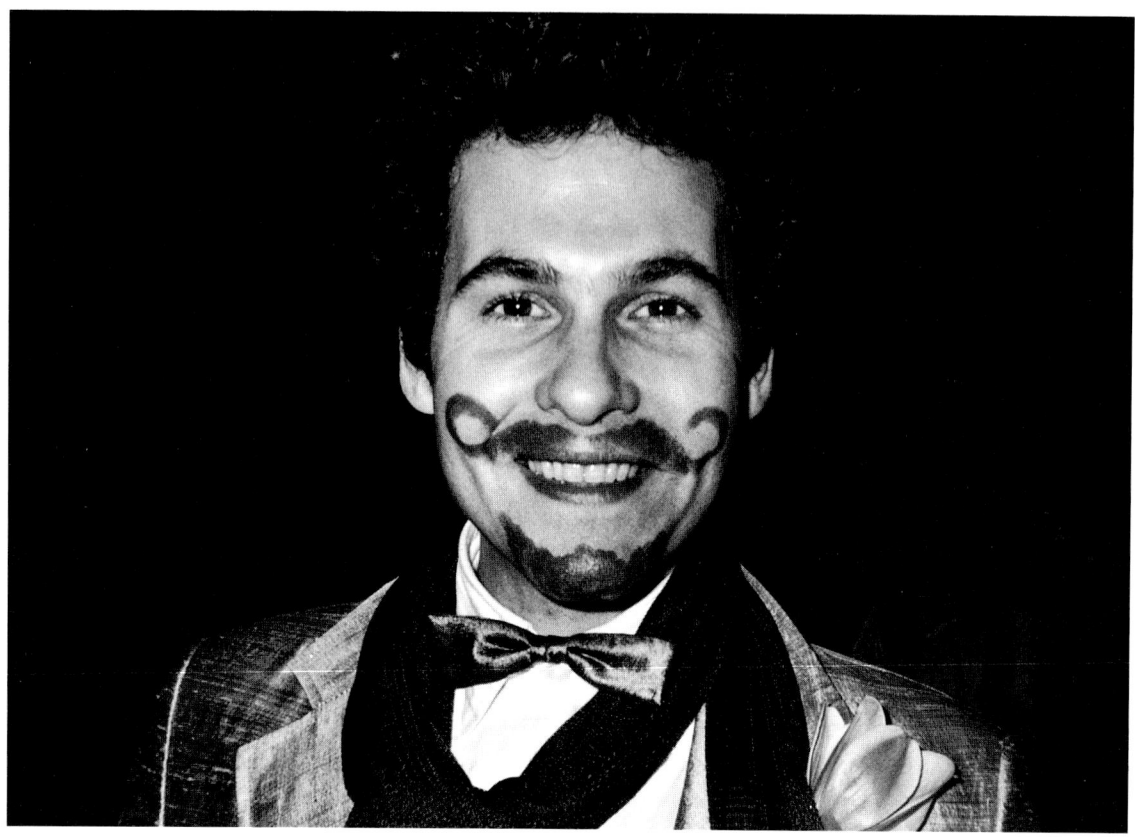

R. COURI HAY

Party boy and gossip columnist R. Couri Hay wrote for the *National Enquirer* and was a regular fixture at Studio. His own parties in the Seventies and Eighties were legendary unto themselves. As a gossip columnist he was both loathed and loved by those he wrote about. Once, in an upscale restaurant in Los Angeles, a plate of food was dumped over his head by an unhappy victim of his reporting. Today he is a successful publicist in New York City.

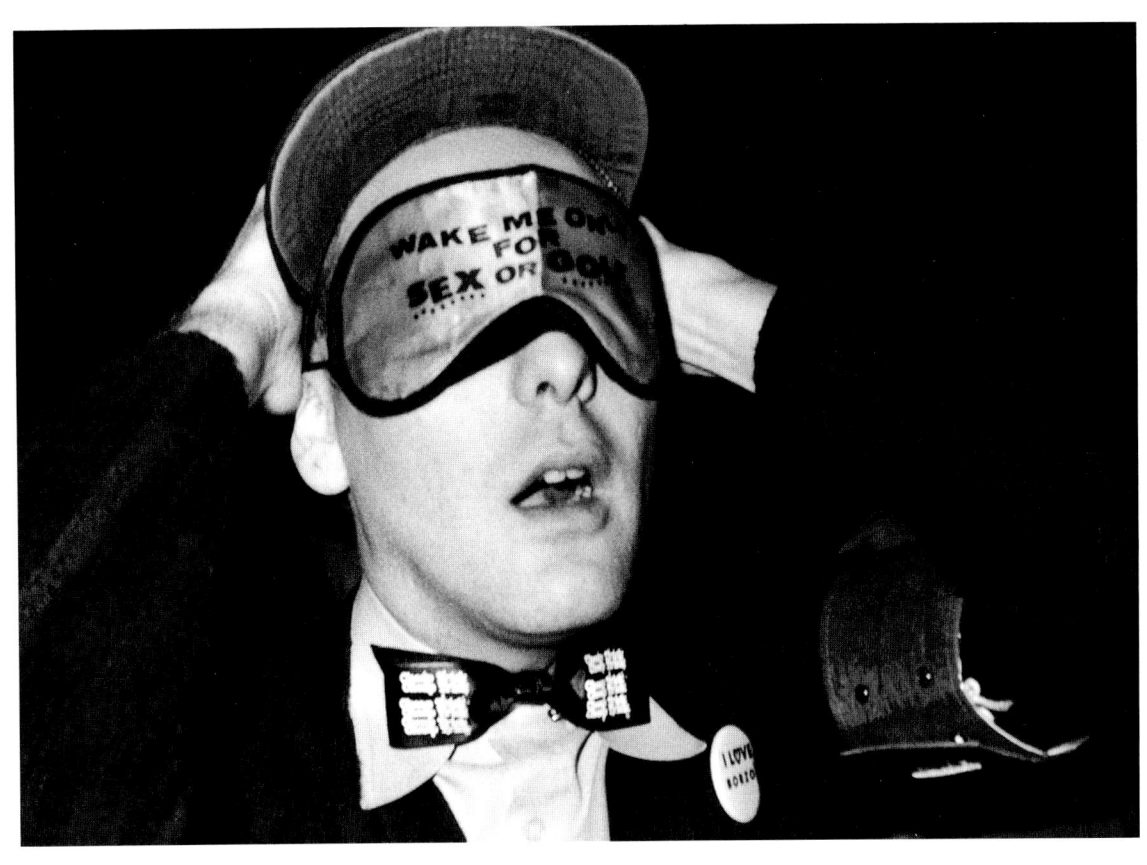

CHEAP TRICK'S RICK NIELSEN

ANN MILLER

A glamorous hoofer with a heart of gold, Ann Miller was from the early Hollywood school and a true legend. At the time this photo was taken, she was starring on Broadway in *Sugar Babies* with Mickey Rooney. Wearing her trademark wig, she came straight from the theater to the dance floor for the *Grease* party and was delighted to have her picture taken. She returned several nights later without her "big hair" wig and had a great time dancing the night away.

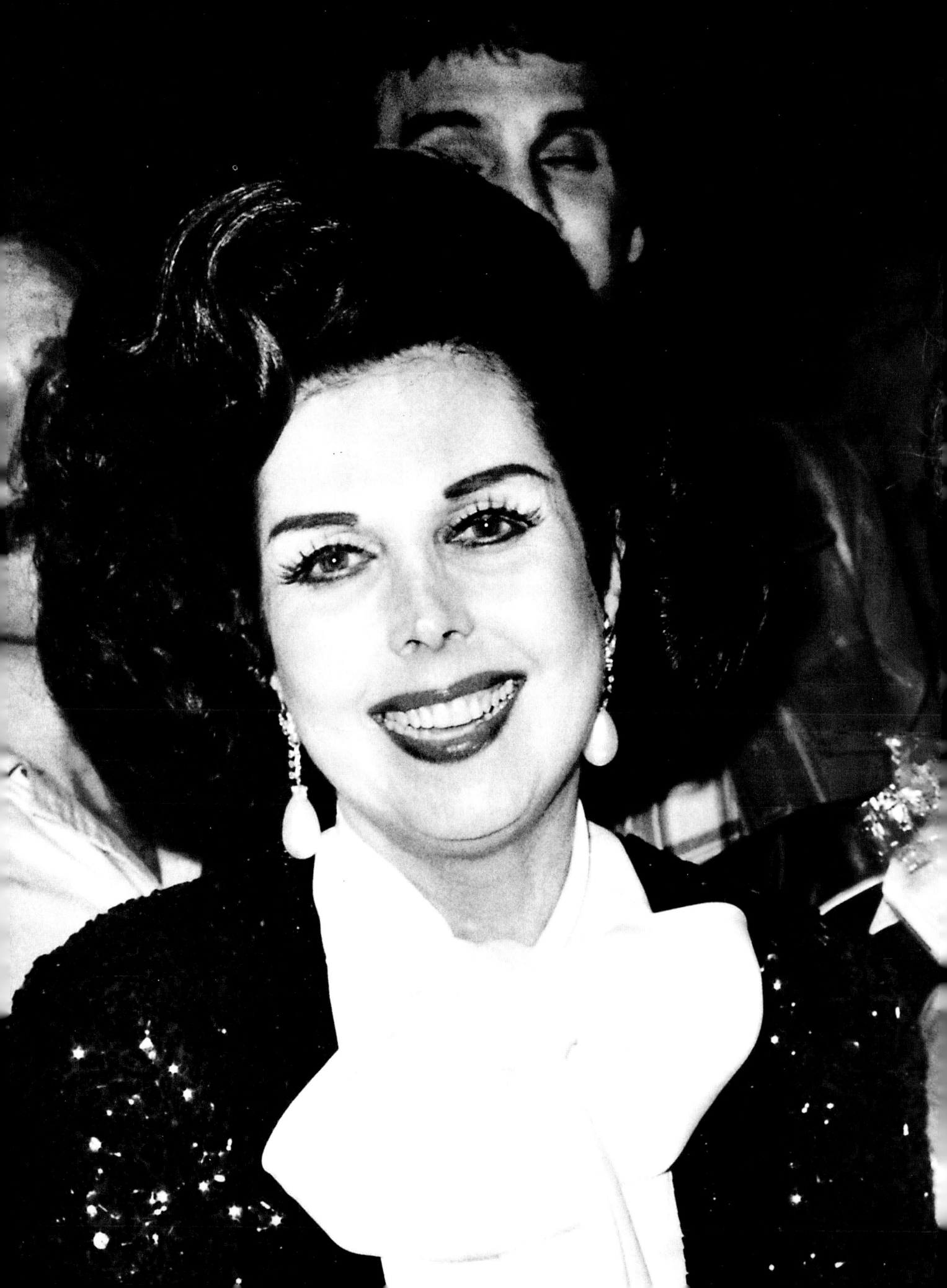

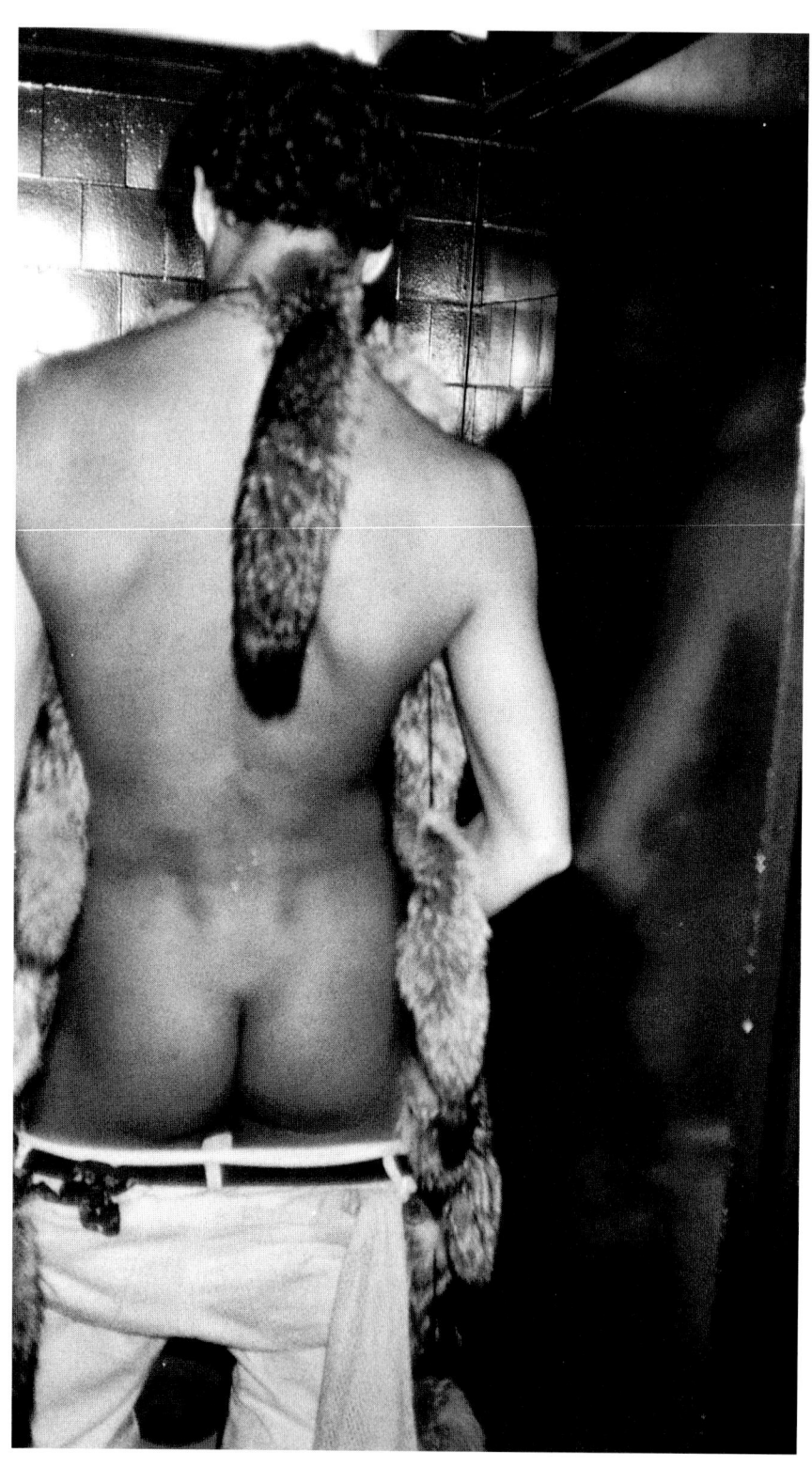

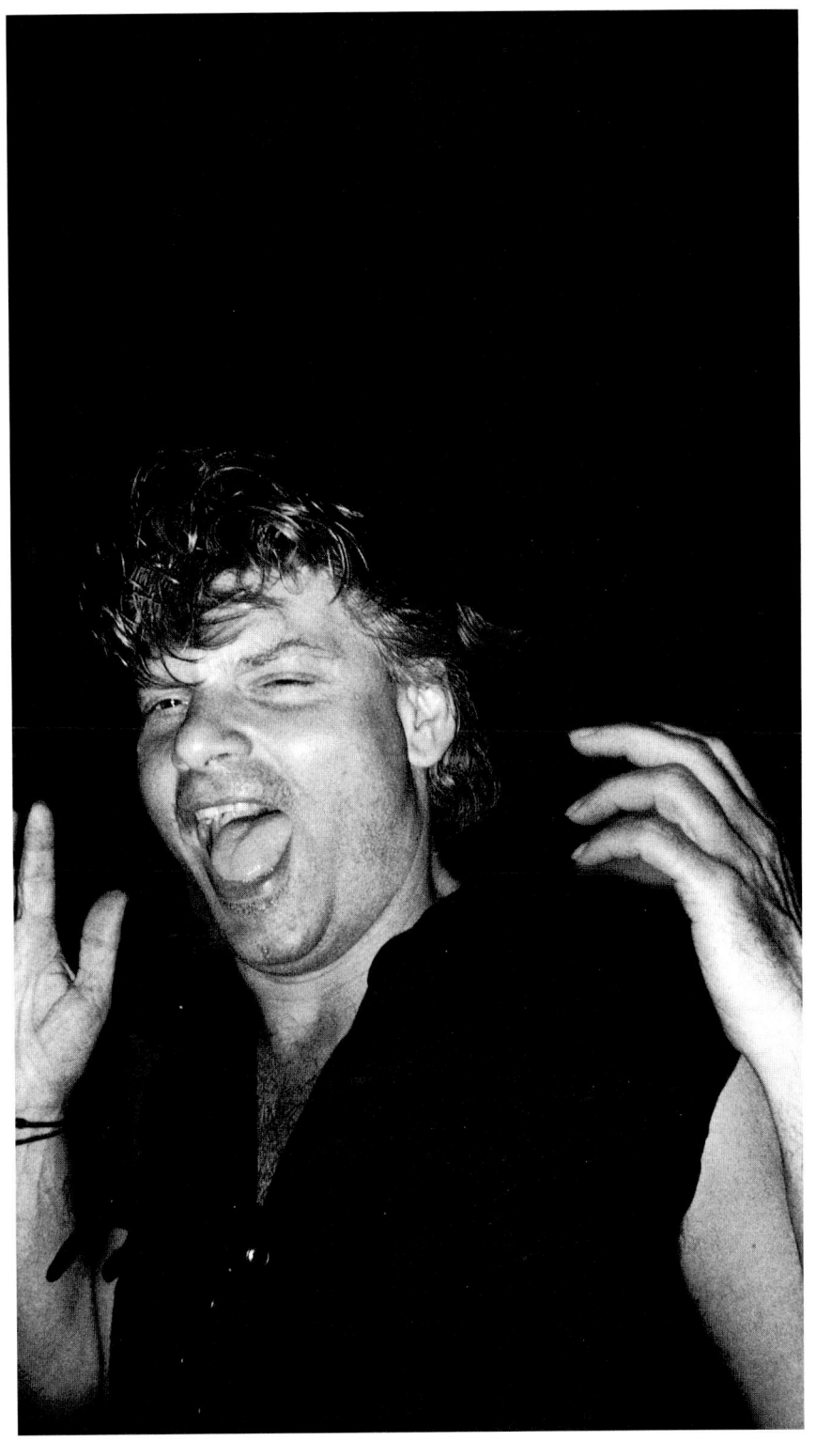

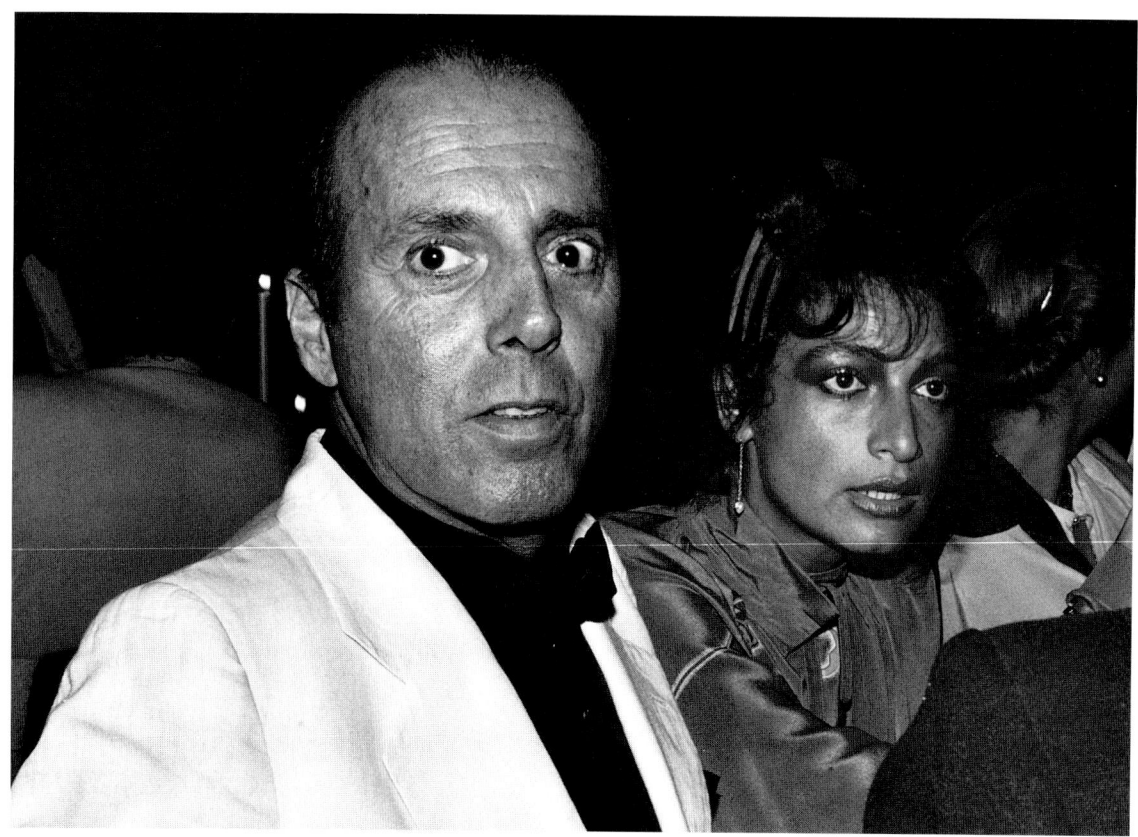

FRANCESCO SCAVULLO AND DANIELA MORERA

No one captured the spirit of the Seventies more than Francesco Scavullo, who as a leading fashion photographer shot all of the greatest personalities and models of the day. He was one of the truly glamorous people of the time. Always dressed to the nines and with a stunning escort, male or female, at his side, Francesco was the most dashing man at the club. And although there were more stars at Studio than in heaven, I never once saw him with a camera in his hand. He was always gracious and polite and acted like a true gentleman to everyone who approached him. In this photo his escort for the evening was the lovely and talented Daniela Morera, an Italian stylist and fashion writer for many of the better fashion magazines.

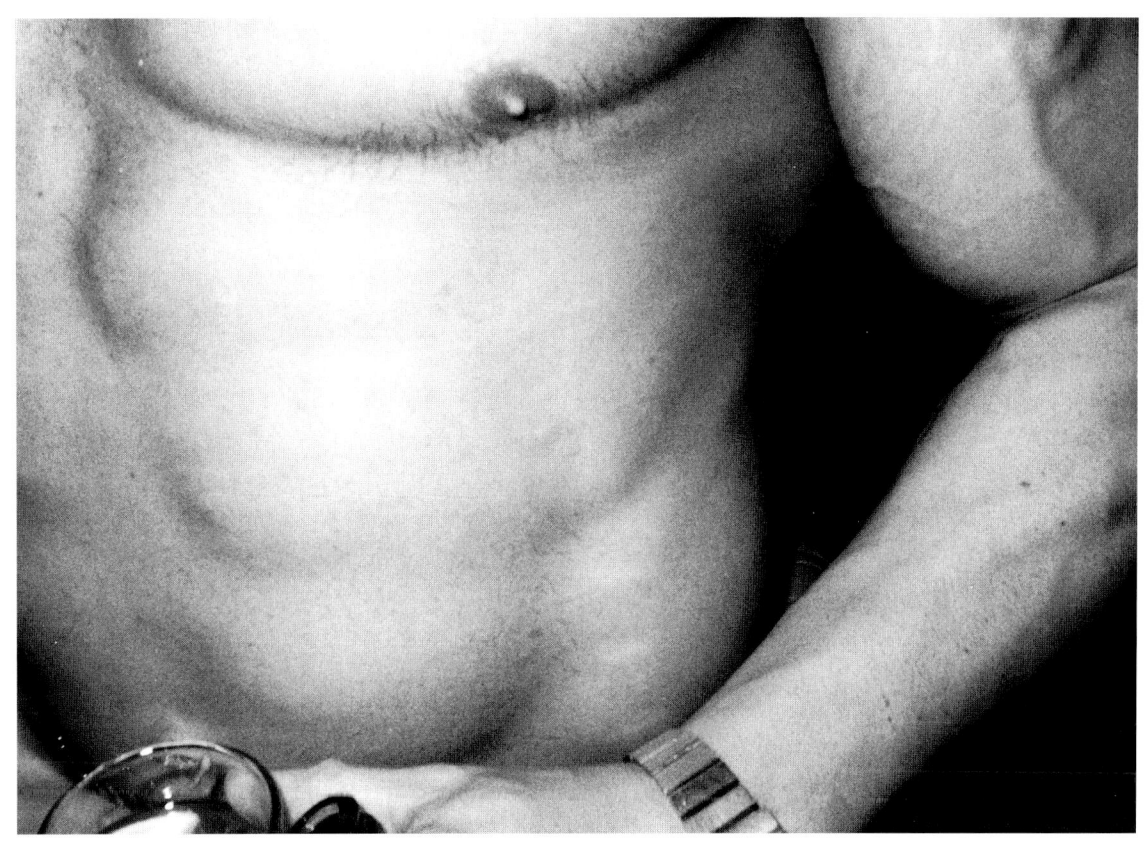

BARTENDER

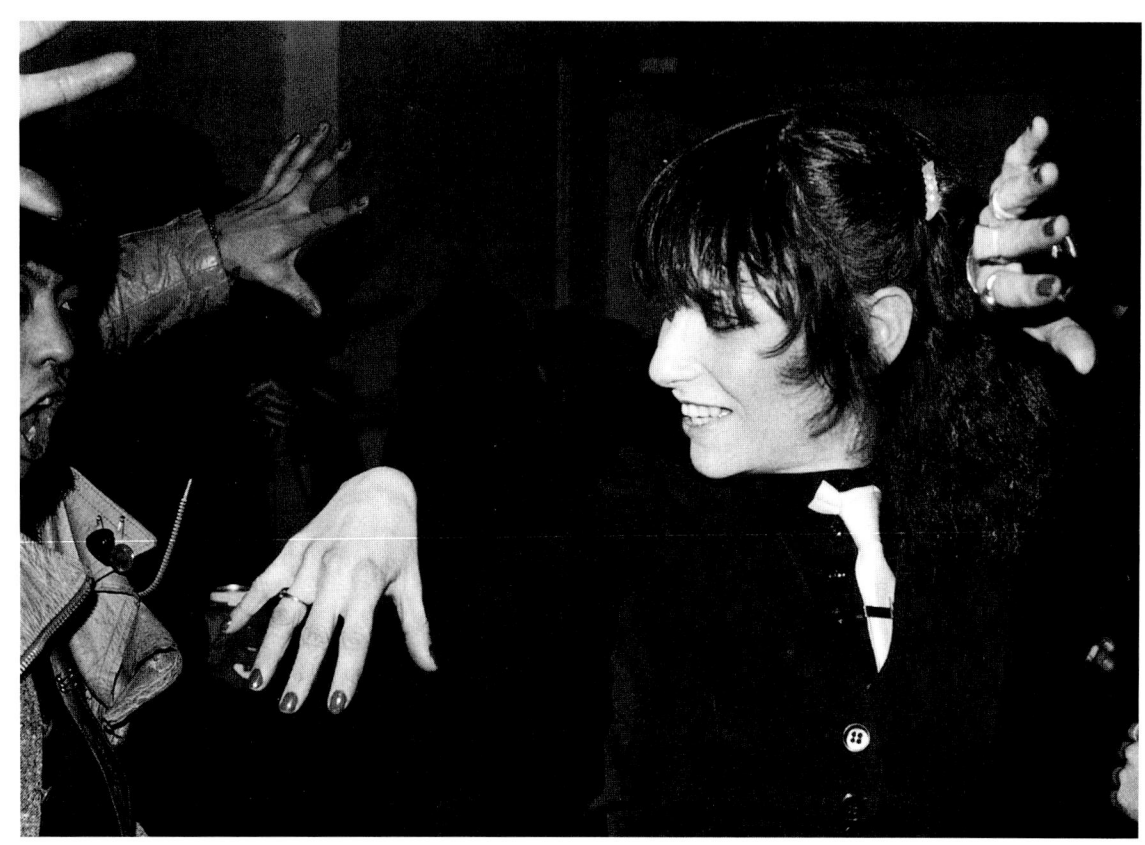

MARCIA RESNICK

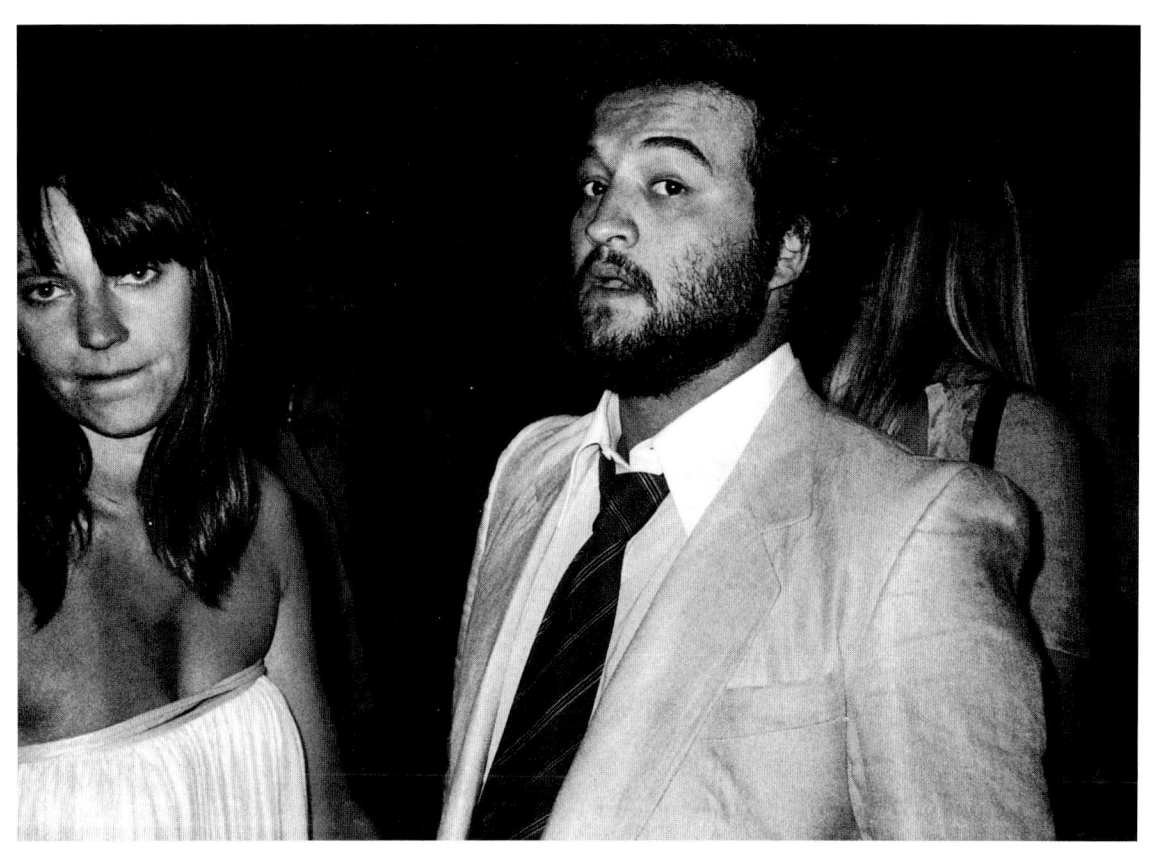

MR. AND MRS. JOHN BELUSHI

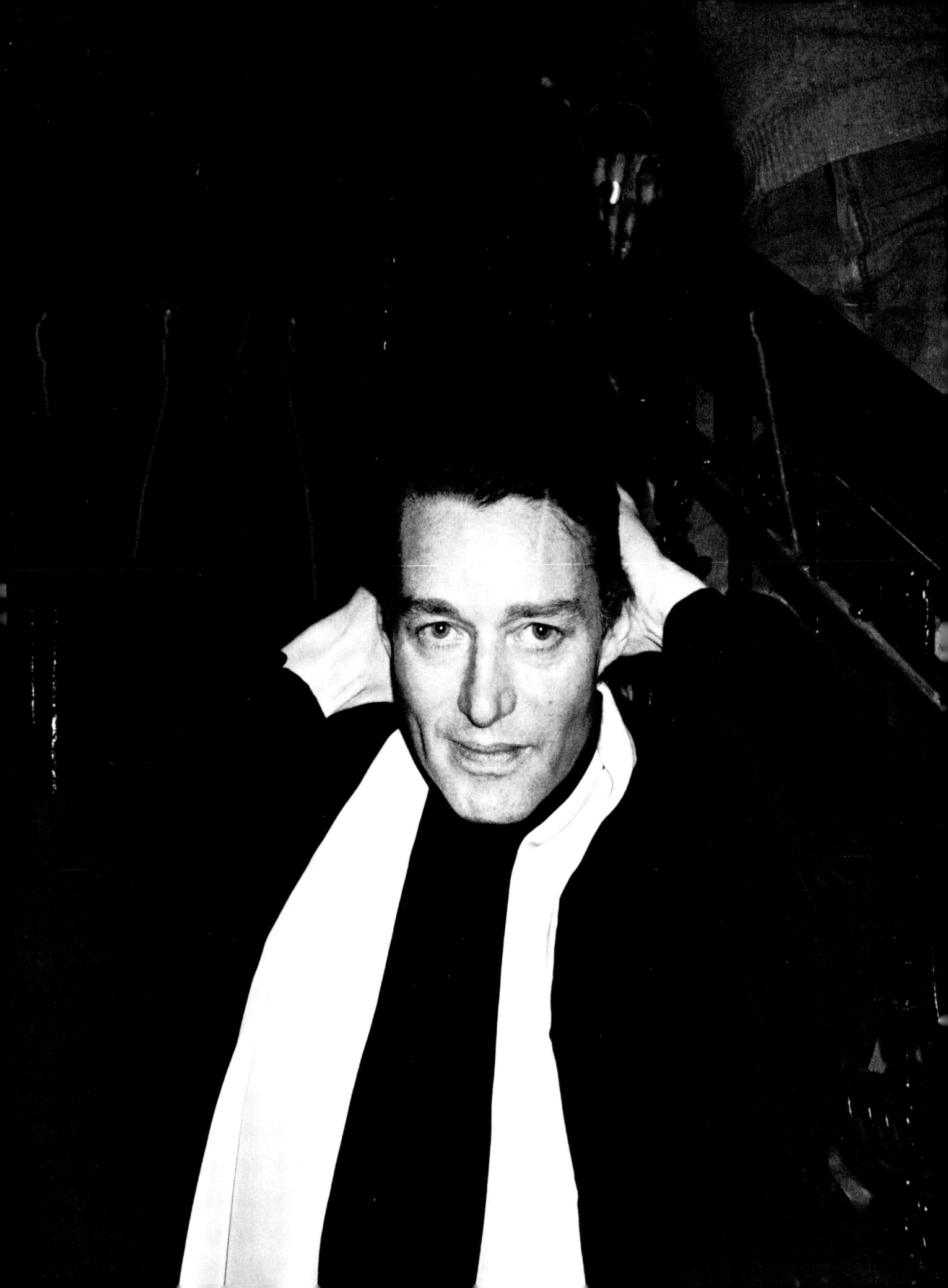

Halston was one of the most famous fashion designers of all time. With a single moniker like Cher, he fancied himself the doyen of style in the Seventies. From his signature black, white, and red palette to his minimalist modern town house and airy atelier/showroom high in the sky, Halston embraced simplicity and bravado at the same time. Not bad for the former Roy Halston Frowick, a hat designer from the Midwest. He was a permanent fixture at Studio from the day it opened its renowned doors. His designs for Liza and Liz helped make him a legend, but when he sold the rights to his name in the Eighties it was to be his undoing. A large conglomerate, Norton Simon, purchased the rights, and Halston disappeared into oblivion until his death in the late Eighties. In this photo, the streaks of light raining down on his head are a rare example of static electricity inside the camera, caused by my feet scuttling across the carpeted floor while rushing to get this shot.

FISHNET GIRL

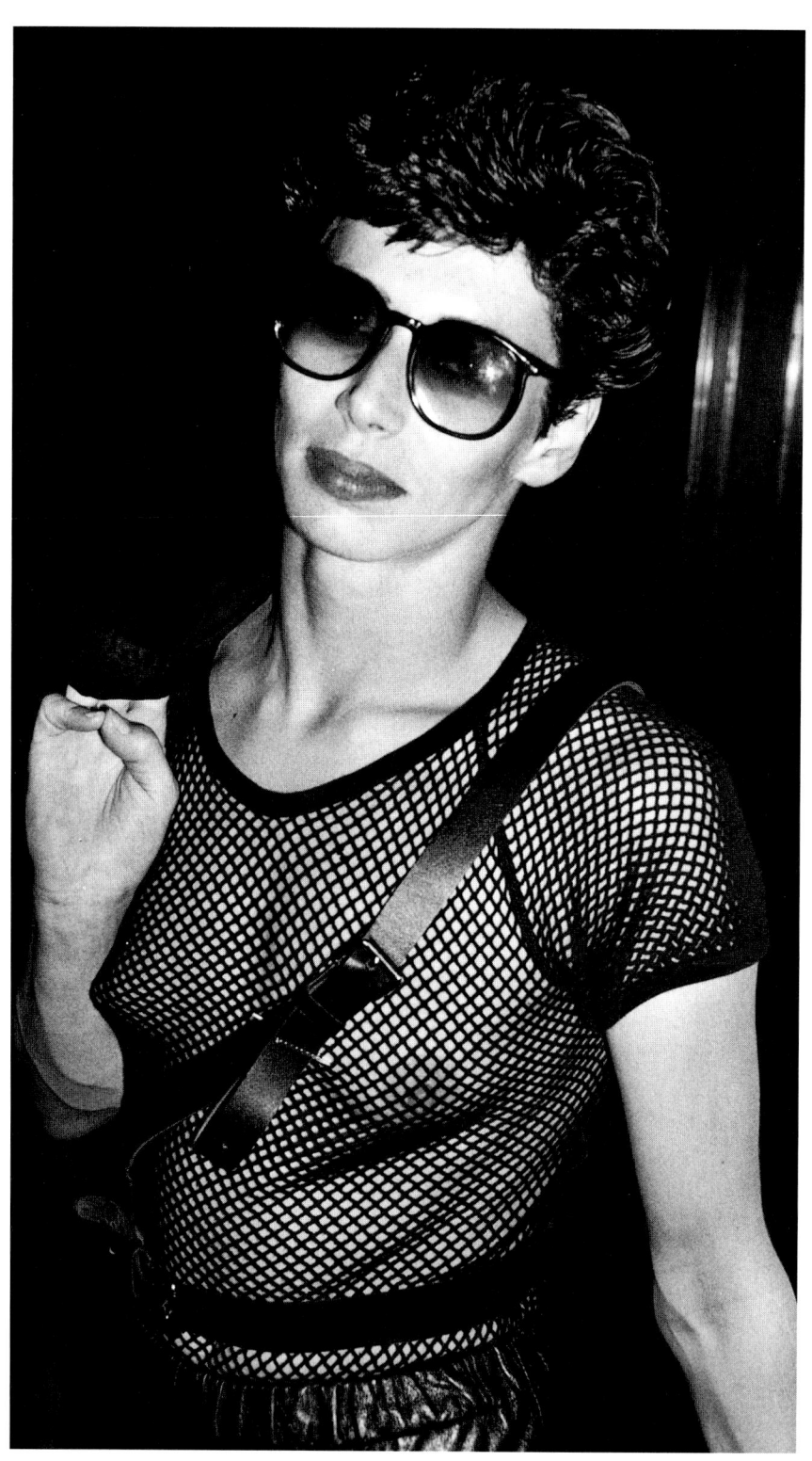

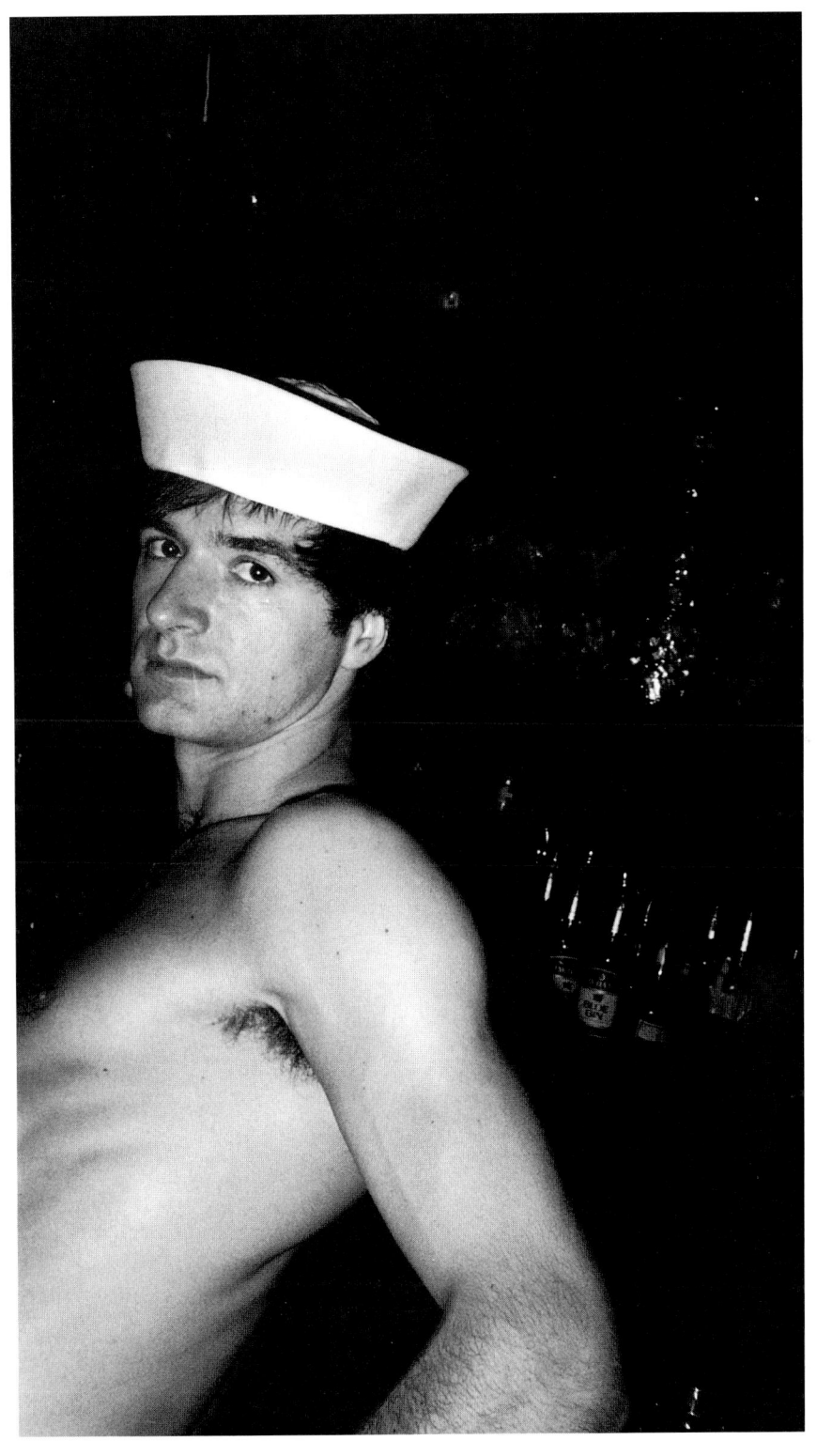

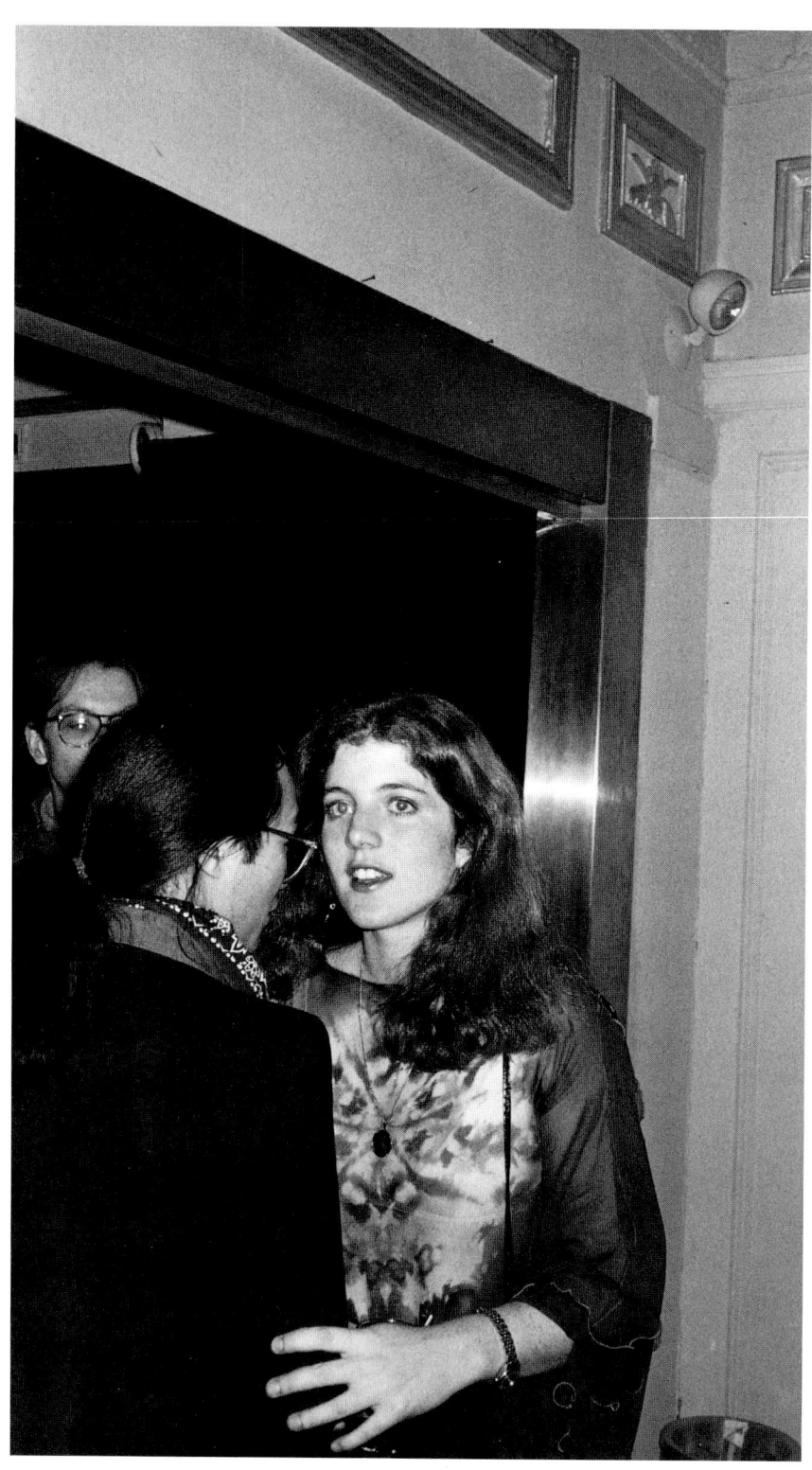

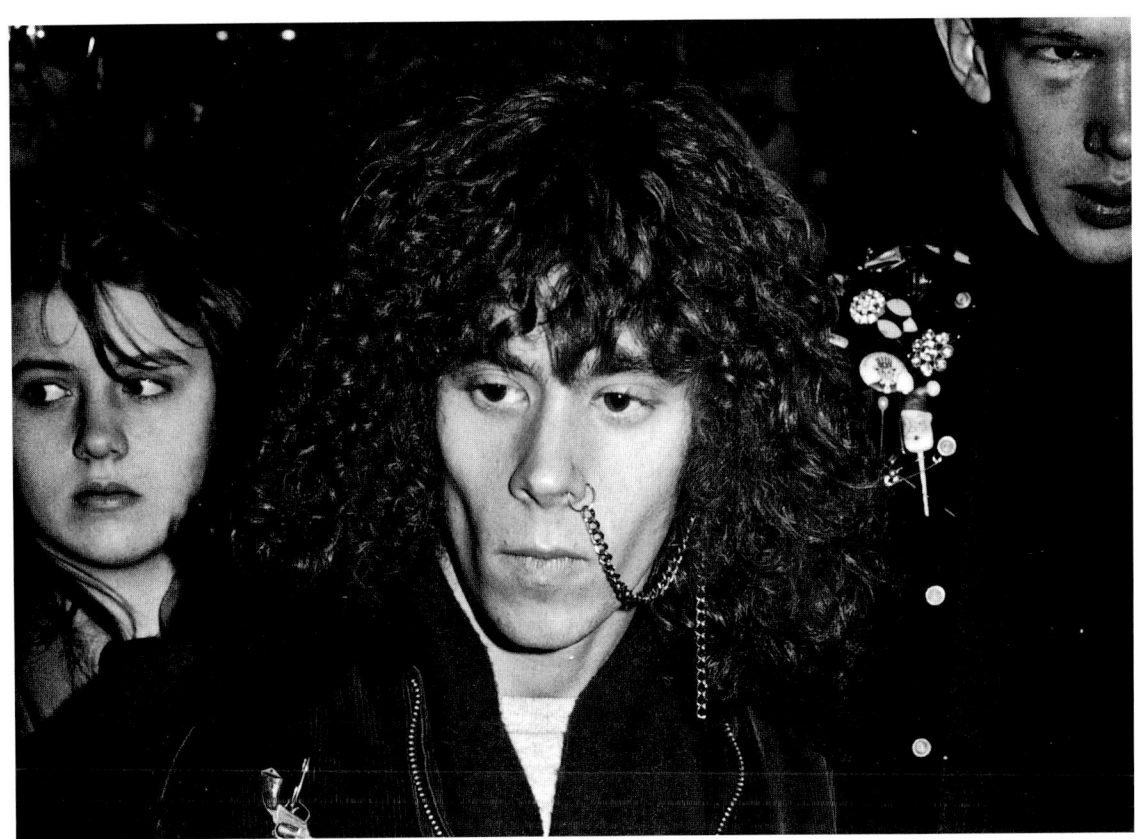

The end of the Seventies brought about dramatic changes in the way many people dressed and behaved. For all of the glamorous types that flocked to Studio, there were also those who expressed their style in a different way and embraced the growing punk movement. It wasn't unusual to find a few of the new punk rockers standing on the sidelines watching the discophiles party the night away. These three kids showed up for Halloween and seemed unimpressed by Studio's glitz.

DISCO GODDESS

This unidentified woman captured the freedom and openness
embraced by so many at Studio.
It wasn't unusual to see women
wearing little to nothing, dancing
alone or in pairs, celebrating the
newly acquired liberation of the
Seventies.

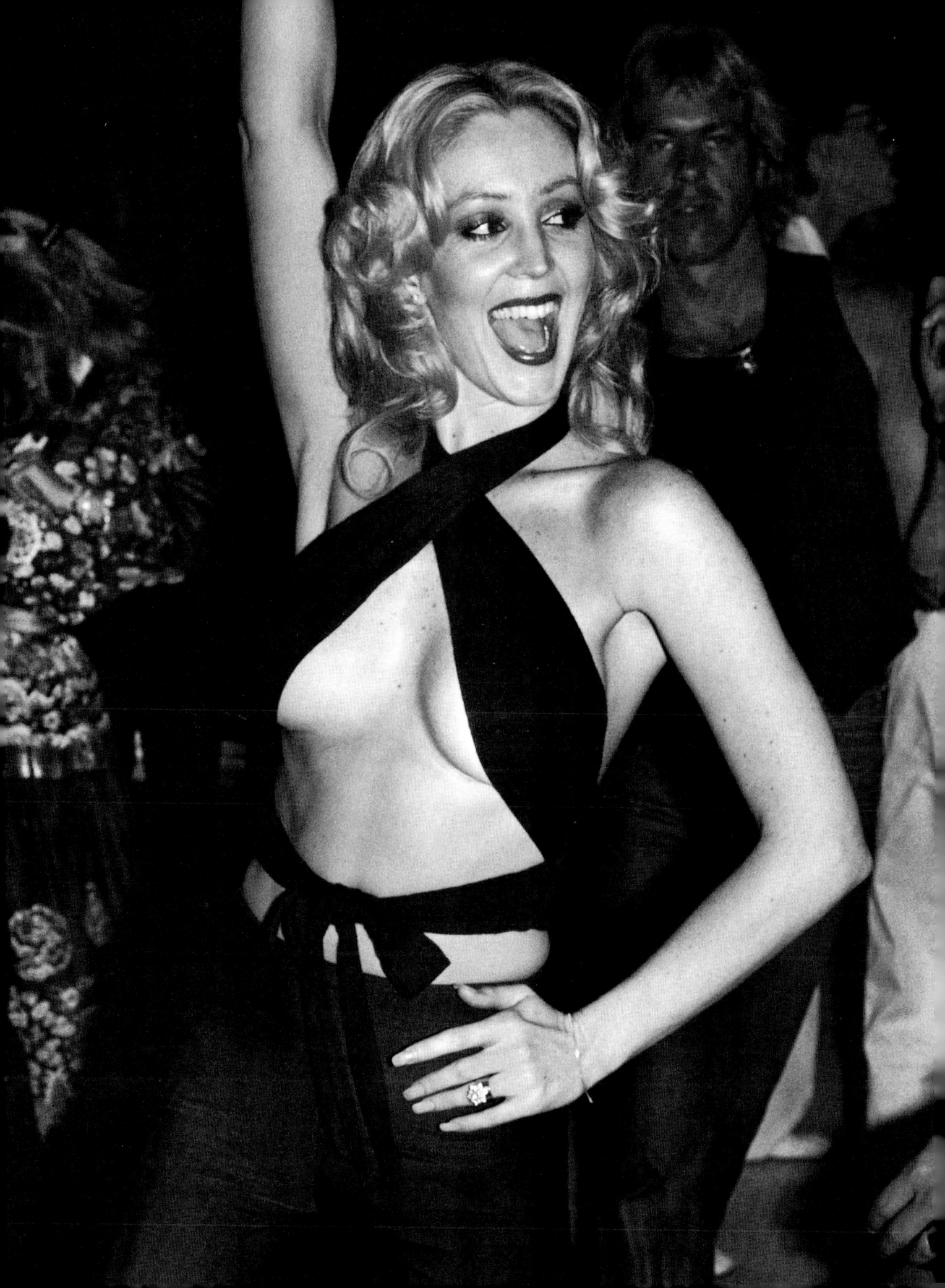

DRAG QUEEN

Drag queens were a common sight at Studio, and there were many who came night after night to entertain, mesmerize, and make people laugh. Some were more well known than others; a few were even legends. Yet despite the wild abandon that permeated the club and the obvious mix of sexuality, queens were often treated as the low "men" on the totem pole. Still, their style and flair made a real impact on the setting—many people had never seen such outrageous people as the drag denizens found there. I will always remember the early queens at Studio for their many innovative and glamorous outfits.

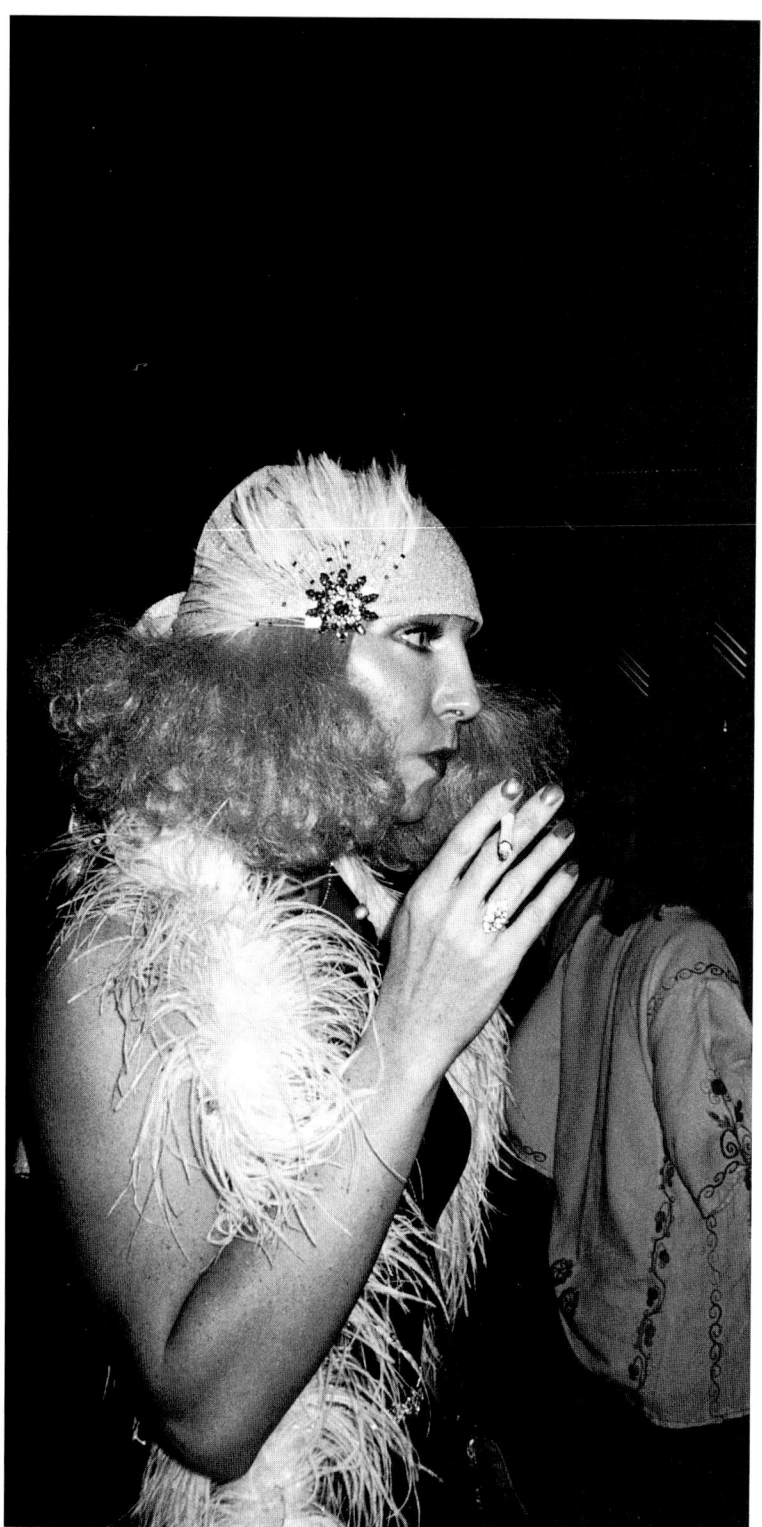

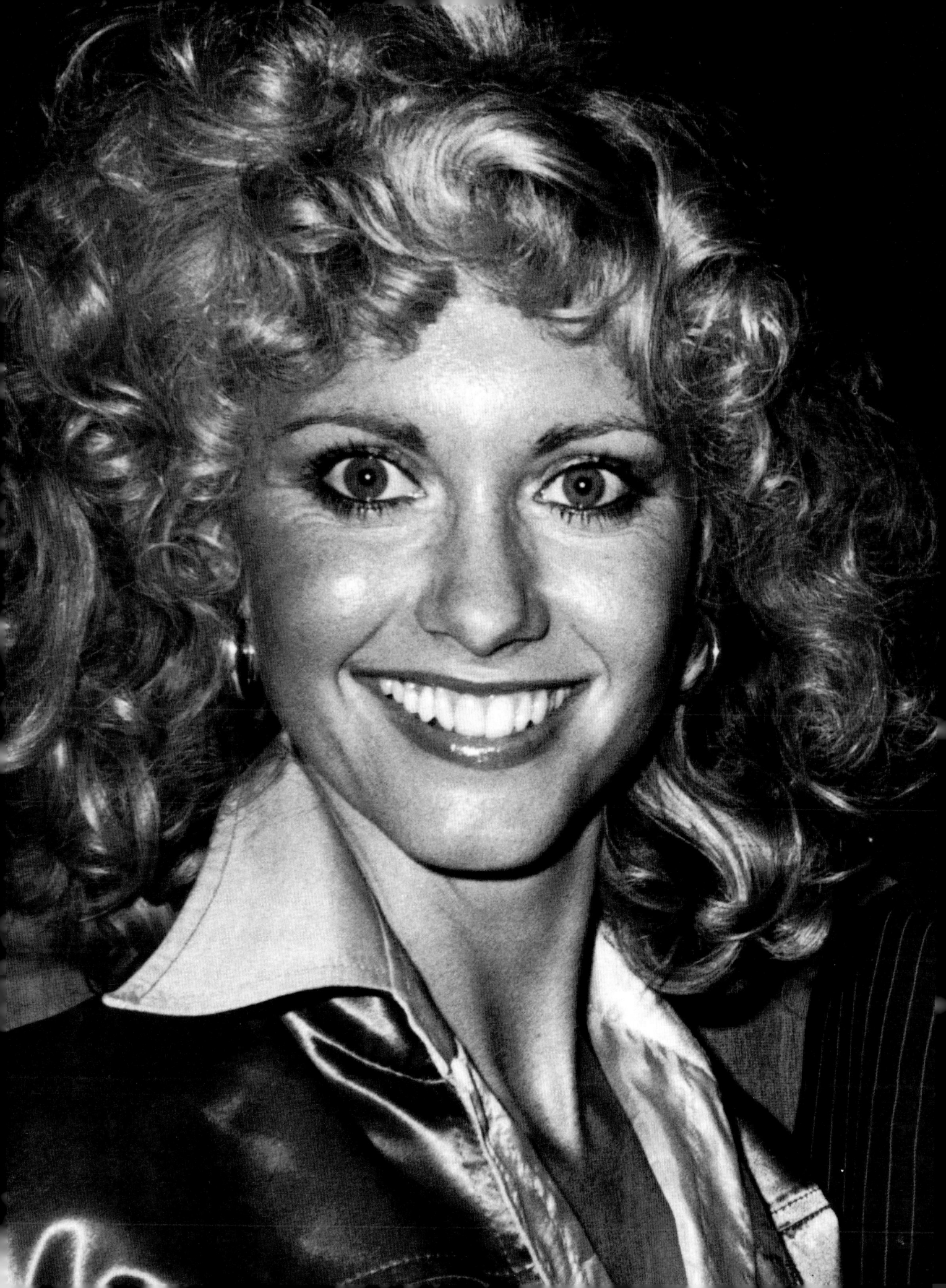

ROD McKUEN

Unofficial Poet Laureate of the Sixties, Rod McKuen was the lyrical voice of a generation of lovesick hippies. Although he published six books of poetry and recorded eight albums of music and spoken word, it was rare to see him in public. But he, like many recluses of the time, was attracted to Studio by its great legend and reputation for an exciting evening out. So many famous people showed up to see Studio for themselves once the word got out. This photograph was taken in the main entrance hall.

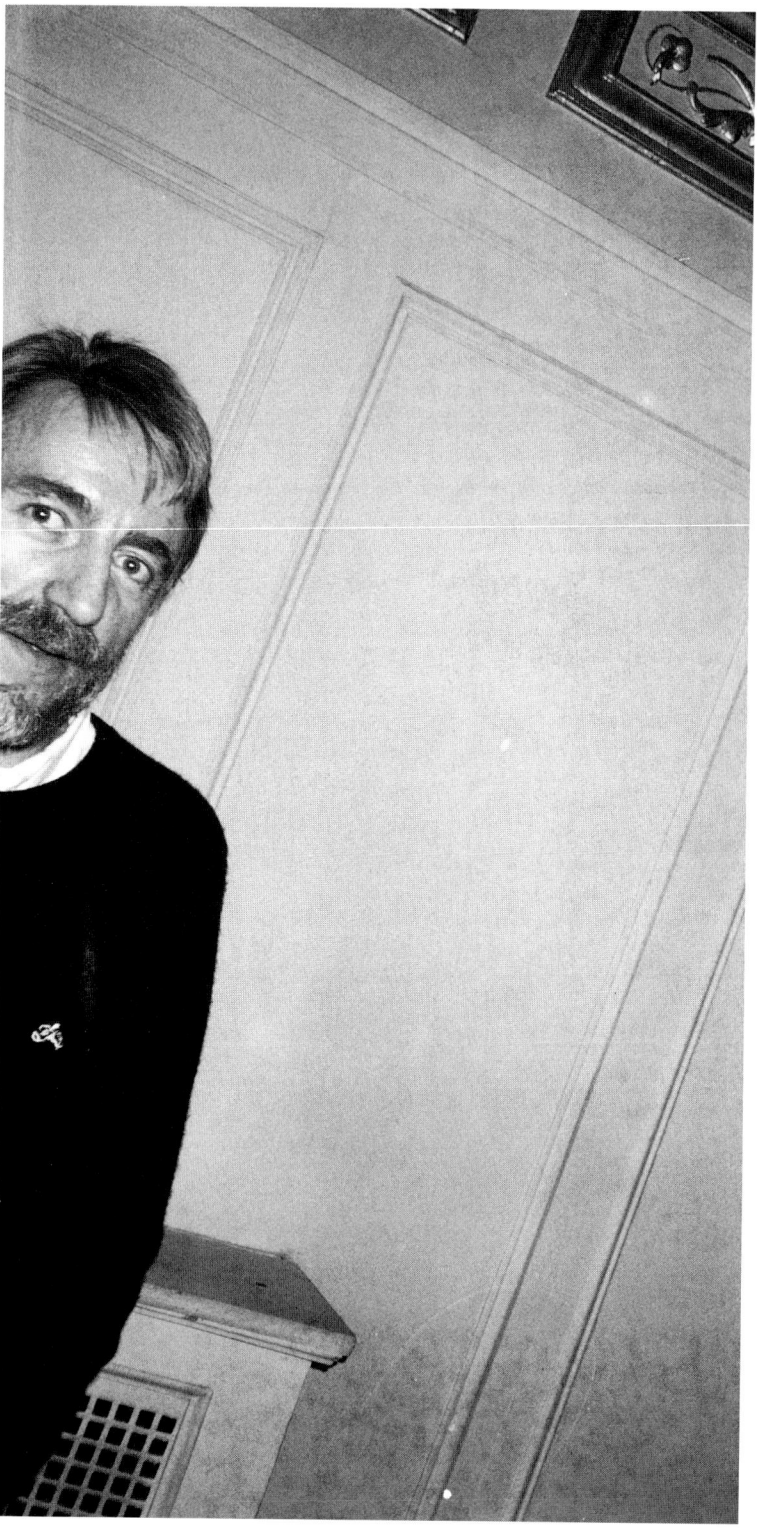

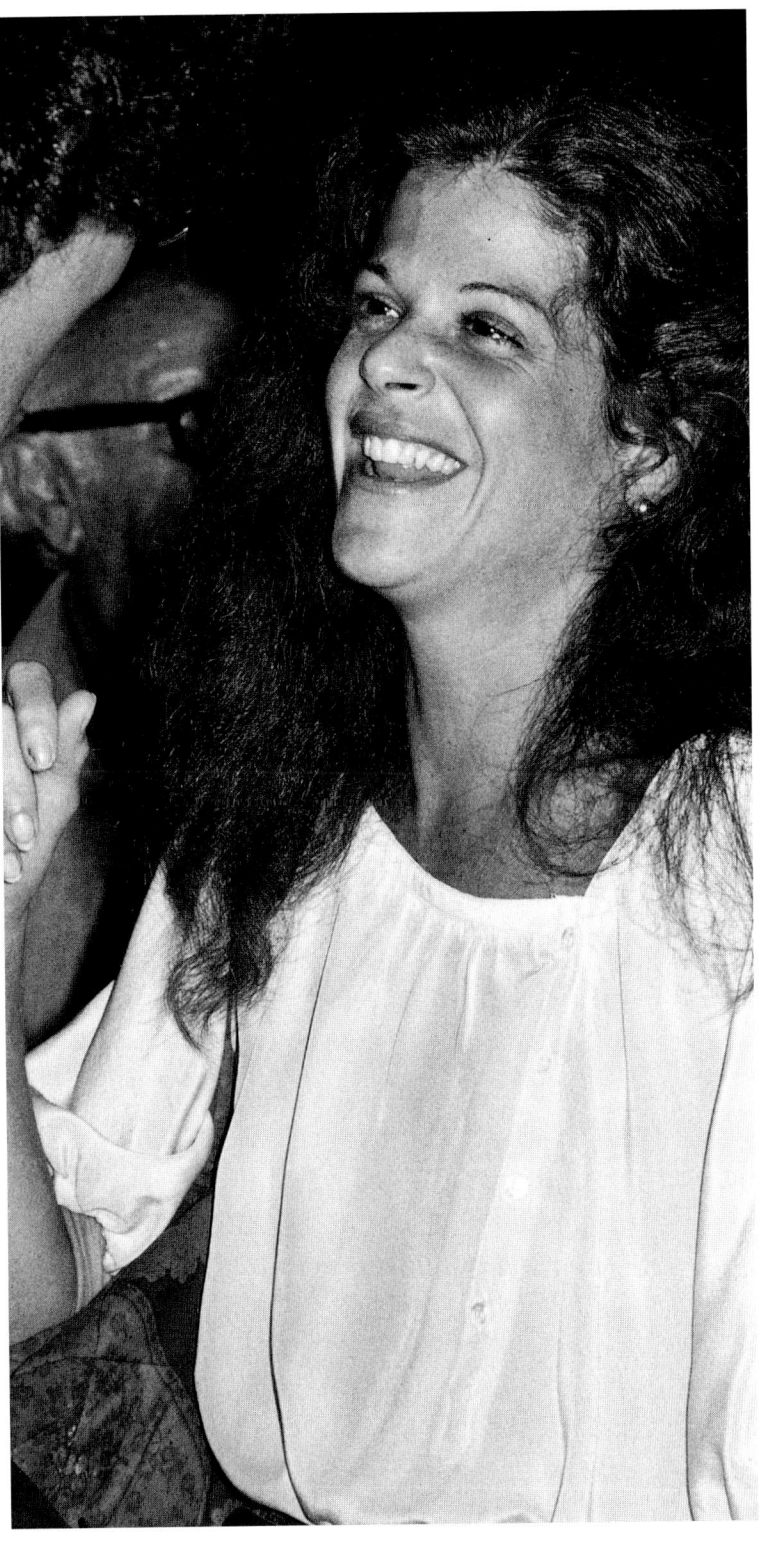

With the success of *Saturday Night Live*, Gilda Radner became a household name. In fact, many of *SNL*'s stars were regulars at Studio. Gilda was friendly and personable and exuded a quiet charm and sweetness.

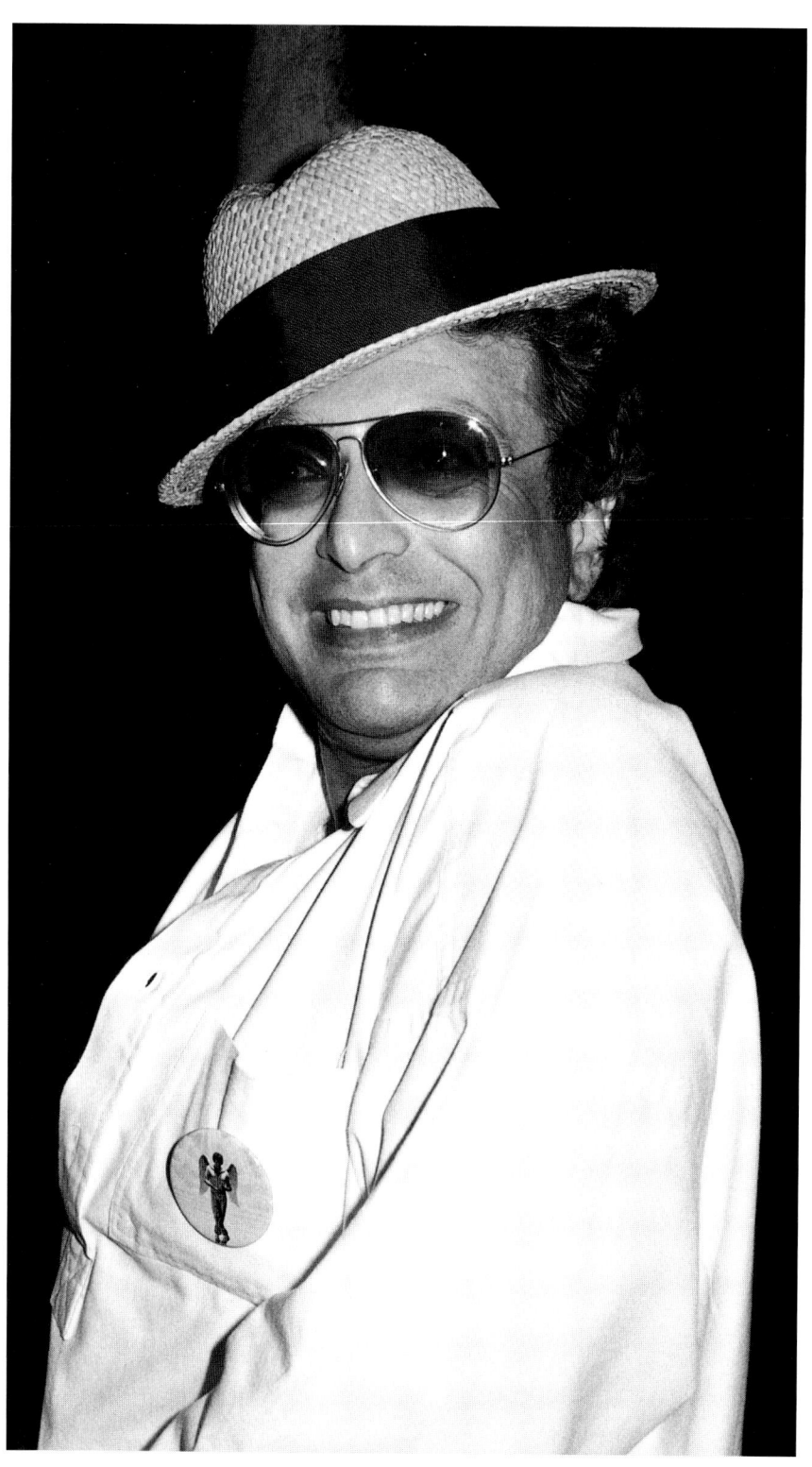

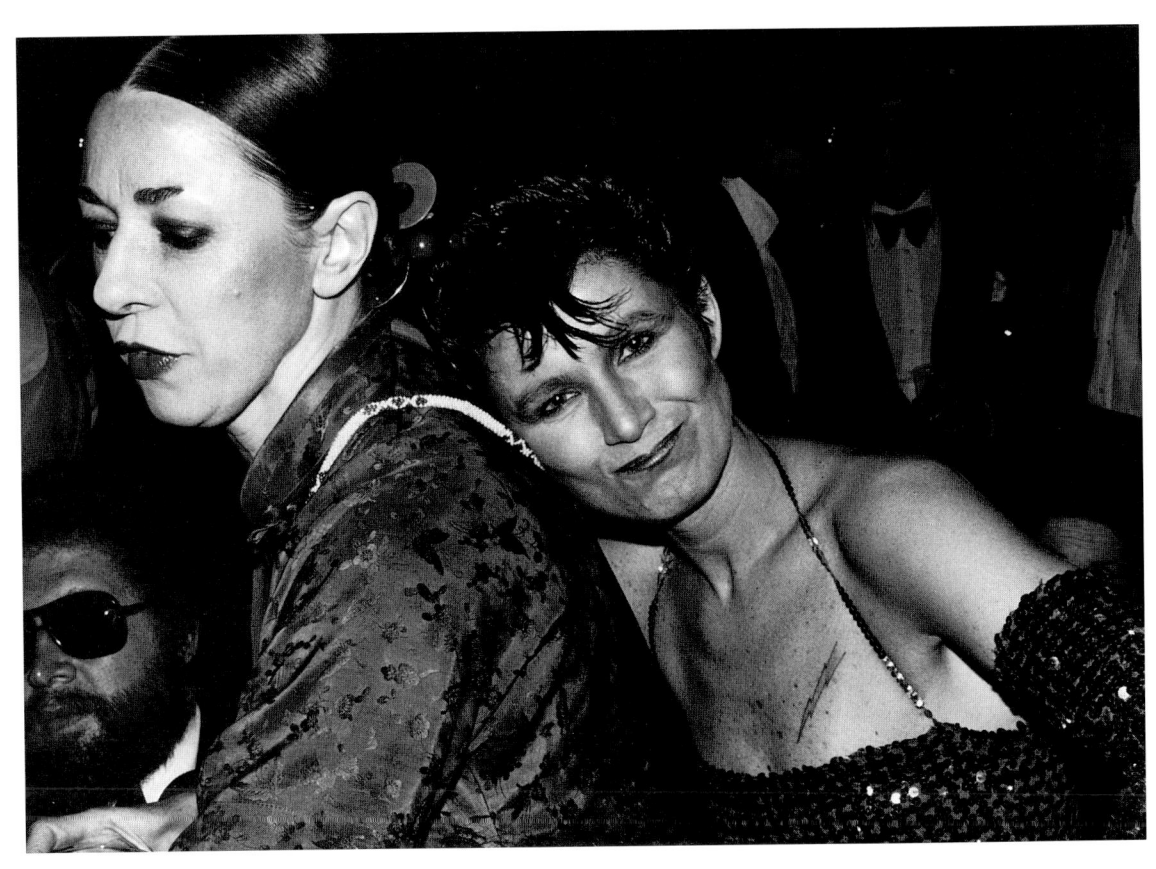

D.D. RYAN AND BETSEY JOHNSON

BOB MACKIE

When one thinks of fashion and the Seventies, it is hard not to think of Bob Mackie first. As designer to the stars, he was made famous by his designs for *The Carol Burnett Show* and *The Sonny and Cher Comedy Hour*. His appearance at Studio was exciting for everyone who loved his dazzling creations.

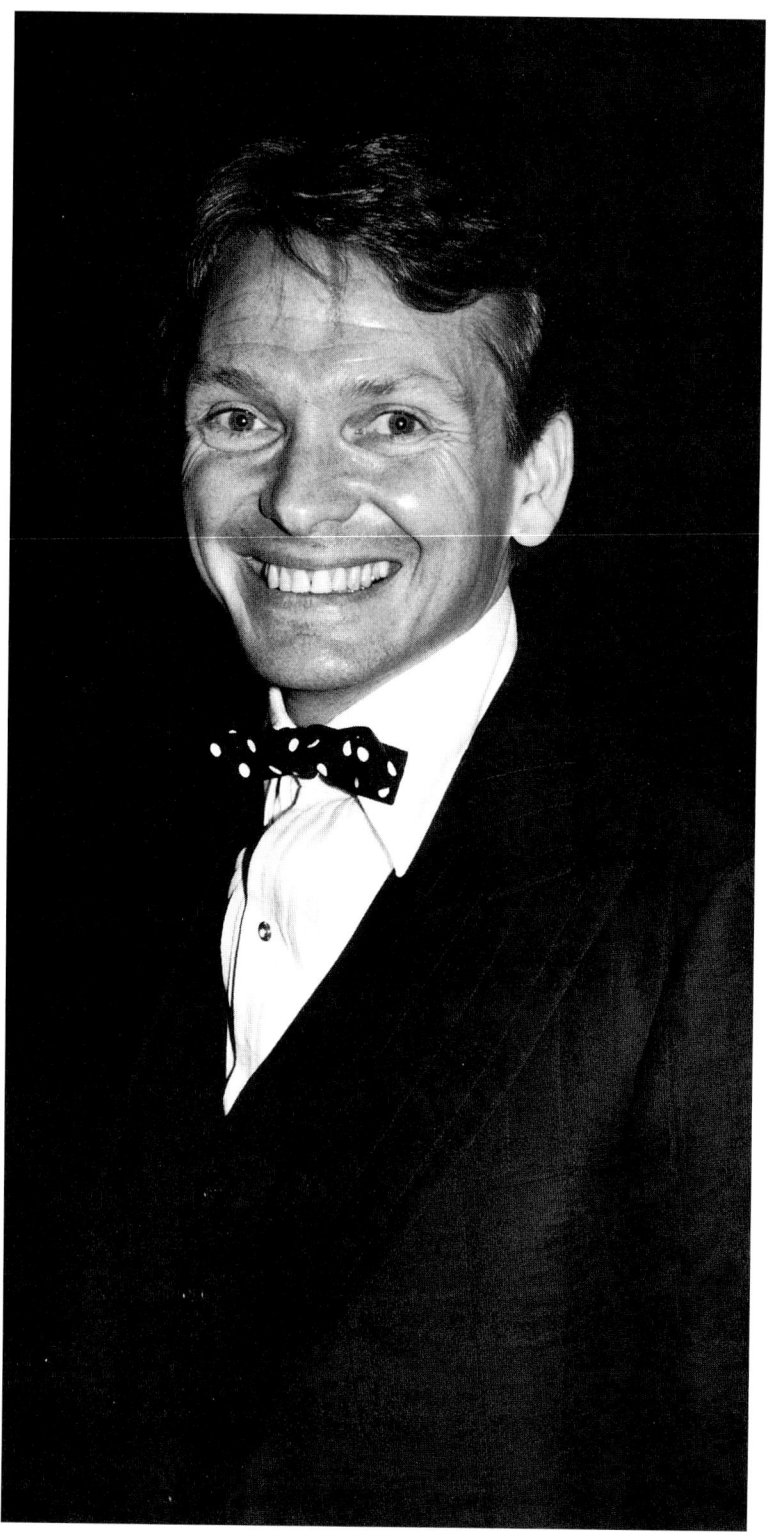

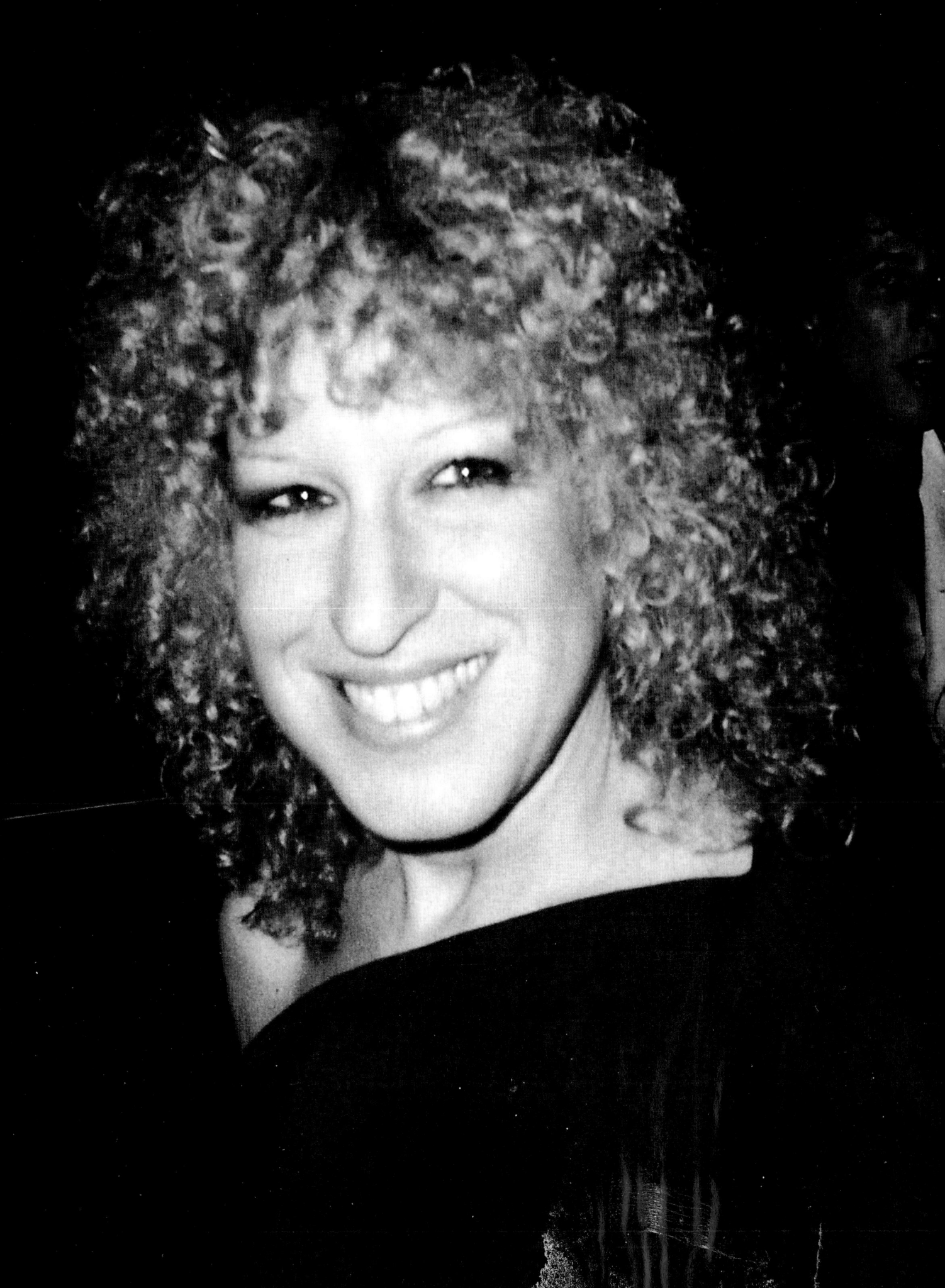

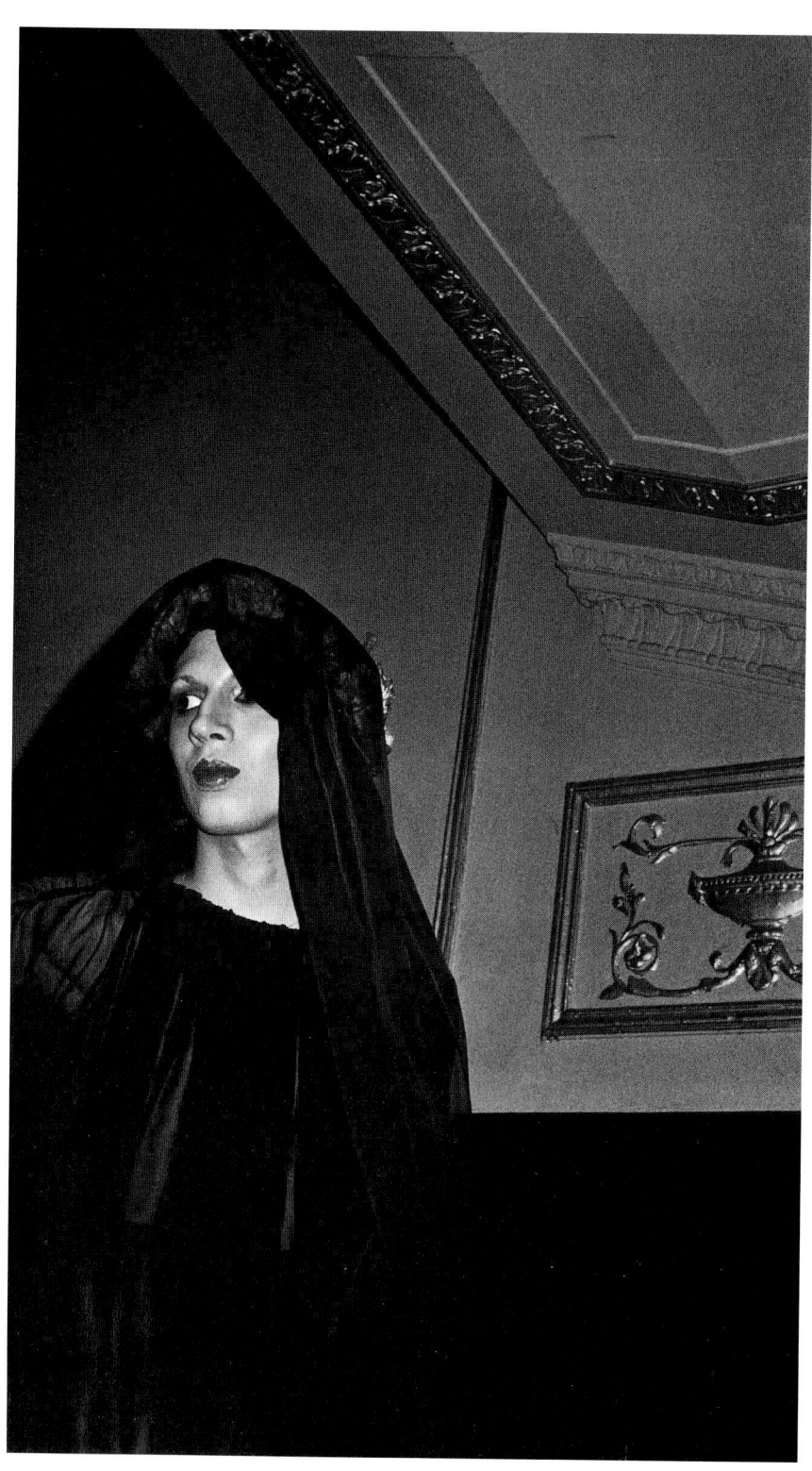

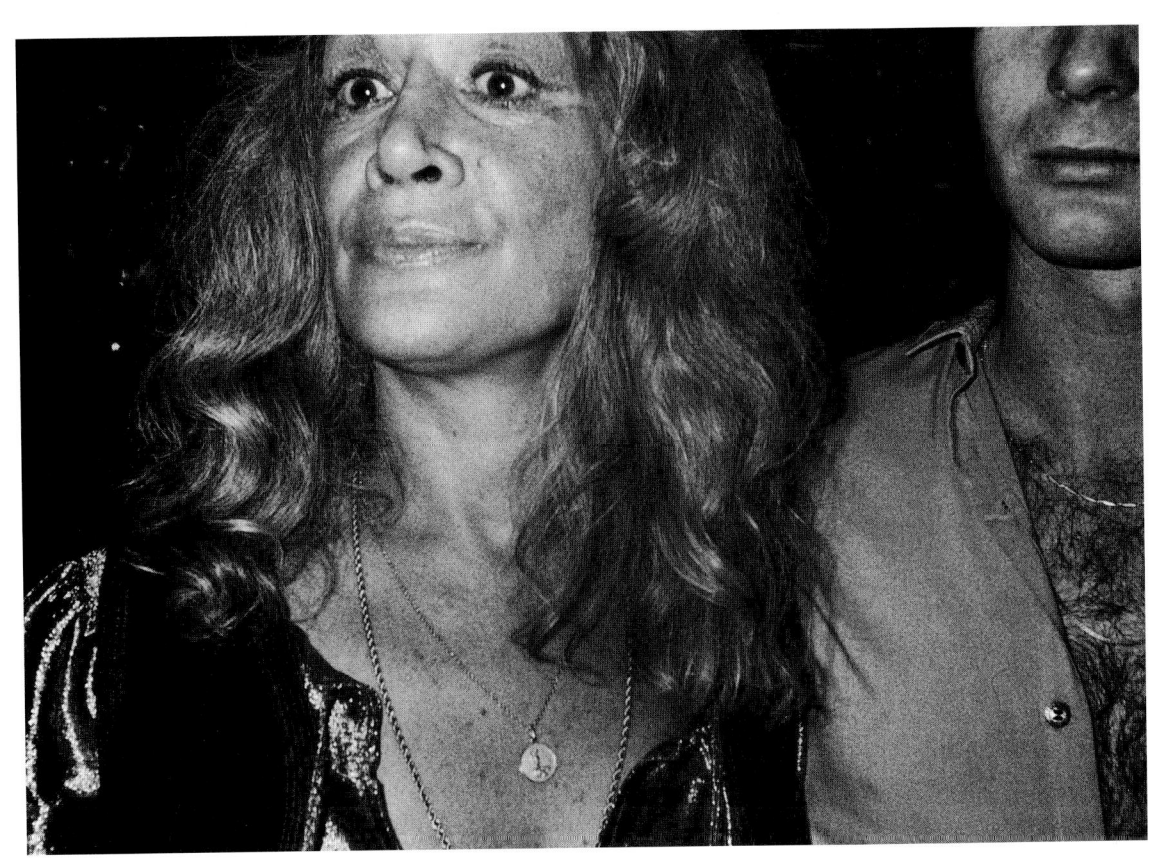

SYLVIA MILES

TAYLOR MEADE

As an actor, Taylor Meade appeared in many of Andy Warhol's early films, including *Lonesome Cowboys* and *Heat*. He was an original habitué of Andy's early Factory and often refers to himself as the illegitimate son of Andy Warhol. He has written several books of poetry and has acted in many underground and feature films. Taylor still lives on New York's colorful Lower East Side and can often be found in many of its cafés and coffee houses.

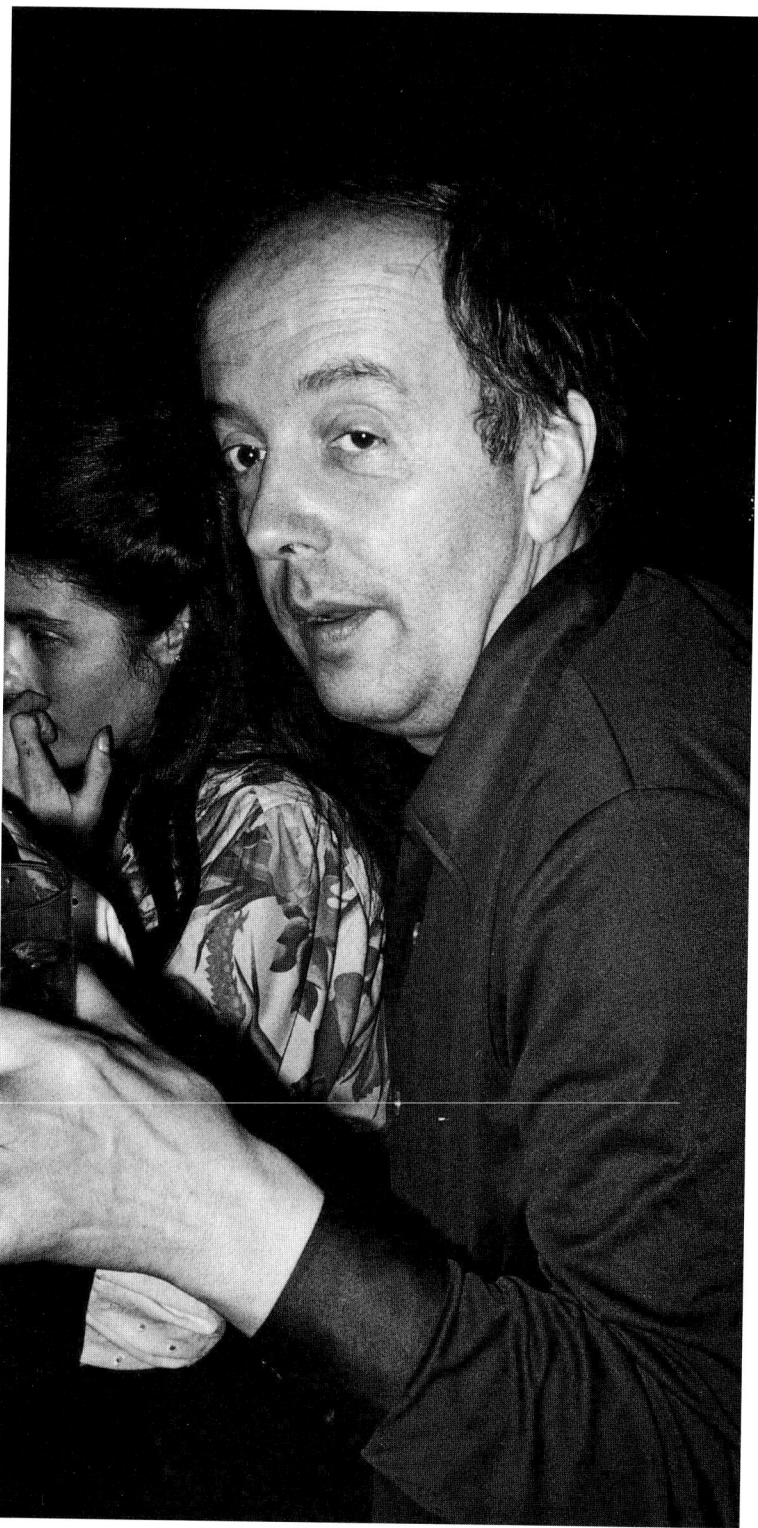

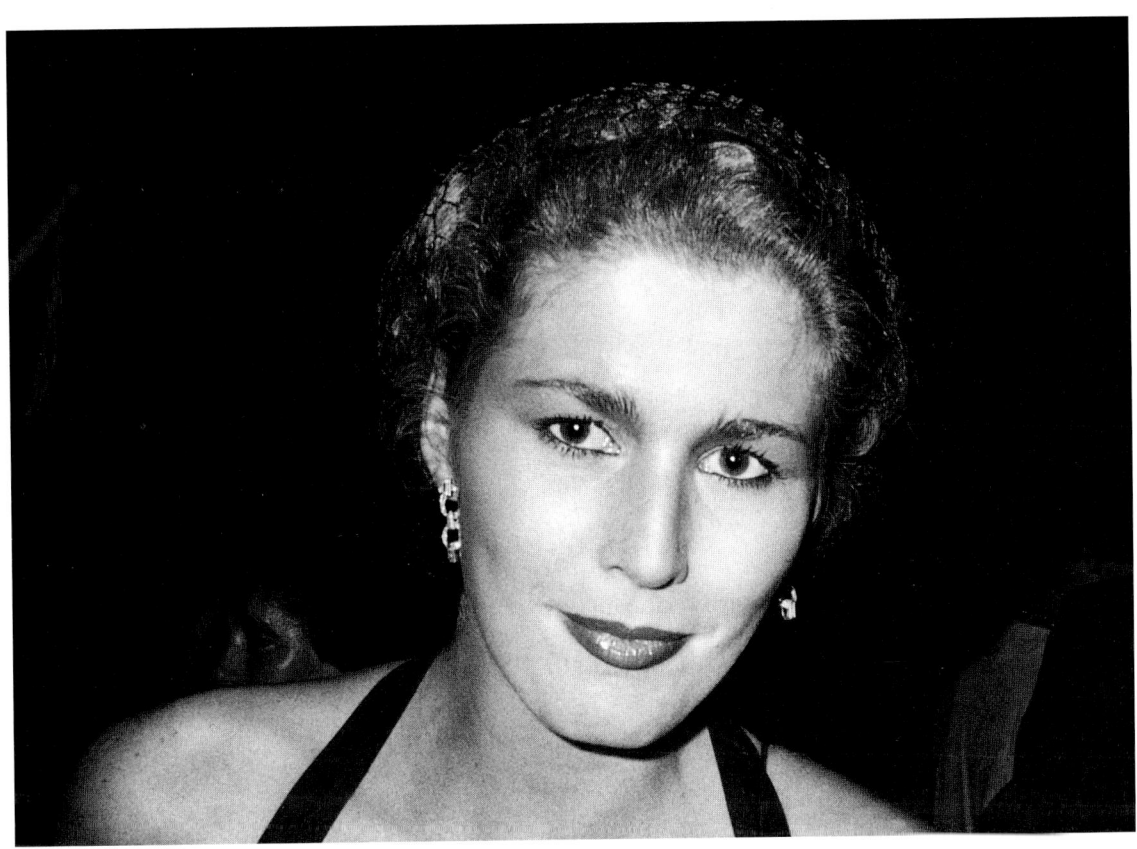

PRINCESS YASMIN AGA KHAN

There was so much royalty at Studio 54 that one might have thought that the red carpet that started at the entrance and led into the club was there for that reason alone. Princess Yasmin Aga Khan is the daughter of Prince Aly Khan and Hollywood queen Rita Hayworth. Active in charities and a prominent part of the social register, the princess was no stranger to Studio. Her beauty and radiance lit up many a night there, and she proved herself both amiable and approachable.

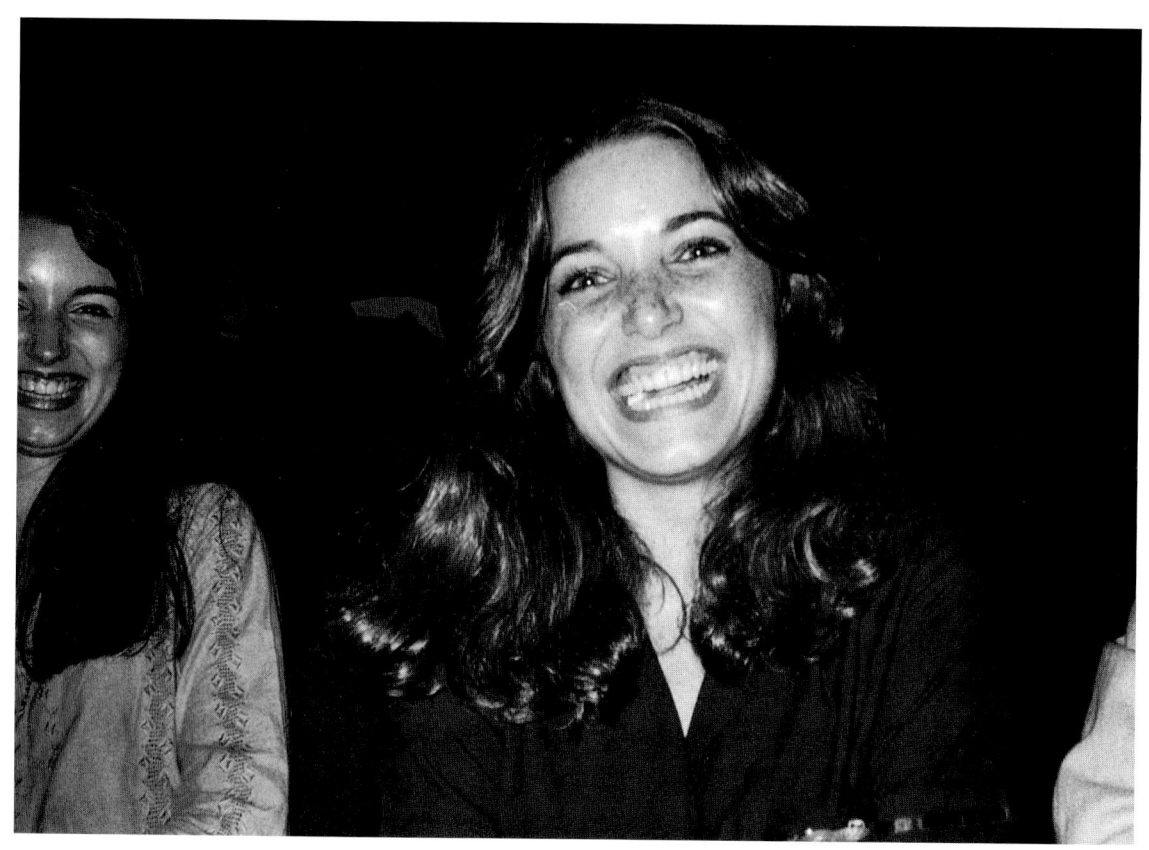

KAREN ALLEN

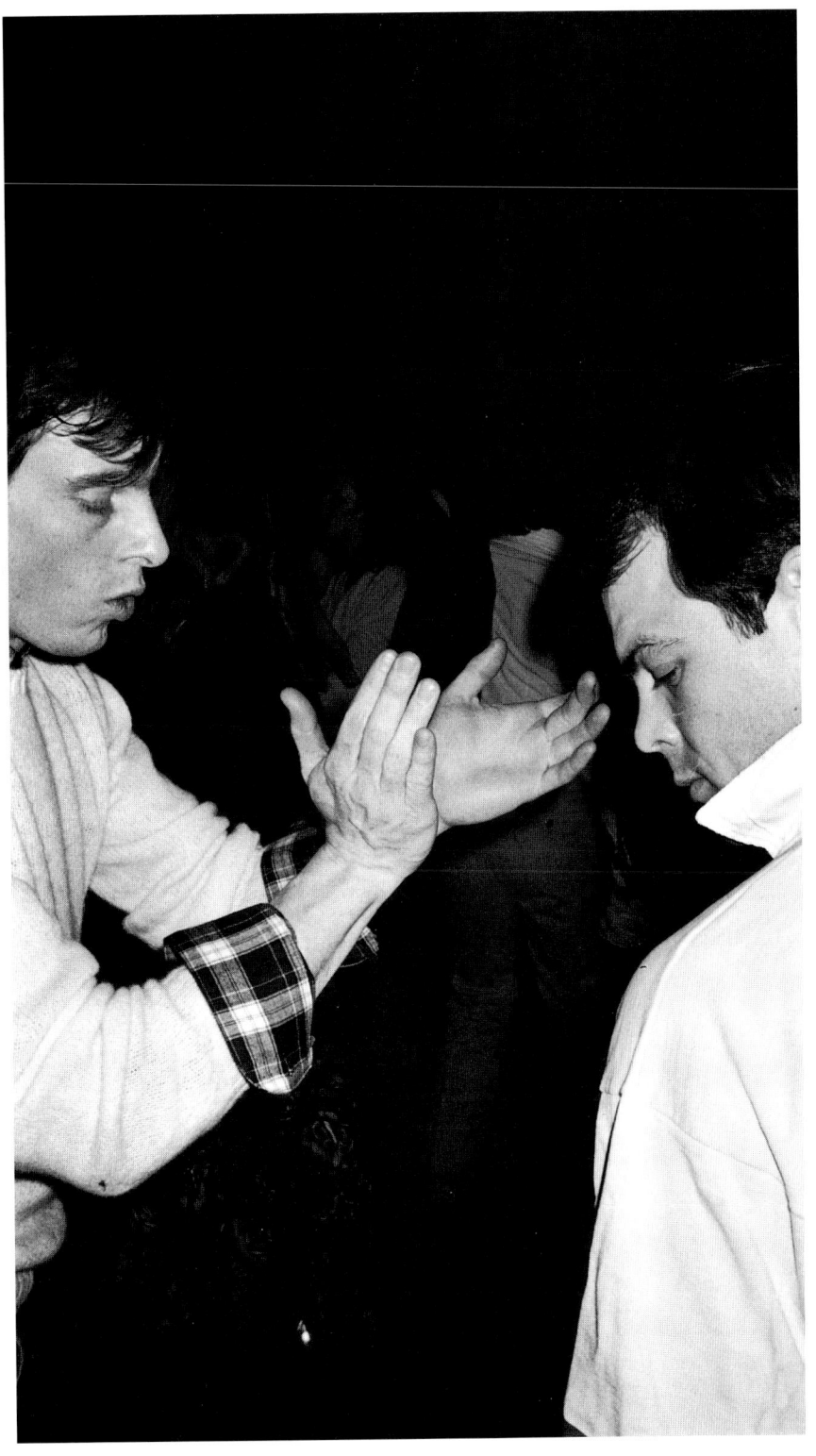

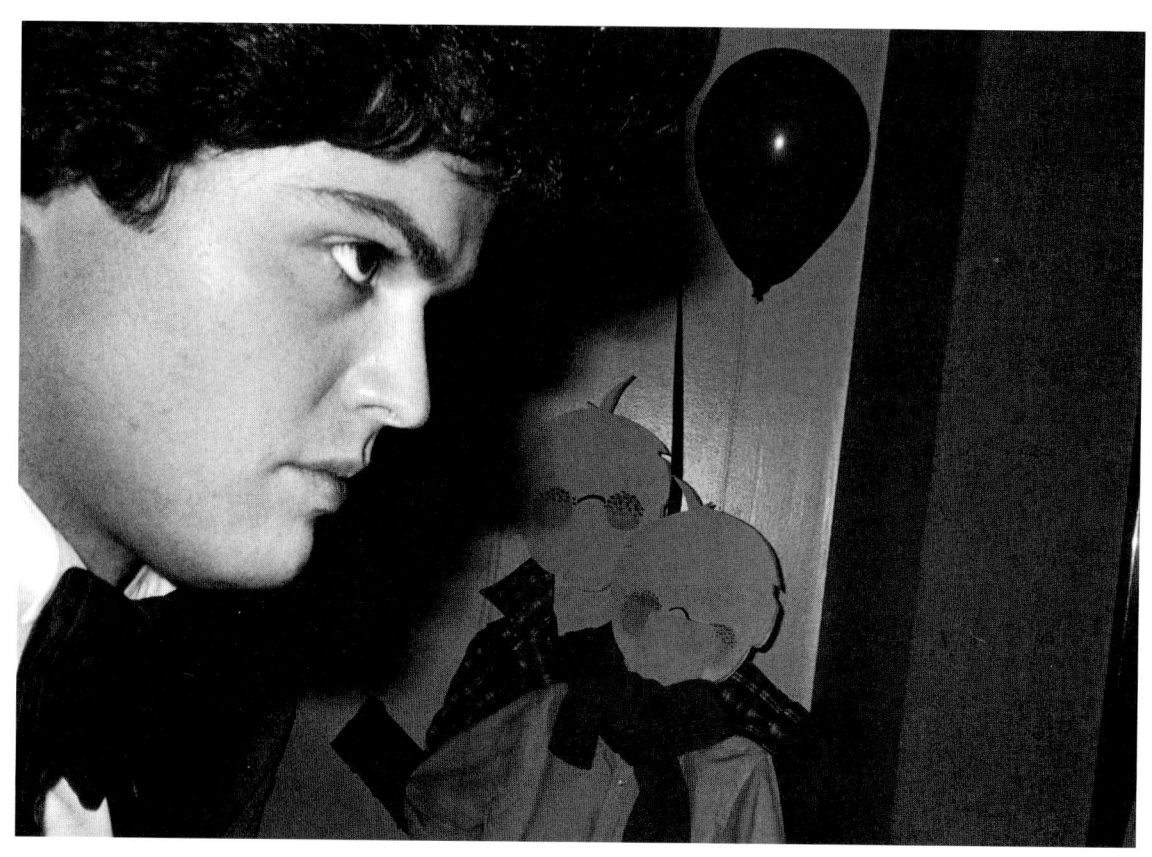

DONNY OSMOND

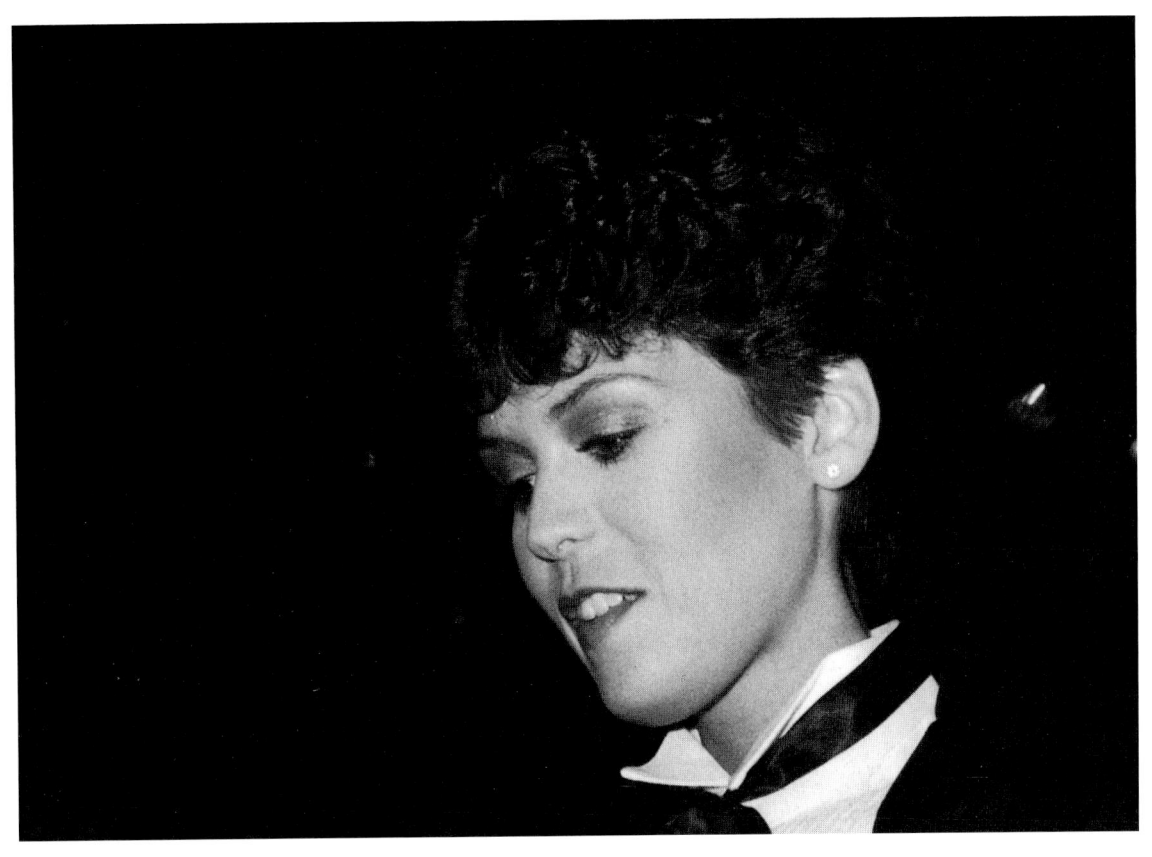

MARIE OSMOND

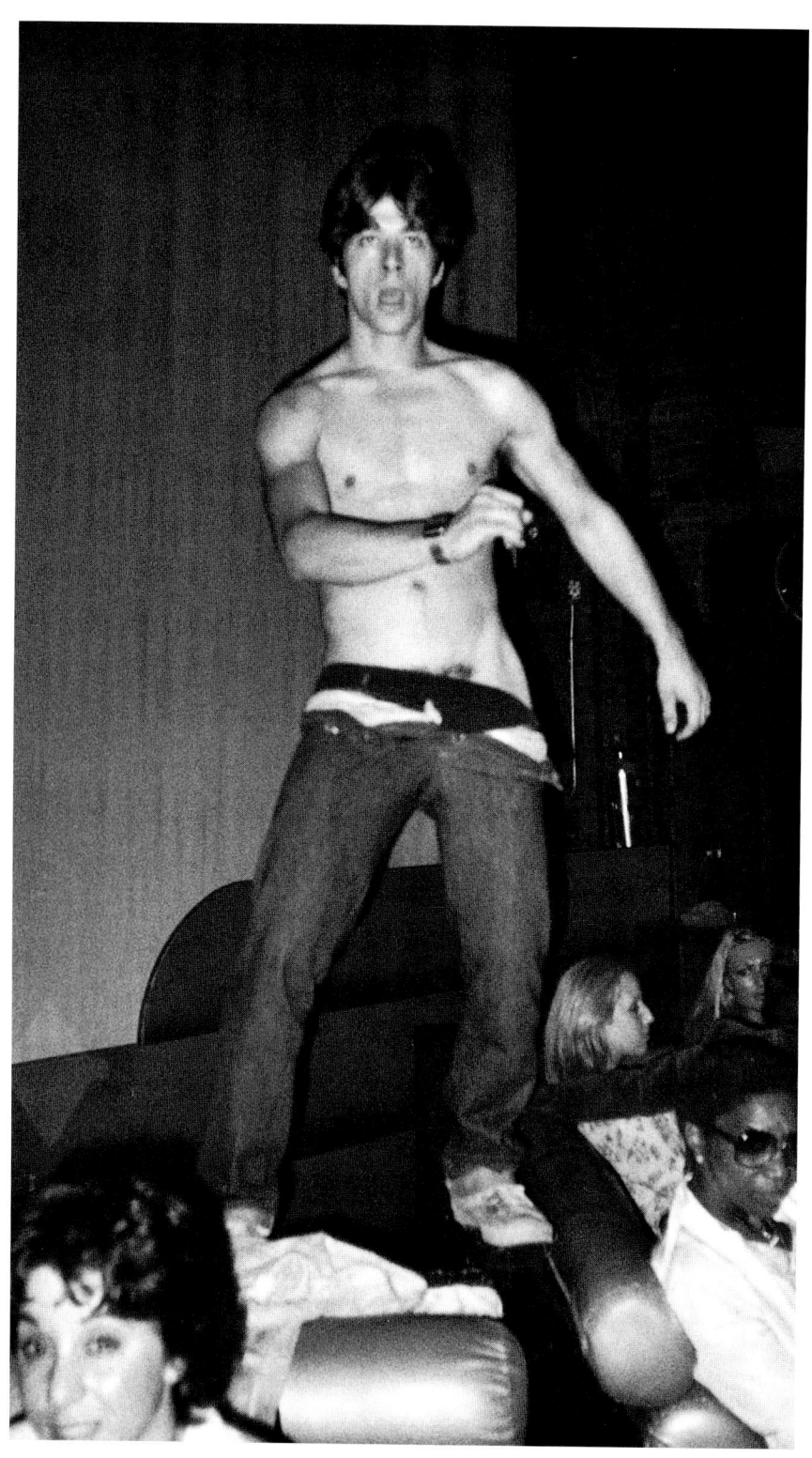

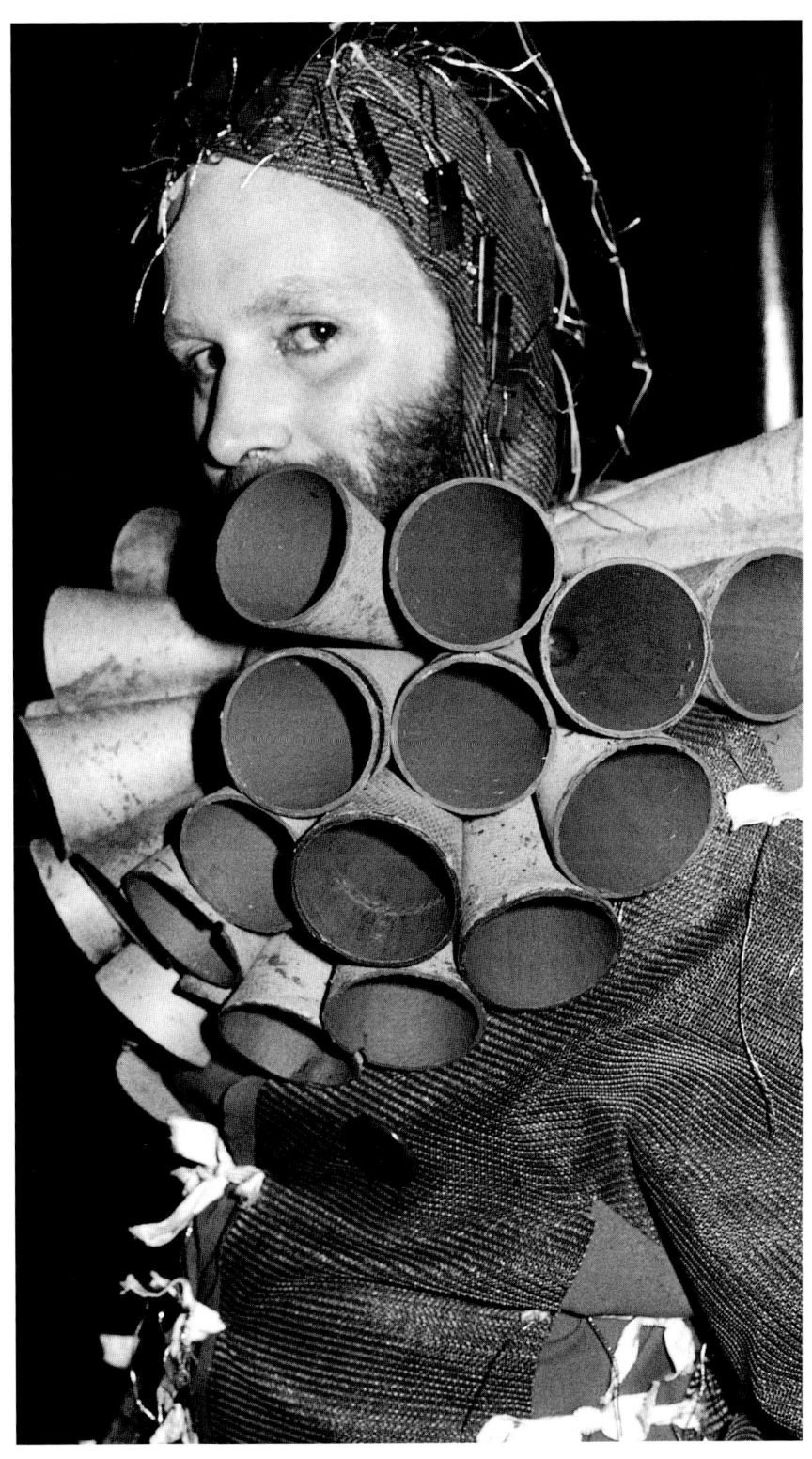

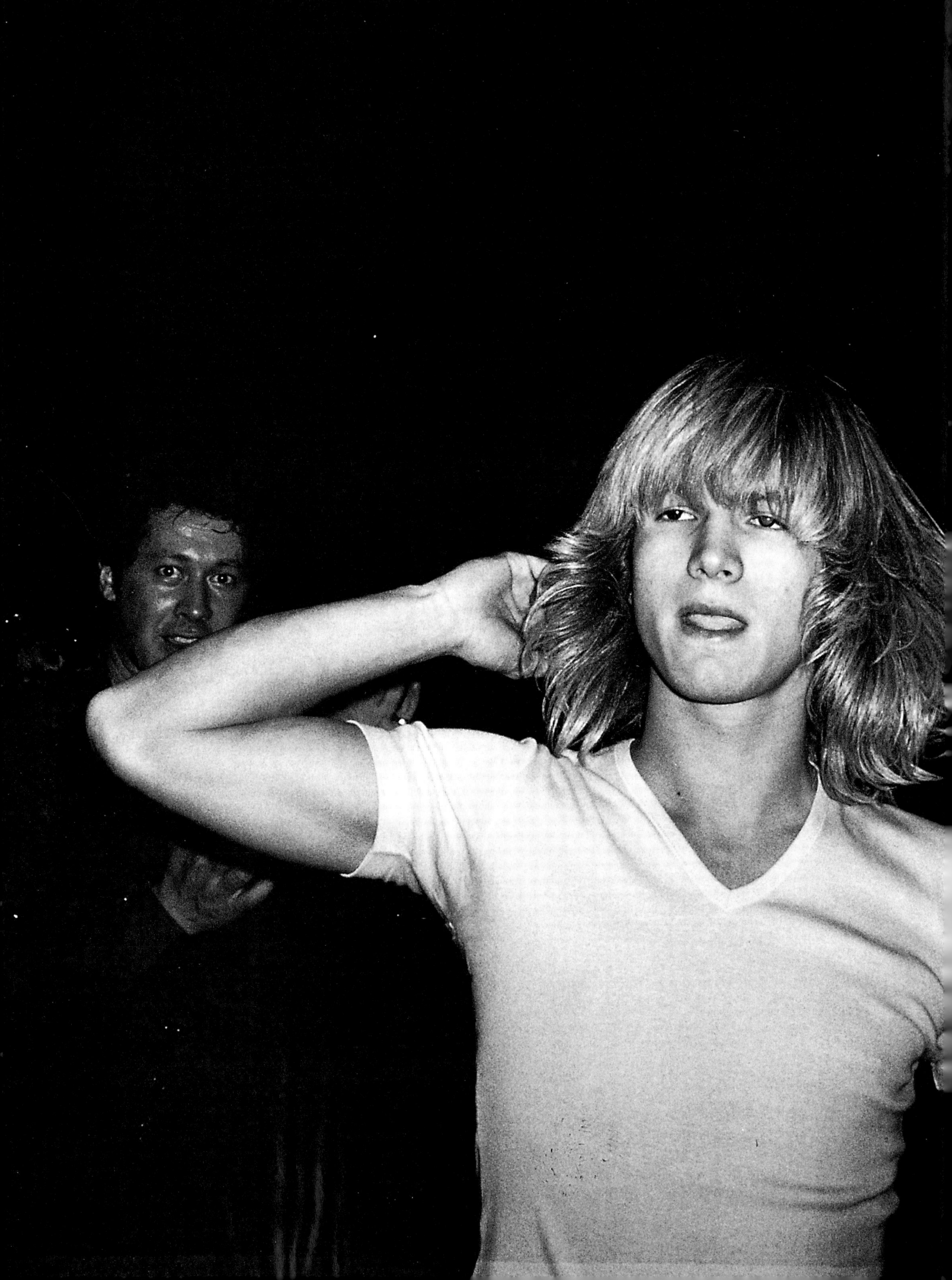

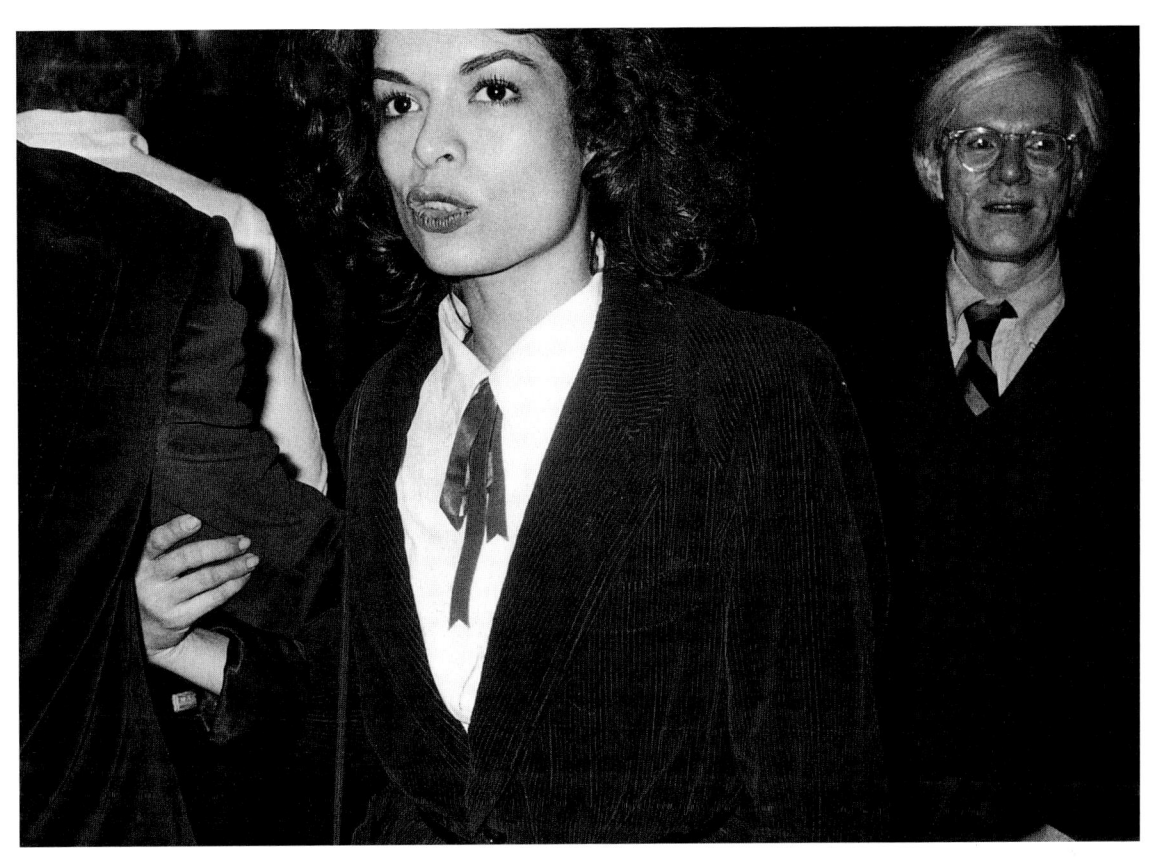

BIANCA JAGGER AND ANDY WARHOL

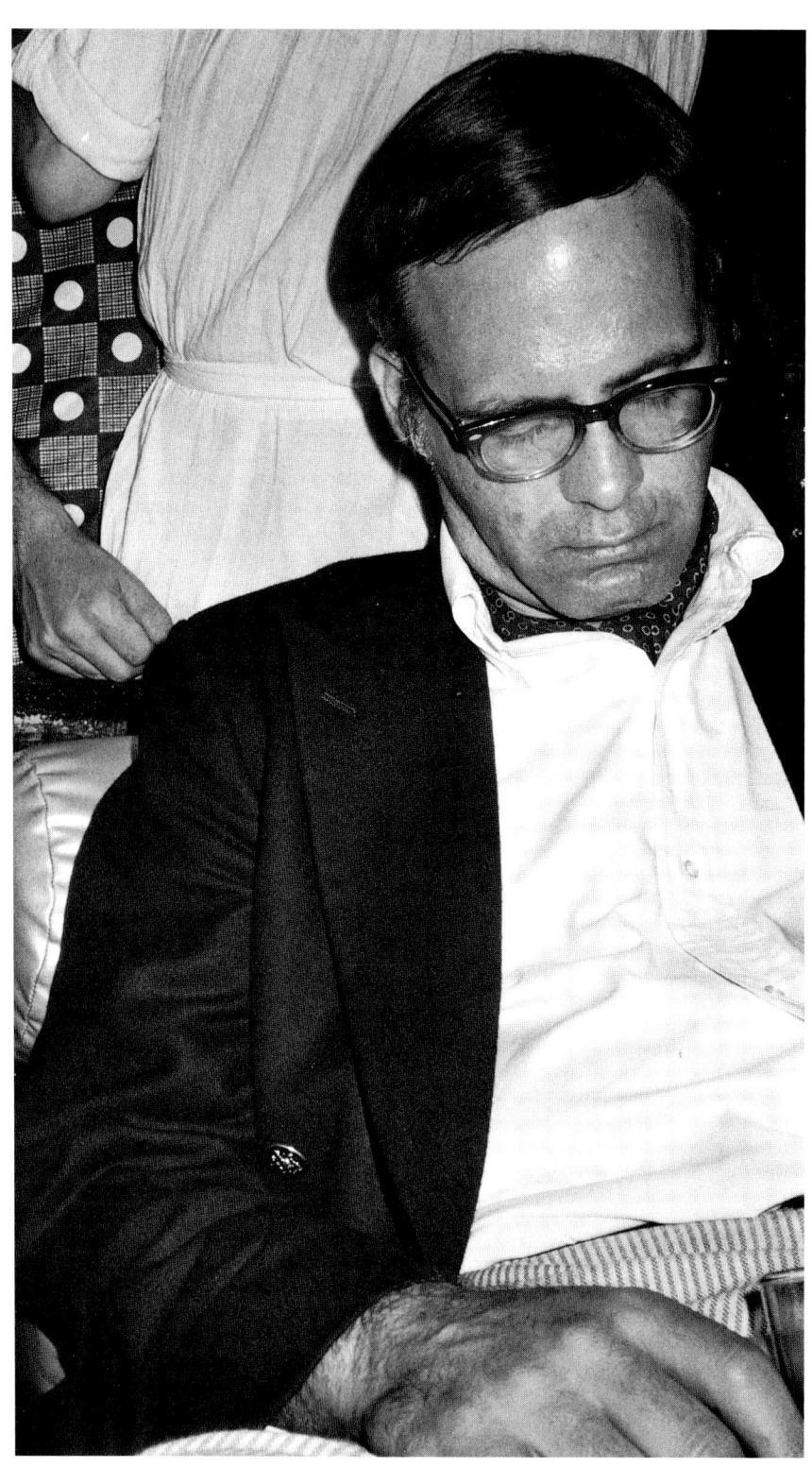

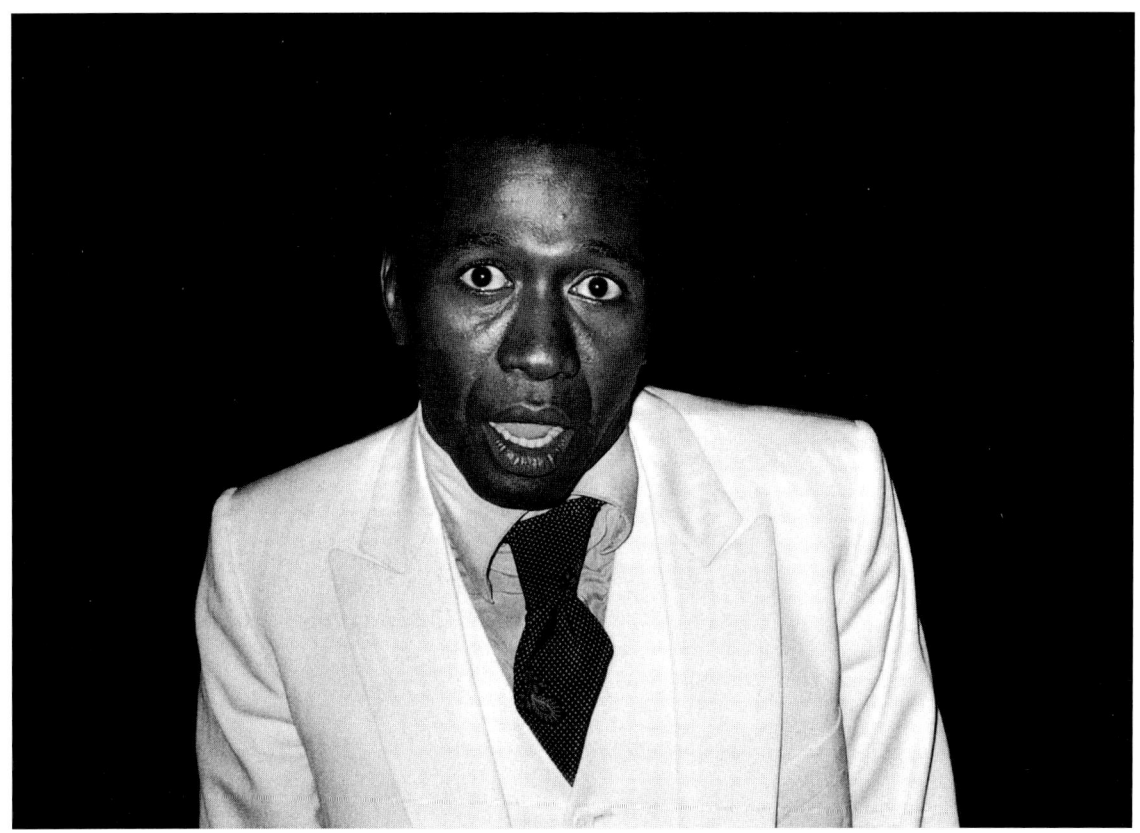

BEN VEREEN

This photo of Ben Vereen was taken on his way out of the club after a long night of partying. From the moment he walked through the door that evening, he insisted that he would be leaving at any time—he had been starring on Broadway and was anxious to get home to bed and sleep. Still, seven hours after his arrival, as the employees were closing up and heading home themselves, he was still going strong and was chased out the door with the rest of us. He had boogied the night away on the dance floor.

BIOGRAPHIES

BOBBY MILLER

Bobby Miller was born in Washington, D.C., in 1952. He began taking photographs in 1976 and studied with the legendary master photographer, Lisette Model. His work has been in such publications as *Newsweek*, *New York* magazine, *Details*, and *The Village Voice*, to name just a few. He lives in New York City with puppeteer Basil Twist.

Aside from his careers in hairdressing, makeup, and photography, Bobby Miller is also a poet and an actor. He has read his work at Alice Tully Hall/Lincoln Center, the Whitney Museum, the New York Historical Society, CMJ Music Festival (1994, 1995, 1996), Bennington College, New York University, American Crafts Museum, ICA/London, Battersee Arts Center/London, CCA/Glasgow, the Rhode Island School of Design, and the Smithsonian Institution. He is also the author of three books of poetry and has been published in *Aloud: Voices from the Nuyorican Poets Cafe*, winner of the 1995 American Book Award, and *Verses That Hurt: Pleasure and Pain from the Poemfone Poets*. He has been seen on PBS's popular series *City Arts* and on the BBC's *Clive James Hour*. The *Village Voice* called him "one of the more interesting spoken word wizards to come down the pike in a while. He mixes the personal, the political, the polemical, and the poetical, adds a touch of sulfur, and conjures up alchemical wonders." He can be heard on the Epic Records double CD *Home Alive,* a compilation with Pearl Jam, Nirvana, Soundgarden, Jim Carroll, and others.

He has organized several successful poetry series in New York City, including Verbal Abuse at Mother on the first Sunday of each month. As an actor he has appeared off-off Broadway in *Forty Deuce* at Theater for the New City, and with Theater Couture in both *The Bad Weed* and *The Final Feast of Lucrezia Borgia*. He is currently developing his one-man show, *Bobby Miller, Bobby Miller.*

VICTOR BOCKRIS

Victor Bockris is a writer and photographer. He has written portraits and biographies of numerous leading figures in the worlds of sports, the arts, music, and literature, including *The Life and Death of Andy Warhol*, *Transformer: The Lou Reed Story*, and *With William Burroughs: A Report from the Bunker*. He lives in New York City, where he continues to focus on the entertainment industry in all its guises.

AMY TRACHTENBERG

Amy Trachtenberg is a writer, editor, and producer of interactive content, and is the Managing Editor at the Mining Company. In addition to producing numerous award-winning Web sites, she has also co-edited an anthology of contemporary urban poetry entitled *Verses That Hurt: Pleasure and Pain from the Poemfone Poets*. She lives in New York City with her husband, Jordan.

Amy Trachtenberg would like to thank:
My dear friend Bobby Miller for giving me the opportunity to work on this very special project; my husband, Jordan Trachtenberg, for his love, passion, and verve; our editor at St. Martin's, Dana Albarella, for believing in this project and fighting to make it the best it could be; my parents, Sonny and Maggie Katzenberg, for their unconditional love and support; the Mining Company, for allowing me to divert some of my attention to this book; and all my friends and family for sharing in my excitement and making this accomplishment all the more significant. My love and respect to you all.

Bobby Miller has special thanks for Amy:
I would like to acknowledge and recognize Amy Trachtenberg for her special involvement in the making of this book. It was she who helped prepare and present the initial proposal for presentation to the publisher. And it was Amy and her husband, Jordan, who brought *Fabulous!* to the eye and attention of my editor, Dana Albarella, at St. Martin's. That started the disco ball rolling. Amy's organizational skills and keen eye for detail helped make this project a successful and pleasant experience for me. She believed in this project from the start and worked earnestly toward its fruition. I quite literally could not have done it without her.

SID KAPLAN AND JIM SMITH

Photographic Printers

Sid Kaplan is a New York legend who began his photographic journey in the South Bronx almost fifty years ago when, as a ten-year-old, he was "hypnotized, almost addicted," he recalls, after he first saw a print come up in the developer. In 1962, Sid ended up working as a black-and-white printer at Compo, a custom lab in New York City that was famous for printing the Family of Man Exhibition at MoMA. At Compo, Sid printed for some of the greatest photographers of the last fifty years, such as Philippe Halsman, Robert and Cornell Capa, Weegee, and most of the Magnum crew, who worked on Edward Steichen's last curated exhibition. The first photographer to set up a darkroom in the shadow of the Flatiron Building in what would later become the photo district, Sid printed "any and everything that came through the door." W. Eugene Smith occupied an adjacent loft for several years. Ralph Gibson introduced Sid to Robert Frank in 1969, and Sid became Robert's printer, a relationship that has continued to this day. Sid's client list grew to include Allen Ginsburg, who also became a neighbor when Sid relocated to the Lower East Side. In 1972, Mr. Kaplan began teaching black-and-white darkroom skills at the School of Visual Arts, where he continues to teach.

Jim Smith has assisted Sid Kaplan on special projects since 1972. As a freelance photographer, Jim has worked in fashion, editorial, and corporate photography and has taught photography and black-and-white printing, from colleges to camera clubs. The bulk of his personal photography consists of four projects over a thirty-year span, including three decades of portraits in the New York City subway system, a documentation of his family's Tennessee farm over the same period, Classic American cars in the American landscape, and 360-degree panoramic landscapes highlighting Americans' impact on their environment. Mr. Smith's work has been published in periodicals such as *Popular Photography*, *Penthouse*, and *Photoworld*, and in books such as *New York at Night*, *The Southerners*, *The Family of Women*, and *The Family of Children*. He has exhibited his work in solo and group shows across the United States and Europe. His prints are included in numerous corporate and private collections.